*W*oolf
*S*tudies
*A*nnual

Volume 21, 2015

PACE UNIVERSITY PRESS • NEW YORK

Copyright © 2015 by
Pace University Press
41 Park Row, Rm. 1510
New York, NY 10038

All rights reserved
Printed in the United States of America

ISSN 1080-9317
ISBN 978-1-935625-19-3 (pbk: alk.ppr.)

Member

Council of Editors of Learned Journals

☉ Paper used in this publication meets the minimum requirements of
American National Standard for Information
Sciences–Permanence of Paper for Printed Library Materials,
ANSI Z39.48–1984

Editor

Mark Hussey — Pace University

Editorial Board

Tuzyline Jita Allan	Baruch College, CUNY
Eileen Barrett	California State University, East Bay
Morris Beja	Ohio State University
Kathryn N. Benzel	University of Nebraska-Kearney
Pamela L. Caughie	Loyola University Chicago
Wayne K. Chapman	Clemson University
Patricia Morgne Cramer	University of Connecticut, Stamford
Beth Rigel Daugherty	Otterbein College
Louise DeSalvo	Jenny Hunter Endowed Scholar for Literature and Creative Writing, Hunter College, CUNY
Anne Fernald	Fordham University
Amanda Golden	Georgia Institute of Technology (Book Review Editor)
Sally Greene	Independent Scholar
Leslie Kathleen Hankins	Cornell College
Suzette Henke	Thruston B. Morton, Sr. Chair of Literary Studies, University of Louisville
Karen Kaivola	Augsburg College
Karen Kukil	Special Collections, William Allan Neilson Library, Smith College
Jane Lilienfeld	Curator's Distinguished Professor of English, Lincoln University
Jane Marcus	Distinguished Professor, CCNY and CUNY Graduate Center
Toni A. H. McNaron	University of Minnesota
Patricia Moran	University of Limerick
Vara Neverow	Southern Connecticut State University
Annette Oxindine	Wright State University
Beth Carole Rosenberg	University of Nevada-Las Vegas
Bonnie Kime Scott	San Diego State University
Brenda R. Silver	Dartmouth College
Susan Squier	Brill Professor of Women's Studies and English, Pennsylvania State University
Peter Stansky	Stanford University
Alex Zwerdling	University of California, Berkeley

Many thanks to readers for volume 21 (in addition to the Editorial Board): Judith Allen (Writer's House, U of Pennsylvania); Michèle Barrett (Queen Mary U of London); Suzanne Bellamy (Independent Scholar); Jessica Berman (UMBC); Emily Blair (Solano CC); Marcia Day Childress (U of Virginia); Karen DeMeester (U of Georgia); Logan Esdale (Chapman U); Brenda Helt (Independent Scholar); Mary Joannou (Anglia Ruskin U); Alice Keane (U of Michigan); Michael Lackey (U of Minnesota, Morris); Holly Laird (U of Tulsa); Karen Levenback (Franciscan Monastery); Helane Levine-Keating (Pace U); Eleanor McNees (U of Denver); Marlowe Miller (U of Massachusetts, Lowell); Makiko Minow-Pinkney (Independent Scholar); Darya Protopopova (UCL/Institute of Education); Steven Putzel (Penn-State Wilkes-Barre); Roberta Rubenstein (American U); David Sherman (Brandeis U); Jacqueline Shin (Towson U); Elisa K. Sparks (Clemson U); Mia Spiro (U of Glasgow); Alice Staveley (Stanford U); Susan Wegener (Purdue U); Michael Whitworth (Merton C, Oxford); Alice Wood (DeMontfort U). And very special thanks to our Review Editor, Amanda Golden.

Woolf Studies Annual is indexed in *Humanities International Complete, ABELL* and the *MLA Bibliography.*

Call for papers for a special issue of the
Virginia Woolf Miscellany

Issue #91/Spring 2017

*Virginia Woolf, Bloomsbury,
and the War to End War*

This issue commemorates the advent of the Great War and its representation by Virginia Woolf and her friends and colleagues in Bloomsbury and beyond (even H.G. Wells, who wrote a 1914 pamphlet called *The War that Will End War*)—noncombatants, combatants, and conscientious objectors; writers of prose, poetry, and drama; fiction and memoirs; criticism, reviews, and social commentary; journalists, historians, philosophers, and humanists. Contributions need not necessarily involve work done during the war, but gauge the war's ongoing effect on a wide range of topics and perspectives: cultural, socio-economic, modernist, feminist, to name the most obvious. How did war-consciousness, for example, affect views of mass culture and consumerism? Articles on other topics (e.g., constructions of self and identity in wartime, and post-war aesthetics) are also welcome.

Please send *inquiries* to Karen Levenback at kllevenback@att.net ASAP and *submissions* of not more than 2500 words by 1 August 2016.

Contents

Woolf Studies Annual

Volume 21, 2015

	viii	Abbreviations
		ARTICLES
Rebecca Wisor	1	About Face: The *Three Guineas* Photographs in Cultural Context
Kristin Czarnecki	50	Melted Flesh and Tangled Threads: War Trauma and Modes of Healing in Virginia Woolf's *Mrs. Dalloway* and Leslie Marmon Silko's *Ceremony*
Bethany Layne	78	The "Supreme Portrait Artist" and the "Mistress of the Phrase": Contesting Oppositional Portrayals of Woolf and Bell, Life and Art, in Susan Sellers's *Vanessa and Virginia*
		GUIDE
	107	Guide to Library Special Collections
		REVIEWS
Darya Protopopova	127	*The Common Reader* translated by Natalya Reinhold; *Night and Day* translated by Natalya Reinhold
Helane Levine-Keating	134	*Translation as Collaboration: Virginia Woolf, Katherine Mansfield, and S.S. Koteliansky* by Claire Davison

Sarah Terry	137	*Virginia Woolf and Music* by Adriana Varga
Kelly Walsh	142	*Modernism and Melancholia: Writing as Countermourning* by Sanja Bahun
Diana Swanson	146	*Ecocriticism and the Idea of Culture* by Helena Feder; *Ecocriticism and Women Writers: Environmentalist Poetics of Virginia Woolf, Jeanette Winterson, and Ali Smith* by Justyna Kostowska
Mark Hussey	151	*The Bloomsbury Group Memoir Club* by S. P. Rosenbaum
Maggie Humm	156	*Virginia Woolf, Art and Life* by Frances Spalding
Claire Battershill	160	*Modernism, Middlebrow and the Literary Canon* by Lise Jaillant
Emily James	163	*The Work of Revision* by Hannah Sullivan
Verita Sriratana	166	*Virginia Woolf and December 1910: Studies in Rhetoric and Context* Makiko Minow-Pinkney, ed.; *Virginia Woolf and the Problem of the Subject: Feminine Writing in the Major Novels* by Makiko Minow-Pinkney
Erica Johnson	171	*Modernism and The Rhythms of Sympathy* by Kirsty Martin
Annalee Edmondson	174	*Feminist Narrative Ethics* by Katherine Nash
Chris Schorr	177	*Virginia Woolf, Jane Ellen Harrison, and the Spirit of Modernist Classicism* by Jean Mills
Stephen Barkway	181	*Virginia Woolf's Garden* by Caroline Zoob

Jennifer Burns Bright	184	*The Bloomsbury Cookbook: Recipes for Life, Love and Art* by Jans Ondaatje Rolls
Dianne M. Hunter	188	*Literary Aesthetics of Trauma: Virginia Woolf and Jeanette Winterson* by Reina van der Wiel
Lorraine Sim	190	*A Mystical Philosophy: Transcendence and Immanence in the Works of Virginia Woolf and Iris Murdoch* by Donna J. Lazenby
Beth Rigel Daugherty	193	*Becoming Virginia Woolf* by Barbara Lounsberry
Randi Saloman	196	*Virginia Woolf: Experiments in Character* by Eric Sandberg
Jay Dickson	200	*Behind the Mask: The Life of Vita Sackville-West* by Matthew Dennison
	204	Notes on Contributors
	209	Submission Guidelines

Abbreviations

AHH	*A Haunted House*
AROO	*A Room of One's Own*
BP	*Books and Portraits*
BTA	*Between the Acts*
CDB	*The Captain's Death Bed and Other Essays*
CE	*Collected Essays* (4 vols.)
CR1	*The Common Reader*
CR2	*The Common Reader, Second Series*
CSF	*The Complete Shorter Fiction*
D	*The Diary of Virginia Woolf* (5 vols.)
DM	*The Death of the Moth and Other Essays*
E	*The Essays of Virginia Woolf* (6 Vols.)
F	*Flush*
FR	*Freshwater*
GR	*Granite & Rainbow: Essays*
JR	*Jacob's Room*
L	*The Letters of Virginia Woolf* (6 Vols.)
M	*The Moment and Other Essays*
MEL	*Melymbrosia*
MOB	*Moments of Being*
MT	*Monday or Tuesday*
MD	*Mrs. Dalloway*
ND	*Night and Day*
O	*Orlando*
PA	*A Passionate Apprentice*
RF	*Roger Fry: A Biography*
TG	*Three Guineas*
TTL	*To the Lighthouse*
TW	*The Waves*
TY	*The Years*
VO	*The Voyage Out*

About Face: The *Three Guineas* Photographs in Cultural Context

Rebecca Wisor

> [E]very image of the past that is not recognized by the present as one of its own concern threatens to disappear irretrievably.
> —Walter Benjamin, "Theses on the Philosophy of History"

I Pass in Review[1]

Jane Marcus's 2006 annotated edition of *Three Guineas* introduced many of Woolf's American readers to the work's five black-and-white photographs, four bearing images of contemporary British patriarchs.[2] Omitted from American editions beginning with the 1963 Harbinger edition, and from British ones with the 1968 printing of the Uniform edition, the photographs were restored to the latter with Michèle Barrett's 1993 Penguin composite edition of *A Room of One's Own* and *Three Guineas*.[3] While the appearance of Barrett's edition generated significant interest in the photographs, their generic captioning prompted scholars to read the images as anonymous, symbolic illustrations of Woolf's written arguments connecting fascism, patriarchy, and war. In 1998, Alice Staveley's archival research yielded crucial information about the subjects' identities, and her subsequent article gestured toward their immense cultural importance to Woolf's contemporary readership:

---

[1] Chapter 11 of US Army TC 3-21.5 identifies "pass in review" as the final step in a ceremonial battalion parade, in which the battalion passes before a reviewing party, rendering honors to the commander of troops and staff. The views expressed herein are those of the author and do not reflect the position of the United States Military Academy, the Department of the Army, or the Department of Defense.

[2] The first issue of the first British edition, published by the Hogarth Press on June 2, 1938, and the second issue of the first British edition (the Uniform edition), published November 1943, included five plates opposite pages 37, 39, 43, 113, and 220. The first American edition, published by Harcourt Brace on August 25, 1938, included five plates opposite pages 30, 32, 34, 94, and 184; see Kirkpatrick and Clarke. These photographs are notably absent from the truncated, Americanized version of *Three Guineas* published as "Women Must Weep" in the May-June 1938 issues of the *Atlantic Monthly*.

[3] Barrett's 1993 Penguin composite edition was the first of these reprints to restore all five plates to their original positions, labeled as "A General," "A University Procession," "A Judge," "An Archbishop," and "Heralds." The second British edition, a 1986 Hogarth photo-offset reprint introduced by Hermione Lee, included four rather than five plates, as did Lee's 1984 composite edition of *A Room of One's Own* and *Three Guineas*; in the latter edition, the photographs were reduced in size and rearranged to appear on two two-page spreads. Morag Shiach's 1992 World's Classics composite edition of *A Room of One's Own* and *Three Guineas* likewise included only four photographs in a two-page spread; see Kirkpatrick and Clarke.

> Far from comprising a series of faded and anonymous snapshots of late great men—a misperception enhanced by the distance of time or place, not to mention the somewhat grainy images reproduced in subsequent paperback editions—these men were not only very much alive in June 1938, they were also the reigning "chiefs" of the patriarchal enterprise spanning Empire, Government, Justice, and Religion. (4-5)

The subjects include former Prime Minister (and Chancellor of Cambridge University) Stanley Baldwin; then current Archbishop of Canterbury Cosmo Gordon Lang; then current Lord Chief Justice Gordon Hewart; Boer War hero and founder of the Boy Scouts General Robert Baden-Powell; and the State trumpeters of the Household Cavalry. That each man's image should have appeared on the 1930s-era cigarette cards that have been reproduced here, alongside the work's original photographs, further reinforces the extent to which these figures would have been recognized readily by Woolf's contemporary audience.[4]

Despite the importance of these subjects to British contemporary culture, and to a politically informed reading of the work, subsequent scholarship has run the gamut from demonstrating a casual disregard for their identities to an outright rejection of their materiality to the work itself, their names typically (if at all) recited as part of a ritualized, obligatory roll call conducted from the margins of the text.[5] Scholarly attention to the subjects themselves, and to the signifying power of their images for Woolf's readership, has been noticeably absent within Woolf studies, with the exception of Stuart Clarke's "The Lord Chief Justice and the Woolfs" which argues that each subject should be recognized "not just a pillar of the establishment, not just a name, not just a representative of the male order of things—but a real person, one whom she [Woolf] had read about in the newspapers, one whom she heard about from relations and friends, and one whom she had watched in action" (24). In their place has emerged a distinct preoccupation with the photographs' "generic," illustrative, parodic, and/or comedic effects in the years

---

[4] Cigarette cards, collectible trading cards issued in series and included by manufacturers to stiffen cigarette packs, were popular from the mid-nineteenth to twentieth centuries. Three of the five cards included here—those depicting Cosmo Gordon Lang (as Archbishop of Canterbury), Gordon Hewart (as Lord Chief Justice), and a State trumpeter of the Household Cavalry—are part of a 1937 Coronation series produced by British cigarette manufacturer John Player and Sons. The cigarette card rendering of Robert Baden-Powell is part of Alick P. F. Ritchie's 1926 "Straight Line Caricature" series, also produced by John Player and Sons, while that of Stanley Baldwin belongs to Phillips Godfrey's 1935 "In the Public Eye" series. Additional images from these, and other, cigarette card series are viewable through the online digital collections of the New York Public Library and the National Portrait Gallery.
[5] See, for example, Black, "Not a novel" 41-43, "Introduction" lvii, and *Virginia Woolf* 170; Knowles 95; Humm, *Modernist* 198 and "Virginia Woolf and Visual Culture" 227.

since the publication of Staveley's article.[6] Attention to the photographs' "strong comic dimension" (Briggs 324) has been especially pervasive, training readers to focus on the photographs' surface dimension and relegating the subjects (both literally and figuratively) to ancillary, decorative, and (ironically) feminized roles in the text.[7] This trend is problematic in light of its potential to erode and gradually erase historical knowledge of these subjects, as the omission of Staveley's findings from some recent studies of the photographs demonstrates.[8]

What is most noteworthy about the photographs that are physically embedded in the work is their subjects' minimal presence in the text, a deliberate strategy that liberates the image from its subordinate status to the written text, creating a visual language that operates in conjunction with, but whose meaning is not contingent on, written language.[9] On the surface, the photographs of British patriarchs seem to belong to a rather dull, because exceedingly familiar, class of images over which the eye is more prone to skim than be arrested. Yet however mute and "silent" (Gillespie 38) the subjects may appear to modern readers, each photograph nevertheless "immediately yields up those 'details' which constitute the very raw material of ethnological knowledge," what Roland Barthes has called *studium* (28). While successful transmission of these details has been impeded heretofore by the subjects' temporal (and, for non-British readers, cultural) remoteness, the problem is one of reception rather than conduction: that is to say, the photographs have lost their ideal audience, but not their ability to signify. Rather than "opaque representations

---

[6] A curious fact underscoring how thoroughly these subjects have been divested of bone and blood is the frequency with which they are reduced to inanimate objects: whether as "satirical *illustrations*" (Gualtieri 165; italics mine); "*illustrations* of masculine spectacle" (Pawlowski, "Seule" 8; italics mine); "*fetishes* of the symbolic. . . . timeless dead *icons* of patriarchy" (Humm, *Modernist Women* 198; "Virginia Woolf and Visual Culture" 227; "Cinema and Photography"; italics mine); "contemporary British *totems*" (Duffy and Davis 128; italics mine); or a *simulacrum* of reality" (Dickey 389; italics mine). For additional examples, see Gillespie; Wussow; Black, "Not a novel"; and Duffy and Davis.

[7] On the comic and/or parodic dimension of the photographs, see Burton; Bell, "A Room"; Briggs; Hartley; Neverow, "Freudian Seduction" and "Documenting"; Dickey; Hinnov; Warner; Sharpe; Black, "Introduction" lxi. Emily Dalgarno and R. S. Koppen, by contrast, call attention to the photographs' ideological and semiotic functions, respectively, while Jane Marcus ("Introduction"), Conor Tomas Reed, and Jean Mills attend to their political significance.

[8] See Berman and Coates.

[9] While Dalgarno calls attention to photographs' ability to "signify independently of the text" (169), she does not consider the implications of this principle to the photographs under consideration here. Moreover, her view of Woolf's subversive aesthetic, whereby image and text are de-coupled, is predicated on a familiar de-historicizing of the subjects: Woolf "deconstructs the relationship of image to text," her argument goes, "when she represents the functions of institutions not as generals, judges, and professors, but as decorations and costumes" (171).

which need the intervention of the text to yield their intended meanings," as has been argued (Gualtieri 175), I wish to suggest that the photographs paradoxically gesture toward the world *off* the page while visually reinscribing recent history *on* the page, and that Woolf relies on them as a kind of visual shorthand capable of triggering readers' associations and memories of the discursive field surrounding each figure—the recent speeches, policies, and/or rulings that would have been immediately accessible and familiar to her readers.[10]

Woolf's 1926 essay "The Cinema" captures her appreciation for how documentary filmmaking not only renders an objective portrait in perpetuity—"We are beholding a world which has gone beneath the waves," she writes in wonderment (2)—but how it functions as an aid to remembering, and thus immortalizing, the prewar past: "The war sprung its chasm at the feet of all this innocence and ignorance but *it was thus* that we danced and pirouetted, toiled and desired, thus that the sun shone and the clouds scudded, up to the very end" (2; italics mine). For Woolf's contemporary Walter Benjamin, documentary images are invested with a kind of moral imperative that their subjects be remembered; by activating the cognitive processes of image recognition, they invite viewers to take part in a preemptive gesture against their historical erasure. The *Three Guineas* photographs extend such an invitation to us, just as they did to Woolf's contemporary audience. "[E]very image of the past that is not recognized by the present as one of its own concern threatens to disappear irretrievably," Benjamin cautions in "Theses on the Philosophy of History" (255). For Benjamin and Woolf, moments both major and minor constitute the true stuff of history.[11] Woolf's reliance on newspapers and women's autobiographies and memoirs as source materials in *A Room of One's Own* and *Three Guineas* registers her sympathy with Benjamin's view that "nothing that has ever happened should be regarded as lost for history" (254). The latter's celebratory vision of a past that has "become citable in all its moments," in which each moment "becomes a citation *à l'ordre du jour*" (ibid.), is an enticing one to entertain in the context of Woolf's fiercely antiwar polemic: the militaristic connotation of "something mentioned in the day's dispatches" (Eiland and Jennings 398) invites us to regard the photographs as a kind of visual evidence, as domestic dispatches that testify to the pervasiveness of fascist, imperialist, and hyper-militarist discourses on the front lines of a soon-to-be-war-torn London.[12]

---

[10] Woolf's liberation of the image can be viewed as a significant anti-patriarchal technique, one of many in this text. For further discussion, see my "'My Country Is the Whole World': *Three Guineas* and the Culture of Pacifist Dissent," Ch. 3; Marcus, "Introduction"; Duffy and Davis; Winterhalter; Black, "Introduction"; and Lilly.

[11] In "Thinking back through Our Mothers," Jane Marcus finds common ground between Walter Benjamin and Virginia Woolf's subversive use of documentary history as a form of social and political resistance.

[12] Howard Eiland and Michael W. Jennings provide the following definitions of *citation à*

Each photograph, then, can be viewed as a citation of a specific individual implicated in the spread of these cancerous ideologies, and whose role in that regard would have been understood immediately by Woolf's contemporary readers. As Stuart Hall's work on documentary photography helps us understand, "the ideological concepts embodied in photos and texts in a newspaper . . . do not produce new knowledge about the world. They produce *recognitions* of the world as we have already learned to appropriate it" (qtd. in Dalgarno 171; italics in original). Thus, this essay is as much an attempt to resurrect (albeit partially) the historical and cultural materiality of these subjects as it is to reconstruct the kind of "*recognitions* of the world" Woolf sought to exploit among her contemporary readership through the deployment of these photographs.[13]

Woolf's only extant reference to the photographs, a diary entry from February 1932 in which she notes having "collected enough powder to blow up St. Paul's. It is to have 4 pictures" (*D4* 77), makes clear that their primary attraction for her lay in their "explosive," rather than comedic, potential. In addition to demonstrating that descriptive labels would have been unnecessary for a contemporary audience, letters that Woolf received from various correspondents following the publication of *Three Guineas* suggest that any comic effect generated by the photos had been produced as a result of their highly specific, rather than purportedly "generic," nature. Alfred Sayers, for example, commented on Woolf's inclusion of "LCJ, Head of Church, Baldwin at their best—a real triumph!" (qtd. in Snaith, "Wide Circles" 33), while Ray Strachey commended her for "pulverizing imbeciles in high places" (23). And while some respondents commented on the hilarity of the photographs, such as Emmeline Pethick-Lawrence, who applauded them as "a work of genius—simply delicious" (64), Judith Stephen, who called them "delightful" (24), and another correspondent, who hailed them "a perfect scream" (65), many others recognized their subversive, "explosive" potential: Nelly Cecil, for one, regarded the photos as "too amusing and deadly" (35), while a second correspondent referred to them as "dangerous stuff. Inflammable material . . . [to] rekindle suppressed and smouldering fires" (73). A review in the feminist journal *Time and Tide* likewise attributed the work's subversiveness to its photographs, remarking how "there are faces that should remain behind a veil . . . and she has dragged the veil away. A terrible sight. Indecent, almost obscene" (qtd. in Marcus, "No More Horses" 286, note 12). The responses of Woolf's contemporaries reveal their acute and immediate appreciation for how, by engineering such "an obvious

---

l'ordre du jour: "a citation to be taken up as (part of) the business of the day," "a citation of pressing concern at a given moment," and, "in a military context, to something mentioned in the day's dispatches" (398).

[13] For a fuller consideration of each subject, see my "'My Country is the Whole World': *Three Guineas* and the Culture of Pacifist Dissent," on which the current article is based.

titular effacement of these well-known men," Woolf was not merely "engaging in subversion," but "flirt[ing] with sedition" (Staveley 5).

The era's widespread curtailment of civil liberties may have provided the impetus for Woolf's turn to documentary photography as a form of cultural critique. Her position as a pacifist author and publisher, and as a champion of civil liberties, had familiarized her with the dangers attached to vociferous speech of the anti-patriarchal, anti-imperialist, and anti-militarist varieties.[14] As Celia Marshik argues in *British Modernism and Censorship*, ownership of the Hogarth Press had heightened the Woolfs' cautiousness about what, and whom, to publish, virtually rendering it "a panopticon wherein . . . [they] were forced to police themselves" (11). Of particular relevance to the Woolfs in this regard was the swelter of controversy—"a major political storm" (Street 216)—surrounding the drafting of the Incitement to Disaffection Bill in 1934, which Leonard would actively protest.[15] The bill was a supplement to the Incitement to Mutiny Act of 1797 that had been drafted in the wake of two mutinies at Nore and Invergordon, hastened by fears that a revolution like that of the French might spread to Britain (Street 215). The original Mutiny Act allowed for the prosecution of those who

> [m]aliciously and advisedly endeavour to seduce any Person or Persons serving in His Majesty's Forces, by Sea or Land, from his or their Duty and Allegiance to His Majesty, or to incite or stir up any such Person or Persons to commit any Act of Mutiny, or to make, or endeavour to make, any mutinous Assembly, or to commit any traitorous or mutinous Practice whatsoever. (MacColl and Wells 354)

Several changes to the wording of the bill in 1934 threatened to expand Government control over civil liberties, emendations of particular consequence to pacifists and publishers of pacifist materials: the change from "duty and allegiance" to "duty or allegiance," in particular, was regarded by many as "expressly directed against pacifist propaganda, which would not endeavour to seduce a man from singing 'God Save the King' (that is, 'allegiance'), but would endeavour to seduce him from dropping bombs on a town in an enemy country (that is, 'duty')"

---

[14] In 1915 she had watched the Lord Mayor of London order her brother-in-law's pacifist pamphlet, *Peace at Once,* be destroyed. She would take an active role in several proceedings regarding free speech in the thirties, speaking out in defense of Radclyffe Hall and Count Potocki de Montalk against obscenity charges, and in support of Rose Macaulay against libel charges. On the latter case, see Stuart Clarke's "Lord Chief Justice."

[15] This bill was roundly denounced by the Council for Civil Liberties, the Labour Party, the Society of Friends, and by several Christian peace organizations, as well as by radical publishers and educators, including Woolf's cousin, H. A. L. Fisher, who maintained that "the powers conferred on magistrates are excessive" ("Sedition Bill").

(MacColl and Wells 355). The second change made it an offense to possess any document the dissemination of which could foment rebellion or mutiny among service members, while a third would expand prosecutable offenses to include "preparations" (rather than "attempts") to seduce (ibid.). As many had feared, these legislative changes resulted in increased censorship of works, particularly those espousing an antiwar perspective. Woolf's deployment of photographs as a form of "visual shorthand" ensured the protection of her readers, whose mere possession of a more verbally explicit work would have left them open to prosecution under this revised bill. Moreover, this strategy allowed her to protect herself: had Woolf voiced her indictments of the particular leaders of Church and State, rather than picturing them "like police posters of the enemies of society" (Marcus, "Thinking Back" 6), she would have left herself vulnerable to charges of seditious libel, defined under British Common Law at the time as

> The expression in some permanent form of opinions made "with an intention to bring into hatred or contempt, or to excite disaffection against the King or the government and constitution of the United Kingdom as by law established, or either House of Parliament, or the administration of justice, or to excite British subjects to attempt otherwise than by lawful means the alteration of any matter in Church or State by law established, or to promote feelings of ill will and hostility between different classes. (O'Higgins 34)

The exceedingly broad terms of this definition made it a veritable "catch-all" for even the mildest forms of dissident speech, enabling it to be "interpreted in such a way that it could catch almost any criticism of the established institutions of society" (O'Higgins 34) during this time—a fact that underscores the potential risk that Woolf managed to circumvent through her strategic incorporation of documentary photographs.

That *Three Guineas* was written in the midst of the nation's heightened sensitivity to its imperial decline, and of increasing anti-British sentiment on the Continent, only would have exacerbated her susceptibility to such charges, given that the text directly violated the dictates of the era's massive, government-sponsored national self-marketing program, which aimed to promote a positive image of Britain abroad (Taylor 127). The seminal text on the dissemination of pro-British propaganda, "The Projection of England," established the guidelines for "project[ing] upon the screen of world opinion . . . a picture of herself" capable of restoring confidence in the modern British empire: of the "national institutions and virtues" deemed fitting for projection are included "The Monarchy," "Parliamentary Institutions," "The British Navy," "In national affairs—a tradition of justice, law and order," and "Oxford and St. Andrews" (Tallents 14-15). These mandates were consistent with those in place for the cinema during this period, compliance with which was overseen by the British Board of Film Censors, which ensured

> [t]hat the film industry depicted only a positive view of Britain for overseas consumption and an uncontroversial one for domestic audiences. Controversial politics, disparagement of public figures and institutions, particularly royalty, or anything likely to encourage disloyalty among native peoples in the Empire or otherwise bring British prestige into disrepute were all banned. (MacKenzie 78)

As the heart of "controversial politics," films possessing pacifist content were especially susceptible to censorship. Among the subjects banned in films were "the portrayal of royalty, judges, Ministers or high officials in an unbecoming or undignified manner; no living individual was to be lampooned, or public characters and institutions disparaged" (MacKenzie 77-78). Similar constraints governed theatre in the thirties: the Lord Chamberlain was authorized to refuse licensing of plays that he deemed "to represent on the stage in an invidious manner a living person, or any person recently dead," "to do violence to the sentiment of religious reverence," or "to be calculated to cause a breach of the peace" (Shellard and Nicolson 63).[16] Situating Woolf's pacifist polemic within the broader context of prohibitions against inflammatory artistic productions during the interwar period invites us to speculate as to the eminently practical considerations that may have informed her decision to deploy photographs in this work. Such a perspective allows us to acknowledge the exceeding importance of these particular subjects to Woolf's argument and the complex discursive and ideological fields that they were, and are, and will be, capable of signifying to Woolf's readers.

II About Face

Sir Robert Baden-Powell, "The Hero of Mafeking" and "The Chief Scout"

    Unlike the book's other photographic subjects, neither name nor title of Sir Robert Baden-Powell is referenced in the text of *Three Guineas*. In its stead are generic place markers: a reference to "dragoons" here (66) and fine-looking horses and cavalry soldiers there (10), with a tip of the hat to general officers added for good measure:

---

[16] See also John Johnston, *The Lord Chamberlain's Blue Pencil,* Chapter 7, and Anthony Aldgate and James C. Robertson, *Censorship in Theatre and Cinema.*

Great-grandfathers, grandfathers, fathers, uncles—they all went that way, wearing their gowns, wearing their wigs, some with ribbons across their breasts, others without. One was a bishop. Another a judge. One was an admiral. Another a general. One was a professor. Another a doctor. (*TG* 74)

Lt-Gen SIR R. BADEN-POWELL, Bart.

However, the book's incisive commentary on the seductive lure of military uniforms, ceremonies, and pageantry to induce young men to become soldiers directly evokes Sir Robert Baden-Powell's controversial paramilitary Scouting movement and the imperialist and militarist discourses surrounding it throughout its history. Central to Woolf's pacifist critique in *Three Guineas* is her staunch refutation of an essentialist view of masculinity: from the opening incantation of Wilfred Owen's poetry to the closing invocation of Prince Hubertus Lowenstein's lines—"it is not true to say that every boy at heart longs for war. It is only other people who teach it to us by giving us swords and guns, soldiers and uniforms to play with"—it is a social constructivist position that frames the text and most directly indicts Baden-Powell's Scouting movement (qtd. in *TG* 221). The "splendour" of military uniforms, she writes, "is invented partly in order to impress the beholder with the majesty of the military office, partly in order through their vanity to induce young men to become soldiers" (27). In *Three Guineas* and the later "Thoughts on Peace in an Air Raid" (1940), Woolf will argue that an antidote to this inducement is women's indifference, since "it is far harder for human beings to take action when other people are indifferent and allow them complete freedom of action, than when their actions are made the centre of excited emotion" (129). Woolf's use of a child to exemplify this phenomenon is particularly suggestive in light of her views on children's susceptibility to external influence: "The small boy struts and trumpets outside the window: implore him to stop; he goes on; say nothing; he stops" (ibid.).

A diary entry dated June 18, 1927 reveals Woolf's criticism of the parading scouts she saw during a trip to Hyde Park. "The church boys [the Church Lads' Brigade] were marching; officers on horses in their cloaks like equestrian statues," she observed. "Always this kind of scene gives me the notion of human beings playing a game, greatly, I suppose, to their own satisfaction" (*D3* 139). The editorial note reveals Woolf's subject to be a procession of 6,000 members of the Church Lads' Brigade, who marched from Wellington and Chelsea Barracks to the parade ground near the Marble Arch, where they were to be inspected by the Prince of Wales.[17] In addition to revealing Woolf's distaste for such military pageantry, her comments suggest a provocative collapsing of the boundaries between military officers and scouts, and between living soldiers and statuary, her invocation of the latter calling to mind the cloaked equestrian statue of the Duke of Cambridge, former Commander-in-Chief of the British Army (1856-95), located immediately adjacent to Horse Guards parade.

The name and image of Robert Stephenson Smyth Baden-Powell, first Baron Baden-Powell, the much-celebrated "hero of Mafeking" and founder of the Boy Scouts and Girl Guides, were well known to Woolf's readers. Best known for having protected the vulnerable border town of Mafeking from Boer attack for 219 days during the Boer War (Warren, "Robert" 114), Baden-Powell was elevated to "demigod" status, and his image given a place in Madame Tussaud's wax museum, after the British had secured a victory (Rosenthal 30-31). By 1918, Baden-Powell's Scouts and Guides had become "established features of national life in Britain and the empire, and, with variations, throughout the world" (Warren, "Robert" 116) while the spectacle of pageantry associated with Scouting during the 1920s ensured that "Baden-Powell loomed far larger in the public imagination than he had previously," winning him a baronetcy in 1922 (Jeal 511, 512). His reputation was so well established

---

[17] Other church organizations such as the Boys' Brigade and the YMCA used as their foundation Baden-Powell's early military manual, *Aids to Scouting* (1899), the product of his many years of scouting and reconnaissance work with the army; incidentally, Baden-Powell had served as VP of the Boys' Brigade in 1903 while planning his own organization (Warren, "Robert" 115).

by 1924 that biographer Eileen Wade did not consider it an exaggeration to describe him as a man "destined to have perhaps more widely reaching effect than that of any man since the founder of Christianity" (qtd. in Rosenthal 15). By 1937, nearly three million Scouts existed in 49 countries worldwide and, upon his death in 1941, he was "lauded as a figure of global significance, having founded the two largest youth organizations in the world" (Warren, "Robert" 117). His influence would extend well beyond his own time: Scouting attracted a membership of 350,000,000 males from its inception in 1908 to the present day (Daniels 22), and his Scouting manual, *Scouting for Boys,* sold "more copies worldwide than almost any other text, excluding the Bible" (Warren, "Robert" 115).[18]

Baden-Powell's critical role in the British victory over the Boers firmly associated him in the popular cultural imagination with a brand of imperial prowess then in decline. The period was characterized by an acute, persistent national anxiety over the strength of the Empire and the quality of British soldiers brought on in part by Britain's lackluster performance in the Boer War and exacerbated by General J. F. Maurice's 1902 statement alleging that the British race had so deteriorated that it could no longer produce men capable of serving as soldiers (Ross 198-200).[19] Given that "Victorian standards of manliness [were] thought crucial for colonial order" (Enloe 48), the perception of a declining masculinity among soldiers became cause for national concern. Despite later attempts to divorce Scouting from its military roots, Baden-Powell conceded that the Scouting movement's emphasis on physical education was a direct response to recruiting statistics that "show that an appallingly large proportion of our manhood is classed as C 3—medically unfit," as he wrote in a *Times* article in 1937 ("Lest We Run"). Inculcating in British youth the skills and qualities deemed essential to the preservation of the Empire, "Scouting and Guiding emerged as particularly potent imperial movements" (Proctor 606) designed to help consolidate imperial power. As Baden-Powell had secured the town of Mafeking during the Boer War, so would his Boy Scouts and Girl Guides secure the safety of England and protect the interests of her Empire.

The Boy Scouts and Girl Guides were established upon the premise that participation in group activities, adherence to a strong moral and spiritual code, and the cultivation

---

[18] Baden-Powell authored numerous books in addition to his most widely read Scouting manual, *Scouting for Boys: A Handbook for Instruction in Good Citizenship* (1910), which sold millions of copies and went into ten editions in his lifetime (Daniels 24).

[19] Such fears, it seems, were not entirely unwarranted, as "stunted stature" and poor dental health were so ubiquitous among British recruits during this conflict that the army had to modify its physical standards (Daniels 23). Among the causes generally blamed for racial deterioration were venereal disease, racial intermarriage, and declining birthrates (Enloe 50). Declining birthrates and anxiety over racial deterioration would prompt the government to introduce programs aimed at improving infant mortality and welfare, which resulted in the emergence of a powerful pronatalist movement at the outset of the Great War (Ross 198-201).

of a sense of brotherhood could create happier individuals and better citizens (Warren, "Robert" 117). Rather predictably, gender would play a central role in defining the very terms of that citizenship. Scouting thus emphasized the necessity for chivalry and bravery among boys, and the desirable aim of "breed[ing] manly men" ("Peace Aim of Scouting"), while Guiding emphasized girls' future roles as wives and mothers, and framed their participation in the preservation of the Empire in terms of the production of healthy children. For Woolf, this gendered vision of citizenship would have called to mind Mussolini's notion of "two worlds in the life of the nation, the world of men and the world of women" (qtd. in *TG* 213), a subject of considerable concern to her.[20]

Woolf's contemporaries, particularly those on the Left, easily recognized the paramilitary nature of the organization, which had been founded and was administered by military personnel and which had its origins in an imperial cadet corps and police force.[21] To these should be added its indebtedness to certain military conventions and traditions, including an emphasis on honor, the use of badges to distinguish rank and achievement, the grouping of individuals into small units or troops, the use of uniforms, and an emphasis on skills drawn from the battle ground, including scouting and reconnaissance.[22] Moreover, the organization has its origins in the Mafeking Cadet Corps and the South African Constabulary (SAC). The

---

[20] The development of the Girl Guides coincided with the emergence of a powerful pronatalist movement in Britain. Baden-Powell and his sister, Agnes (who would run the Girl Scouts until the post was assumed by his wife, Olave), laid out the principles of Guiding in *How Girls Can Help Build up the Empire: A Handbook for Girl Guides* (1912) (Warren, "Robert" 115-6). Both Woolf and Baden-Powell recognized the importance of child-bearing to the nation: while Baden-Powell held that girls' future roles as wives and mothers bestowed upon the Girl Guides "greater national importance than the Boy Scouts" ("Lest We Run"), Woolf urged women to resist pronatalist propaganda as a political gesture, noting how "one method by which she [the educated man's daughter] can help to prevent war is to refuse to bear children" (147); see also MHP B16.f, Vol. 3: 4.

[21] Criticism of Scouting's paramilitary aspects was rife during the 1920s and 1930s, particularly among the British Left. The Prince of Wales commented that "disciplined physical training is a form of 'militarism' or conducive to it" ("Peace and 'Pacifism'" 15) while Ramsay MacDonald refused in 1923 to serve on the Scout Council over concerns that those running the movement had intentions to militarize it (Springhall, "Baden-Powell and the Scout Movement" 940). Lady Shena Simon, in a Letter to the Editor included in Woolf's scrapbooks, similarly expresses concern over Lord Stanhope's appointment as President of the Board of Education given his connections with the military, and over whether "'the new drive for physical fitness in the schools is to be developed in close connection with the fighting Services'" (MHP B16.f, Vol. 3: 8).

[22] For further discussion of the idea that Scouting was created to form a new generation of soldiers, see Springhall, "Baden-Powell and the Scout Movement," "The Boy Scouts, Class and Militarism," and *Youth, Empire and Society*; Hynes; Gillis; Summers; Rosenthal, and MacDonald. For the opposing view, see Jeal and Warren.

former was comprised of boys from ages nine and up who would perform various duties in town—carrying messages, acting as orderlies, delivering mail, and serving as look-outs—thus freeing up the town's men for their military activities (Rosenthal 53). *Scouting for Boys* (1908) makes clear that these cadets served as exemplars of the kind of defensive service that Boy Scouts might be called upon to render in future conflicts (Rosenthal 162-63). Not coincidentally, the skills to be learned in Scouting were precisely those required for national defense: thus "every boy ought to learn how to shoot and obey orders, else he is no more good when war breaks out than an old woman" (qtd. in Rosenthal 162). As one historian observes, the South African Constabulary—"the world's largest mounted police force," which, by 1902, had become "a force of imperial control"—served as "the testing ground for many ideas later used in the Scouts and Guides" and as inspiration for Scouting's use of awards and medals, its moral code of honor, its uniform (it was SAC constables who first wore the trademark khaki shorts and shirts and Stetson hats associated with Boy Scouts), and its motto, "Be Prepared"—the initials of which are Baden-Powell's own (Proctor 608).[23]

The image of a militaristic organization was further promoted by the highly publicized military connections of its leaders. In 1910, 140 of the movement's 250 Presidents and Commissioners could be classified as either active or retired military officers, a number that had increased to 247 out of 352 by 1912 (Springhall, *Youth* 128; qtd. in Rosenthal 206). Chief among them was Sir Robert Baden-Powell, whose military exploits read like a list of imperial conquests. Much of what successfully associated Scouting with militarism in the popular imagination, however, was the fact that

> The outward and visible signs of Scouting were military: Scouts were organized in troops, and sub-divided into patrols; they wore uniforms, had parades, and did a little drill, they were led by officers, scoutmasters, patrol leaders, corporals. . . . Scouts' activities were also often military: they practised signaling, carried dispatches, went on trek, posted sentries around camp, and fought mock battles. (MacDonald 186-87)

Scouts were frequently referred to within the Press as Baden-Powell's "Model Army," while their image often appeared in advertisements, cigarette cards, picture books, paintings, and war posters in a military context, or accompanied by a military caption (MacDonald 188, 188-202). It must have outraged Woolf to learn that Baden-Powell had been selected as recipient of the 1937 Wateler Peace

---

[23] See Kathy Phillips's *Virginia Woolf against Empire* for a discussion of Baden-Powell's imperialist rhetoric as it relates to the character of Captain Brace in Woolf's short story "Scenes from the Life of a British Naval Officer" (235, 237-38).

Prize, granted to the individual "who had rendered the most valuable services to the cause of peace or had contributed to finding means of combating war" ("Wateler Peace Prize")—particularly in light of her views, discussed above, of how such "outward and visible signs" of militarism could lead directly to war.

The popular association of Scouting with militarism and patriotism was only further cemented through the Boy Scouts' visible involvement in the Great War. The war provided Scouts an opportunity to demonstrate their willingness to "[make] themselves into fine, reliable men, ready to take the place of those who have gone away to fight and who have fallen at the Front" (Baden-Powell, *Young Knights* 13). Recognizing that "a war requiring mobilization of the nation's resources created opportunities for trained civilian war-service by boys and girls" (Warren, "Robert" 116), Baden-Powell offered the Scouts' services to the government prior to the outbreak of war, and their help was enlisted in protecting communications lines and "coast watching" (Jeal 450). In addition to assisting the Coast Guard, Scouts were also active in guarding telephone and telegraph lines and railway bridges, carrying messages, and acting as wounded soldiers for VAD nurses in training (MacDonald 199). Trained in "cunning and unobtrusive" methods, it was argued that Boy Scouts could make themselves "essential to the war effort" since they could "act as gatherers of intelligence about enemy movements, and as message bearers across enemy lines" (Daniels 25). For their service on the home front during wartime, Scouts could even earn a "war service badge" for performing twenty-eight days of voluntary service (Rosenthal 228). The Great War also saw the founding of Baden-Powell's Scout Defense Corps, whose aim was to provide Scouts aged fifteen to seventeen with advanced training in shooting, signaling, entrenching, and basic infantry techniques, and for which training they would receive a red feather to be worn on their hats (ibid.). Scouts' contributions to the war effort were widely recognized; they received accolades from Prime Minister David Lloyd George and even had a chapter written about their heroic efforts in *The Times History of the War* (Jeal 456; MacDonald 201-2).

Scouts' service to the Empire virtually ensured that the movement would come to signify patriotism and nationalism and "the national symbols of the flag, the King, and Britannia" (MacDonald 195), an association strengthened by the well-publicized support they received from prominent politicians and members of the royal family. Among their supporters were the King, the Prince of Wales, the Archbishops of Canterbury, York, and Westminster, the Lord Chief Justice, Kitchener, and the Lord Mayor of London (MacDonald 196).

A letter from Woolf to Ottoline Morrell reveals her own association of Scouting with nationalism and organized religion: "I must break off, chiefly owing to the Boy Scouts who have camped in our field. . . " she writes. "They have a Union Jack, and go to Church. I wish one liked these things naturally" (*L2* 542). Woolf's reference to her inability to "naturally" like either one reiterates her view of militarism as a product of social conditioning, extending that logic to religion as well. Woolf was impatient with the ready collapsing of distinctions between God and Empire, repudiating the easy association made between the two on numerous occasions.[24] She would expose the institutionalization of this practice in *Three Guineas*, going so far as to expose the Church of England as a political instrument complicit in the perpetuation of war and the persecution of pacifists, a damning indictment that is evoked largely through the text's image of the Archbishop of Canterbury, Cosmo Gordon Lang.[25]

"The Voice of England": William Cosmo Gordon Lang, Archbishop of Canterbury [26]

In 1928, then Archbishop of York William Cosmo Gordon Lang assumed the highest religious position in the Church of England, becoming the 95th Archbishop of Canterbury and "the foremost representative of Christianity in England" (Ollard, Crosse, and Bond 321). Lang was to hold this position longer than any other Archbishop of Canterbury in the twentieth century, resigning only in 1942. His tenure, however, was distinguished by more than its exceptional length: his talents as a speaker, combined with the technological advances of radio broadcasting and an active involvement in matters of church and state, made him both a highly visible and highly audible figure in thirties' England. During his lifetime it was said that "the name of the Archbishop of Canterbury is to-day a household word throughout the inhabited globe" (Wilkinson 459).

That several events of great national and religious significance took place during his tenure no doubt added to his visibility: these included the 1930 Lambeth Conference, the death of King George V, the abdication of King Edward VIII, the coronation of King George VI, the rise of fascism, and the beginnings of the Second World War. He had close, well-publicized connections with monarchs and statesmen alike and his reputation as a public figure of national importance perhaps equaled that of his reputation as a religious one. His entry in the *Oxford Dictionary of*

---

[24] The connection between nationalism and religion is made concrete in a passage of *Three Guineas* in which she acidly remarks, "You will have to wear certain uniforms and profess certain loyalties. If you succeed in those professions the words 'For God and the Empire' will very likely be written, like the address on a dog-collar, round your neck" (85). In a footnote to this passage, she remarks how "those who thus ticket themselves see some connection between the Deity and the Empire, and hold themselves prepared to defend them" (194). "Is God English?" she had asked herself rhetorically in her typewritten notes for *Three Guineas* (MHP B16.f, Vol. 1: 39).
[25] See Wisor for a discussion of pacifism and the role of the Church of England during the interwar period.
[26] Stanley Baldwin, qtd. in Hastings 248.

National Biography attributes much of his visibility in the thirties to such public roles, noting how "His bell-like voice at the coronation had become familiar through film and wireless. He had close relationships with public figures, including Baldwin, Chamberlain, and Halifax. But it was above all his involvement in international questions and royal affairs which made him well known to the public" (Wilkinson 459). When King George V died, Lang presided over the funeral ceremony and it was his voice that was "clearly heard throughout the world" (Lockhart 395); when Edward VIII abdicated the throne, it was again Lang whose broadcast Baldwin claimed represented "the voice of England"; and when George VI became King, it was Lang who "produced" and officiated at his coronation.[27]

Of the many faces that Lang appeared capable of conjuring, however, "it was the proud, pompous prelate that, by the thirties, appeared to the world to have long prevailed" (Hastings 250). This impression was only strengthened when, on 13 December 1936, he made a radio broadcast on the abdication of King Edward VIII which was perceived by many as being highly critical of Edward, "like kicking a man when he was down" (Wilkinson 460). Despite Stanley Baldwin's assertion that Lang had spoken the "voice of England" in his broadcast, "such emotional

[27] Lang's familiarity with the royal family was unprecedented (Hastings 248; Wilkinson 457): he was made honorary chaplain to Queen Victoria in 1896; baptized Queen Elizabeth II as Archbishop of York; and boasted close connections to King George V, Queen Mary, and King George VI. Upon King George V's death in 1936, Lang would eulogize him as "a very dear friend" ("Convocation of Canterbury, Loyal Tributes"). The relations were perhaps closer than many imagined: it was Lang who had drafted the King's last two Christmas broadcasts and his Silver Jubilee broadcast, as well as the messages given by Queen Mary following his death and the abdication of her son, Edward VIII (Wilkinson 459).

moralizing at a moment when everyone felt bruised and in need of silence was far too histrionic to be the voice of England, too judgmental to be authentically Christian" (Hastings 248). This speech, moreover, left the nation with the impression that Lang had played a far more significant role than was the case in getting King Edward to abdicate, thereby igniting animosity in the hearts of many Britons, who booed him when he arrived at Downing Street to visit Baldwin on December 6, 1936 (Wilkinson 460). He acquired a reputation for having a "prelatical" side and a "weakness for people of rank or importance" (Lockhart 328), and his personality was said to combine "unctuousness with snobbery in a way that left a bad taste in many people's mouths" (Hastings 251).

The Archbishop's love of ceremony and elaborate costumes, along with his important social connections, were well known to the public: he was the first Archbishop of Canterbury since the time of the Reformation to wear cope and mitre (Lockhart 315; Ollard, Cross, and Bond 321-2) and the first to standardize the cope as "normal liturgical dress for bishops and archbishops" (Hylson-Smith 273). Among church historians, Lang is known for having "catholicized" the Church of England by implementing ceremonial changes known as the "Six Points," which introduced the wearing of Eucharistic vestments, the lighting of candles on the altar, the use of wafers rather than bread for Communion, the eastward positioning of the celebrant, the ceremonial mixing of water and wine in the chalice, and the use of incense (ibid.). In light of these facts, it is significant that the Archbishop makes his appearance in *Three Guineas* wearing "full canonicals" and presiding over an elaborate ceremony involving the Lord Mayor, "with turtles and sheriffs in attendance, tapping nine times with his mace upon a stone" (120).[28] Woolf's scrapbooks contain additional verbal and visual illustration of religious finery, including a photograph of the Pope on his throne (MHP B16.f, Vol. 2: 44) and a typewritten description of a church service at St. Paul's, in which she remarks on the canon's sermon, on "tradesmen who deal in the paraphernalia of religion," that this is "true of the canon" as well, who, she observes, is wearing "different hood, red bands. Some have satin or plush" (MHP B16.f, Vol. 2: 55).

Lang presided over two particular events that revealed his affinity for ceremony, ritual, and pageantry: his "enthronement" as Archbishop of Canterbury and the coronation ceremony of King George VI.[29] "Delight[ing] in the ancient rites of Church and State," Lang's orchestration of, and officiation at, George VI's coronation ceremony won the attention of the nation (Ollard, Cross, and Bond 321-2). After eight rehearsals in Westminster Abbey, the coronation took place on May 12, 1937,

---

[28] Woolf's scrapbooks contain a description and photograph of the pageantry surrounding the Lord Mayor's Show (MHP B16.f, Vol. 3: 61).
[29] For more on the ritual and symbolic changes made to Lang's enthronement ceremony, see Lockhart and Carpenter.

the first ever to be filmed and radio broadcast (Lockhart 414). Lang noted afterward that some said truthfully that he had "produced" the coronation, and reflected as to "whether any event in history has ever been so *realised* throughout the whole world" (Lockhart 415, 421). Observing Britons' declining interest in the church, Lang regarded the coronation as an opportunity to wed church and state and even masterminded an evangelistic campaign, "A Recall to Religion," to coincide with it, asking people to "dedicate themselves with their King to the service of God and their country" (Lockhart 398). Woolf's comments in her scrapbook on the canon's sermon record, in telegraphic shorthand, the archbishop's message:

> Primate's message. Whither are we going? Losing or holding the foundations of our nations [sic] life. Our blessins [sic] (money) depend on touch with him. all together must fight for the soul of England. What can we do? Primate says you each one can be a link in the chain that binds England to God. So simple. Pray habitually; open the mind daily, public worship on Sunday through the ennobling and enabling power of Jesus be a link that binds. (MHP B16.f, Vol. 2: 55-56)

Despite Woolf's notoriously poor typing, her impressions of the sermon, and the archbishop's message, are fairly clear: "Mere fulsome and filthy playactoring feeble rhetoric," she commented.[30]

The church's intransigent position on the subject of women's ordination and the historic role played by the church in women's personal and public subordination to men, however, form the two heads of the large bone that Woolf wanted to "pick" with Lang in *Three Guineas.* The church's position on women's ministry was made public in a series of published reports that emerged from the Lambeth Conferences of 1920 and 1930 and from the subsequent committee appointed by the Archbishops of Canterbury and York to "'examine any theological or other relevant principles which have governed or ought to govern the Church in the development of the Ministry of Women'" (qtd. in *TG* 143). While the 1930 Lambeth Conference can be said to have taken a remarkably progressive (and well publicized) position on contraception, it simultaneously reasserted marriage laws and restricted women's capacity to serve within the Church of England (Lockhart 349-50, 398). Moreover, the report produced by the 1930 Conference included a long paragraph detailing the theological grounds for objections to women's admission to the priesthood; while recommending that women's role in the church be enlarged, it simultaneously restricted their role to that of deaconesses rather than increasing their rights and privileges (Lockhart 347, 352). Church historians identify the 1930 Lambeth

---

[30] The original reads: "Mere fultosme [sic] and fltithy [sic] p ayactoring [sic] feeble rhetoric" (MHP B16.f, Vol. 2: 56).

Conference as having dealt "a severe blow" to women (Petre 25) for reasons that stem from the decade's previous Conference, when the preparatory committee had determined the order of deaconess to be a holy order, with the result that many women ordained in the twenties had believed themselves to be receiving holy orders (ibid.). Further confusion resulted from the committee's ambiguity as to the actual role of deaconesses within the church: while they were allowed to "lead in prayer" and "instruct and exhort the congregation" with the permission of the bishop, they were not permitted to read from the gospel or to assist with the chalice, as these tasks were reserved explicitly for male deacons. Seeking to clarify this confusion, the 1930 Lambeth Conference declared deaconesses to be "outside the historic order of the ministry," a move that would effectively disenfranchise women in the church.[31]

Woolf's discussion of this historic debate over women's exclusion from the ministry is rooted in her arguments about the professionalization of the priesthood. She is careful to point out that in the early church, the priesthood "was originally open to anyone who had received the gift of prophecy. No training was needed; the professional requirements were simple in the extreme—a voice and a market-place, a pen and paper" (*TG* 146-7). She goes on to show how the resulting professionalization of the priesthood would ensure the "extinction" of prophetesses, the erasure of their existence from religious history books, and the eradication of any further role for women as paid ministers of the church. Several clippings in Woolf's scrapbooks pertain directly to her argument: one about a meeting of the Anglican Group for the Ordination of Women, at which "custom" was identified as the sole "barrier to the admission of women to the ministry" and another in which clergymen's wives are referred to as "the unpaid curates of the Church" (MHP B16.f, Vol. 3: 49, 48).

The recently published findings of the third Commission would form the foundation of Woolf's arguments as to the existence of both a "money motive" for the exclusion of women from the priesthood and the existence of an "infantile fixation" among its male leaders. Her intensive analysis of the *Report of the Archbishops' Commission on the Ministry of Women* yields extensive evidence of the lengths to which church leaders and committee members would go—in blatant disregard for the teachings of the New Testament and the traditions of the early church—in order to attempt to justify their exclusion of women and thereby secure their own status and livelihood. Woolf viewed women's exclusion from "that profession which, since it is the highest of all, may be taken as the type of all, the profession of religion" (143) as emblematic of women's broader exclusion from the professions, including "the priesthood of medicine or the priesthood of science" (151-52).

---

[31] It would not be until the 1968 Lambeth Conference that the role of deaconess would be officially recognized as a holy order and November 11, 1992 that women obtained the right to be ordained as priests in the Church of England (Petre 25).

Women's exclusion from the priesthood exemplified the machinations of the "infantile fixation" at work in the world: "'Miss' may carry with it . . . the savour of scent or other odour perceptible to the nose on the further side of the partition and obnoxious to it. What charms and consoles in the private house may distract and exacerbate in the public office. The Archbishops' Commission assures us that this is so in the pulpit" (62). As proof, she supplies the conclusion of the Archbishops' Commission that "it would be impossible for the male members of the average Anglican congregation to be present at a service at which a woman ministered without becoming unduly conscious of her sex" (191) and their conclusion that "the general mind of the Church is still in accord with the continuous tradition of a male priesthood" (148).[32]

Women's exclusion from the profession of the priesthood calls to Woolf's mind, and to the reader's attention, a further wrong committed by that body in the past: for "the influence of religion upon women's education, one way or another, can scarcely be overestimated," she writes (180). Citing the biographies of Mary Astell and Mary Butts, Woolf recounts the church's active efforts in centuries past to intervene in the education of women, both by obstructing the founding of women's colleges and by espousing the view that "desire for learning in woman was against the will of God" (ibid.). She goes on to show that the scriptural basis for the church's exclusion of women in the past—St. Paul's view of chastity as expressed in his Letter to the Corinthians—remains the basis upon which women continue to be excluded from educational opportunities. In what is surely one of the text's most dramatic moments, she connects the figure of Paul—and with him the whole of the church's authority—with the figure of fascism, remarking how "he was of the virile or dominant type, so familiar at present in Germany, for whose gratification a subject race or sex is essential" (198).

Stanley Baldwin, "The Most Respected Figure in British Public Life" [33]

Stanley Baldwin, leader of the Conservative party from 1923 to 1937 and Prime Minister in 1923-24, 1924-29, and 1935-37, appears frequently throughout the text of *Three Guineas*. That Baldwin is referred to in Woolf's essay "This is the House of Commons" as "a country gentleman poking pigs" (59) invites us to imagine him, along with Maynard Keynes, as a potential source of inspiration for Woolf's correspondent in *Three Guineas,* who, "instead of turning on your pillow and prodding your pigs," is "writing letters, attending meetings, presiding over this

---

[32] Woolf attributes the dwindling number of female churchgoers with their exclusion from the church (*TG* 139, 212). The Monks House scrapbooks contain further evidence of Woolf's interest in women's absenting themselves from the church as a political gesture (MHP B16.f, Vol. 1: 63; Vol. 3: 49; and Vol. 1: 54).
[33] Williamson, "Reputation" 131.

and that, asking questions, with the sound of the guns in your ears" (6).³⁴ The text of *Three Guineas* is laced with evidence of Baldwin's activities during the thirties, which included writing letters to *The Times* soliciting funds for Newnham College; hosting meetings at 10 Downing Street for the same cause; and delivering speeches and radio broadcasts on subjects as diverse as universities, women's professions, the British Empire, and fascism. Woolf's correspondent, we are told, "began . . . . [his] education at one of the great public schools and finished it at the university" (ibid.)—a detail that further aligns him with Stanley Baldwin, who attended Harrow and Cambridge, and who assumed the Chancellorship of Cambridge University in 1930 (Middlemas and Barnes 574). Including a photograph of Baldwin in his capacity as Chancellor allows Woolf to gesture toward the pageantry and ceremony central to these institutions and to invoke contemporary discourses regarding educational and professional opportunities for women, imperial decline, and the fascist threat to democracy.

Given that most citizens "could only 'know' and respond to political leaders through their constructed and projected public characters, especially as revealed by speeches and media presentation," and since "politicians are what they speak and publish" (Williamson, *Conservative* 15), Baldwin's public character was largely established through the image he projected in his speeches and addresses, many of which were delivered via radio broadcast and reprinted verbatim in national, local, and organizational newspapers, or printed as pamphlets (Williamson, *Conservative* 154).³⁵ The advent of radio broadcasting during this time meant, furthermore, that

---

[34] The trivia question that appears at the bottom of the cigarette card bearing Baldwin's image suggests that his reputation as a gentleman farmer was known widely in 1935, the year in which this card was issued by Phillips Godfrey.

[35] Selections from his speeches were published in four volumes that appeared just prior to

in contrast to Lloyd George and Bonar Law, "the personalities of Baldwin and MacDonald, as matters of public interest and inquiry, probably occupied the time and readership of the electorate more than any since Gladstone and Disraeli in the infancy of the modern political system" (Middlemas and Barnes 479).[36] Thus, during the General Strike of 1926, "the first occasion in Britain when a national crisis was acted out on the radio," Woolf would record in writing those features of his speech that she connected with the presence of an increasingly violent "male political authority" within the government (Lee, *Virginia Woolf* 534-5):

> Baldwin broadcast last night: he rolls his rs; tries to put more than mortal strength into his words. "Have faith in me. You elected me 18 months ago. What have I done to forfeit your confidence? Can you not trust me to see justice done between man & man?" Impressive as it is to hear the voice of the Prime Minister, descendant of Pitt & Chatham, still I can't heat my reverence up to the right pitch. I picture the stalwart oppressed man, bearing the world on his shoulders. And suddenly his self assertiveness becomes a little ridiculous. He becomes megalomaniac. No I don't trust him: I don't trust any human being, however loud they bellow & roll their rs. (*D3* 81)

In addition to her gifts of mimicry and wit, one recognizes in this criticism her view of men's public speech as a form of game playing or posturing involving the use of excessive verbal force: here, Baldwin exemplifies that "monstrous male, loud of voice, hard of fist, childishly intent upon scoring the floor of the earth with chalk marks" (*TG* 125). The connection between such acts of speech and the warlike preparations being made by Baldwin's government in response to the General Strike would have been readily apparent to Woolf, and further illustration of the inseparability of the private and public realms.[37]

and during the period under discussion: these included *On England and Other Addresses* (1926), *Our Inheritance, Speeches and Addresses* (1928), *This Torch of Freedom* (1935), and *Service of Our Lives, Last Speeches as Prime Minister* (1937). These volumes sold well, and were reprinted in cheap editions between 1935 and 1938. *On England* was reissued in paperback by Penguin in 1937, while extracts from the last three volumes, edited by R. Bennett, appeared in 1937 under the title *This Torch I Would Hand to You* (Williamson, *Conservative* 154, 366).

[36] Two events, in particular, would place Baldwin at the center of considerable public controversy during the mid-thirties: his support for the 1935 Hoare-Laval Pact that proposed the partitioning of Abyssinia—about which then Secretary of State for War Duff Cooper wrote, "I have never witnessed so devastating a wave of public opinion" (193)—and his refusal to introduce a bill in favor of morganatic marriage in December 1936, which was perceived by the public as having unceremoniously forced Edward VIII's hand in favor of abdication.

[37] "Baldwin's government organised as for war, energised by a ferociously anti-working-class

Woolf's arguments regarding women's educational opportunities often give the appearance of having been composed in direct conversation with Baldwin himself. Her attention to the sacrifices made by the daughters of educated men on behalf of their brothers' education can be read as a feminist revision of Baldwin's view of University history. Absent from his public remarks on University members' debts to their predecessors, for example, is any mention of their indebtedness to their sisters, mothers, and grandmothers:

> Great have been your privileges; learning, old and new, has been yours to grasp and you have unconsciously been drinking in the traditions of the ages and breathing the influence of centuries of high endeavour. On you above all of your generation, on you, members of the universities, it rests to repay, as far as you are able, and each in his vocation the debt you owe to those who have gone before you, and who, by their piety and forethought, made it possible for you to obtain these blessings. You go out into all the world—in the Church, in Medicine, and in Law, in the Civil Service of this country, of India, and of the Colonies, in a hundred trades and businesses. And wherever you go you will influence your fellows because of your sojourn here. ("Freedom and Discipline" 285)

Here, of course, are the central themes of the first chapter of *Three Guineas*: how access to such tradition, influence, and privilege is extended to the sons of educated men, but refused the daughters of educated men; how such benefits are obtained at the expense of those same daughters; and how educational opportunity leads directly to professional opportunity, wealth, and influence.

The "fabulous proportions" (33) of the incomes of Oxford and Cambridge, detailed in several places throughout *Three Guineas*, serve as a stark reminder of the financial destitution of women's colleges, whose treasurers relied on public fundraising appeals to raise money for the renovation and expansion of their facilities. Woolf's scrapbooks abound with evidence of her interest in the contrasting state of financial affairs at men's and women's colleges, often positioned in close proximity to one another.[38] In contrast with men's colleges, women's colleges

Churchill (Virginia Woolf saw his armoured tanks on the streets, and heard the rumours about his plans for using tear gas) and a reactionary Home Secretary, Joynson-Hicks" (Lee, *Virginia Woolf* 532). Much of the Strike's impact on onlookers would have been the result of the fact that "the war was so recent" and that "so many of the strikers, and the workers who helped to break the strike, had fought for their country" (Lee, *Virginia Woolf* 533).

[38] The index to Volume Two, for example, includes the heading "Newnham wants money to rebuild" in close proximity to entries detailing "Oxfords [*sic*] income" and "More money for Universities" from the state (MHP B16.f, Vol. 2: 14, 19). Volume One reveals a similar

suffered doubly from the relative poverty of their alumni: "The old students are supporting their college generously," one such solicitation letter from Newnham College ran, "but they are not themselves wealthy" ("Newnham College" 10). In his position as Chancellor of Cambridge, Baldwin was involved actively in soliciting much-needed funds for both Girton and Newnham College ("Women at Cambridge"; "Newnham College"), including the campaign spearheaded by Woolf's friend and Principal of Newnham, Pernel Strachey. Strachey's letter of February 1936, included among Woolf's scrapbooks (MHP B16.f, Vol. 2: 7), would serve as the real-life basis for the "fictional" letter from an honorary treasurer "asking for money with which to rebuild her college" in *Three Guineas* (39). The poverty of women's colleges, women's exclusion from the public sphere, and the perpetuation of war are conjoined in this letter, which announces a meeting to discuss Newnham's fundraising campaign to be held at the center of British political life: "the Prime Minister, who is also Chancellor of the University of Cambridge, has most kindly consented to arrange for a Meeting concerned with the needs of Newnham College to be held under his Chairmanship at 10, Downing Street on March 31st" (MHP B16.f, Vol. 2: 7).

A footnote to *Three Guineas* directing the reader to "compare Mr. Baldwin at Downing St. (March 31st, 1936.)" (181) draws attention to Baldwin's advocacy of women's education and their employment in the Civil Service.[39] The comparison Woolf prompts the reader to make here is with Walter Bagehot, who had refused Emily Davies's request to assist in the founding of Girton College and who supported women's employment only "as *labourers* or in other *menial* capacity" (ibid.). Baldwin's comments supporting women's employment in the Civil Service also form the rhetorical centerpiece of the mock trial of *Baldwin* v. *Whitaker* staged by Woolf in the second chapter of the book. She uses his personal testimony as to women's "industry, capacity, ability and loyalty" (60) in the Civil Service profession to disprove her conjecture that the economic disparity in men's and women's earning potentials may be due to some deficiency on women's part: "it may be, to

preoccupation with the financial and physical state of women's colleges, juxtaposing on a single page a report of a room at Somerville "over run with mice" with a second report that "Somerville received with pathetic gratitude the £7,000 which went to it last year from the Jubilee gift and a private bequest" (MHP B16.f, Vol. 1: 46).

[39] Although Woolf was not in attendance at the March 31, 1936 meeting at which his remarks were made—she notes in her diary, "I wished I had gone to Downing St. to hear Baldwin on Newnham" (*D5* 21)—it appears that she later requested information on this speech from the Women's Service Library. In a letter dated July 3, 1937, the librarian, Vera Douie, writes, "I am sending you a copy of the report on Mr. Baldwin's speech about women in the Civil Service which appeared in the 'Daily Telegraph' on April 1st, 1936" (Pawlowski, "The Virginia Woolf and Vera Douie Letters" 11). Woolf quotes extensively from this report throughout the second section of *Three Guineas*.

speak bluntly, that the daughters are in themselves deficient; that they have proved themselves untrustworthy; unsatisfactory; so lacking in the necessary abilities that it is to the public interest to keep them to the lower grades" or that they are intellectually inferior to men (59). Woolf uses the evidence supplied by Baldwin's personal testimony to contrast the reality of women's ability with the reality of how they continue to be treated by their brothers, a distinction that demonstrates the persistence of the separate spheres doctrine and the existence of the "infantile fixation." Since "both boards and divisions transmit human sympathies, and reflect human antipathies," it is "quite possible that the name 'Miss' transmits through the board or division some vibration which is not registered in the examination room. 'Miss' transmits sex; and sex may carry with it an aroma" (62). The existence of this aroma "allows us to decide in the case of *Baldwin* v. *Whitaker* that both the Prime Minister and the *Almanack* are telling the truth. It is true that women civil servants deserve to be paid as much as men; but it is also true that they are not paid as much as men" (64).

The advent of imperial radio broadcasts and frequent imperial "gatherings" in the thirties meant that, by 1937, Baldwin "was regarded in the Dominions as well as Britain as the foremost *imperial* statesman of his time" (Williamson, *Conservative* 260; italics in original). That Woolf regarded him in much the same way is suggested by her decision to include in her scrapbooks a newspaper clipping detailing his final speech as Prime Minister on the occasion of the Empire Day and Coronation banquet, in which he "revealed his intense personal faith in the triumph of its [the Empire's] ideals" (MHP B16.f, Vol. 3: 7). His speeches regularly evoked celebratory images of a unified, patriarchal Empire whose "greatest days . . . still lay ahead" (qtd. in Williamson, *Conservative* 261) despite indications to the contrary. The preservation of imperial prowess was regarded in these speeches as essential to the preservation of peace, for "no greater blow could befall the peace of the world than the disablement of the British Commonwealth of Nations" ("Unto Whomsoever" 27).

If the health of the British Empire was seen as pivotal to world peace, then the health of Britain was regarded as the sole guarantor of freedom against the threat of totalitarianism. In a letter to Tom Jones, Baldwin maintained that "we are the only defenders left of liberty in a world of Fascists" (qtd. in Williamson, *Conservative* 319) and, in a 1935 speech, he claimed that more than any other nation, "we are today the guardians and the trustees for democracy [and] ordered freedom" (qtd. in Williamson, *Conservative* 332). Williamson notes that Baldwin's concern with the threat of totalitarianism surpassed that of the ordinary, and became the "keynote in a series of valedictory addresses on leaving office in 1937" (*Conservative* 317). Because Baldwin was always sensitive to the threat that "imported foreign ideas"—key among them fascism and communism—potentially posed to British democracy and freedom, a "sense of international infection" became a "principal feature of Baldwin's public doctrine, and his most favoured political instrument" (ibid.) during this time. Thus he would refer to fascism and communism—those "alien plants—for they neither have their roots in England" ("Our Freedom" 23)—as external threats against which Britons must protect themselves. *Three Guineas* supplies evidence in direct refutation of such claims, arguing instead that the dictator "is here among us, raising his ugly head, spitting his poison, small still, curled up like a caterpillar on a leaf, but in the heart of England" (65). The lines that follow take on added significance when we consider that they may, after all, have been addressed to Baldwin himself. "Should we not help her to crush him in our own country before we ask her to help us to crush him abroad?" she asks her male correspondent. "And what right have we, Sir, to trumpet our ideals of freedom and justice to other countries when we can shake out from our most respectable newspapers any day of the week eggs like these?" (65-6).

"His name . . . a household word throughout the land": Sir Gordon Hewart [40]

Of the photographic subjects who appear in *Three Guineas,* the identity of Gordon Hewart has received the most extensive historical restoration for a contemporary audience, thanks to Stuart Clarke's 2003 article in *Virginia Woolf Miscellany.*[41] His piece documents the Woolfs' references to several prominent cases over which Hewart had presided during the twenties and thirties: namely, the much-publicized murder trial of Edith Thompson and Freddy Bywaters (1922) and the libel trials of Marie Stopes (1923), Count Potocki de Montalk (1932), and Rose Macaulay (1936).[42] Limiting his attention to those trials for which we possess "direct evidence" (15) of Woolf's interest (in the form of diary entries and letters), however, Clarke is forced to omit many of Hewart's significant cultural interventions that would have been familiar to Woolf and her contemporaries.

Gordon Hewart was known widely as a skilled, learned orator, who had by the 1920s earned a reputation as "the best after-dinner speaker in London" (Jackson 291): "a well-known establishment figure for his public pronouncements" (Clarke, "Lord Chief Justice" 15) as much as for his judicial ones, both of which appeared frequently in the press. Hewart's figure is evoked most notably in *Three Guineas* in Woolf's extensive quotation of his toast before the Royal Society of St. George, celebrating England as the "home" of liberty and democracy. Hewart's

---

[40] Lord Caldecote, qtd. in "Lord Hewart: Tributes at the Law Courts."
[41] Woolf's decision to include Hewart's photograph is briefly addressed in Alice Wood's recent *Virginia Woolf's Late Cultural Criticism* (2013), 77-78.
[42] Clarke identifies Woolf as a signatory to two letters sent to the newspaper on the subject of obscenity, and a third on the subject of libel, "Authors and the Law of Libel: A Plea for Reform" published in *The Times* ("Lord Chief Justice" 24, 20).

LORD CHIEF JUSTICE OF ENGLAND

speech provocatively establishes a causal connection between men's educational and professional opportunities and their patriotic obligation, observing how "Englishmen are proud of England. For those who have been trained in English schools and English universities, and who have done the work of their lives in England, there are few loves stronger than the love we have for our country" (qtd. in *TG* 12). The transcript of Hewart's remarks is included in two separate newspaper clippings that Woolf archived in her scrapbooks (MHP B16.f, Vol. 2: 3, 12), a fact that further suggests the importance of the "Lord Chief Justice's point of view" (*TG* 13) as a springboard for her inquiries into whether the educated man's sister shared the same obligations as her brother in light of her impoverished educational and professional opportunities.[43] As the head of the British legal system, Gordon Hewart is, moreover, the figure closest to the physical embodiment of Law, and it is in this role as creator and enforcer of the Law that Hewart is cast by Woolf as a modern-day Creon, who "held that 'disobedience is the worst of evils,' and that 'whomsoever the city may appoint, that man must be obeyed, in little things and great, in just things and unjust'" (*TG* 201). "It is easy to squeeze these characters into up-to-date dress," she continues, a reference no doubt to Hewart's actual photograph and to the verbal portrait of him included in Woolf's scrapbook, in which

---

[43] "The educated man's sister—what does 'patriotism' mean to her? Has she the same reasons for being proud of England, for loving England, for defending England? Has she been 'greatly blessed' in England? History and biography when questioned would seem to show that her position in the home of freedom has been different from her brother's .... Therefore her interpretation of the word 'patriotism' may well differ from his. And that difference may make it extremely difficult for her to understand his definition of patriotism and the duties it imposes. It seems plain that we think differently according as we are born differently; there is a Grenfell point of view; a Knebworth point of view; a Wilfred Owen point of view; a Lord Chief Justice's point of view and the point of view of an educated man's daughter" (*TG* 12-13).

he is described as "wearing scarlet and ermine robes and full-bottomed wigs surmounted by black caps" (MHP B16.f, Vol. 3: 61).

Hewart retains the reputation of having been "one of the least satisfactory holders of the office" (Blom-Cooper and Morris, 123 note 38), "a formidable pocket despot whose benevolence was a veneer" (Jackson 295). He is remembered by historians for having been "perhaps the worst Lord Chief Justice of England since the seventeenth century" on account of his "arbitrary and unjudicial behavior," which had "somewhat tarnished" the highest juridical position in the land by the close of his tenure in 1941 (Heuston 603-4). Leonard Woolf, who had attended Count Potocki de Montalk's obscenity trial, regarded Hewart as "a typical example of a High Court judge suffering from the occupational disease of sadistic, vindictive self-righteousness. His treatment of the unfortunate Mr Y [Count Potocki de Montalk] was disgraceful" (*Downhill* 137). Hewart's ruling in the case was deemed a "judicial injustice" and "a grossly inequitable judgment" stemming from bias (*Downhill* 212). This "tendency to take sides in cases that came before him" (Jackson 157) was one well-noted by his contemporaries: in 1929, Hewart's behavior at the much-publicized trial of William Cooper Hobbs "confirmed in the Temple a feeling that on occasions the Chief was far too hasty in his judgments. From the start of the trial, the Chief took a violent dislike to the plaintiff, and all through seemed determined to frustrate his attempt to obtain justice. His conduct of the trial was testy, vindictive, and far from impartial" (Jackson 199). Moreover, his "autocratic and irascible bearing in court" had become "more and more noticeable by 1928," resulting in his public censure by the Bar Council in that same year (Jackson 197-99). His longstanding record as a supporter of women's suffrage and advocate of divorce and marriage law reform notwithstanding, it was Hewart's renowned temperament that made him an ideal modern-day stand in for the autocratic figure of Creon.

Hewart's direct involvement in cases that led to the significant expansion of state powers, the erosion of individual civil liberties, and the suppression of political dissent during the interwar period, moreover, allows Woolf to signify these discourses through his figure. Serving as Attorney General in Lloyd George's coalition government, a position he held from 1919-22 immediately preceding his promotion to the position of Lord Chief Justice in 1922, Gordon Hewart was instrumental in reversing and amending war time legislation (Jackson 87). In 1920, Hewart moved for a second reading of the Official Secrets Act of 1911; while the 1911 Act had referred quite clearly to espionage, the vaguely worded changes proposed in the 1920 Act were widely denounced as potentially threatening to civil liberties and freedom of the press (Anderson 15-16). As General Secretary of the Council for Civil Liberties Ronald Kidd pointed out, in spite of such theoretical assurances by Hewart and others of the bill's supporters, in practice the Act was used as "a convenient instrument for the assertion of bureaucratic authority, . . . for political purposes, to check the freedom of the Press and even to limit free discussion in the House of Commons" (91). In 1937, the National Campaign for Civil Liberties undertook a campaign against "misuse" of the law, which led lawmakers in 1939 to amend its language, thereby restricting its applicability to "acts of espionage" (Anderson 22, 19).[44]

Several additional trials with which Hewart was associated are likely to have been of interest to the Woolfs: namely, his successful (and highly unpopular) prosecution of Trade Union leader Tom Mann in 1912 under the Incitement to Mutiny Act for his efforts to persuade soldiers to disobey orders to break strikes (Jackson 54), and two appeals cases over which he presided in the Divisional Court that would directly involve him in controversy over the suppression of individual civil liberties in the mid-thirties—two of the "great quartet of public order cases in English law" (Williams 118).[45]

In the first of the two appeals cases, police refused to leave a peaceful protest organized by Alun Thomas, a member of the Communist Party, protesting the Incitement to Disaffection Bill that was then under parliamentary review in 1934, despite the fact that just two months earlier the Home Secretary, Sir John Gilmour, had affirmed before the House of Commons that police were barred from attending such meetings "unless they have reason to believe that an actual [as opposed to an anticipated] breach of the peace is being committed in the meeting" (Williams 118-19).[46] Hewart quickly dismissed the case, maintaining that police entry to private property was justified in circumstances in which an officer has "reasonable ground for believing that an offence is imminent or is likely to be committed" (Williams 122).[47] The second of these important trials extended to police the authority to ban public meetings that were seen as being likely to cause a breach of the peace. In 1934, Katherine Sinclair Duncan, a member of the National Unemployed Workers'

---

[44] Twenty-eight prosecutions resulted between the years 1933 and 1938; see Anderson 18 and Kidd 90-107 for further discussion. Hewart presided over a highly controversial case in 1938, in which a journalist, Ernest Lewis, was prosecuted under the Official Secrets Act of 1920 for declining to reveal his sources—a decision that led to an outcry among Members of Parliament (Jackson 324).

[45] See Ewing and Gearty; Williams; E. C. S. Wade; Goodheart; and Kidd for summaries of both cases. Williams identifies the others as *Wise v. Dunning* and *Beatty v. Gillbanks* (118).

[46] Sir John Gilmour's articulation of police policy before the House of Commons in June 1934, following upon the heels of the violent B.U.F. rally at Olympia that took place earlier that month, appears to have been a defense of what many regarded as a failure on the part of police to intervene in a situation in which a breach of peace clearly *had been* taking place (Kidd 124-25; Goodheart 22).

[47] This decision reiterated an earlier one regarding a similar series of events at Glamorgan, which many constitutional authorities maintained was based on a flawed interpretation of the law (Jackson 290).

Movement, was arrested for refusing to move her platform during a public meeting outside a training center for unemployed workers on the topic of "defend[ing] the right of free speech and public meeting" (E. C. S. Wade 179). The legal issue in *Duncan v. Jones* hinged on the question of whether, and in what circumstances, police possessed the authority to prevent a political meeting from taking place, since "before this decision, the police could intervene to prevent a meeting being held only when a breach of the peace actual or contemplated at the meeting then assembled was in issue" or when a gathering obstructed traffic (E. C. S. Wade 179). As a September 22, 1934 article in the *New Statesman* explained, "her arrest was justified on the ground that she might have said something, had she been allowed to speak, which would have led to a breach of the peace" (qtd. in Kidd 23). Hewart again was to dismiss the appeal after only a hasty hearing, effectively establishing the police "as the arbiters of what political parties or religious sects shall and shall not be accorded the rights of freedom of speech and freedom of assembly" (Kidd 24). What made this ruling particularly problematic was its notably uneven application, as police were more likely to intervene in meetings of the Communist Party, unemployed workers' groups, and anti-war groups than those of fascist organizations like the B.U.F.[48] Although largely unknown to modern readers, this episode in British juridical history "is as noteworthy today for the vacuity of its reasoning as for its long term deleterious effect on civil liberties. The case is well known for the latter, and frequently applied by the police, though its historical context has long been forgotten" (Ewing and Gearty 265). The theoretical and practical consequences of this decision, which provided "a source of open-ended police power to restrict civil liberties" (Ewing and Gearty 274), were as devastating for the private individual as for groups holding marginalized views. As Ronald Kidd writes, this decision "establishes the precedent that the police have power to ban any political meeting in streets or public places at will. . . . The police are set up by this judgment as the arbiters of what political parties or religious sects shall and shall not be accorded the rights of freedom of speech and freedom of assembly" (24). An

---

[48] This discrepancy in the application of the law is made further apparent in the events surrounding the much-publicized B.U.F. rally held at the Royal Albert Hall in 1936. While approximately 2,000 officers were positioned at the anti-Fascist demonstration outside where the rally was taking place, only thirty officers were positioned inside the hall itself; eyewitness accounts maintain, moreover, that those thirty officers repeatedly refused to intervene amidst escalating Blackshirt violence, despite being asked for assistance by several members of the crowd (Kidd 126-27; Ewing and Gearty 295-302). It is interesting to note that Gordon Hewart had presided over Sir Oswald Mosley's libel case against *The Star*—"a political *cause célèbre* of first magnitude" (Jackson 244)—and came out strongly in favor of the Fascist leader, securing from the jury damages in the nearly unprecedented amount of £5,000 (Jackson 242-48). One of Mosley's attorneys in the case was the Woolfs' friend, St John Hutchinson.

effect of this decision was to further disenfranchise those with limited economic resources, as another legal commentator has noted:

> Since *Duncan v. Jones* the net has closed entirely upon those who from lack of resources, or for other reasons, desire to hold meetings in public places. The result is that there is now no assurance, unless police permission is secured in advance, that a meeting can be held anywhere in a public place. (E. C. S. Wade 179)

The decisions of the Divisional Court on both matters was to confer an unprecedented authority upon the state to intervene in civil affairs, leading one commentator to reflect that "had the police sought a general power of this nature from the Legislature, no House of Commons in the twentieth century would have been willing to grant it. . . . Both *Thomas v. Sawkins* and *Duncan v. Jones* are certainly powerful weapons in the hands of the Administration" (ibid.).

Woolf's emphasis on those "cheap and so far unforbidden instruments" that the Outsider might use to "put her opinion into practice" (*TG* 116) can be read as an acknowledgment of the above recent legislation, and as a grassroots attempt to circumvent it. "The private printing press is an actual fact, and not beyond the reach of a moderate income. Typewriters and duplicators are actual facts and even cheaper," she remarks (ibid.). Private meetings, furthermore, may take the place of public ones, now that "you have a room, not necessarily 'cosy' or 'handsome' but still silent, private; a room where safe from publicity and its poison you could, even asking a reasonable fee for the service, speak the truth" (116). It is from this place, and through these means, that women of even the most limited means can learn to "speak freely as free people should" (148). Her inclusion of Hewart's photograph is an attempt to indict one of the individuals most directly responsible for the curtailment of civil liberties and expansion of police powers during the interwar period.

"Prancing down Whitehall on a War-Horse": State Trumpeters of the Household Cavalry [49]

To date, the most ubiquitous reading of the photograph picturing the State Trumpeters of the Household Cavalry focuses on "the notable visual (and textual) omission at the heart, or the top, of this hierarchy," as Alice Staveley writes:

> [T]he Heralds stand regally to attention—the monarch [sic] coat of arms with its motto, "Dieu et Mon Droit" visible on their ensigns—trumpeting a monarch whose very absence marks the sort of presence that, in the wake of the recent Abdication Crisis, provided its own equivocal commentary on the inviolability of the old order. (5)

---

[49] "[Orlando] thanked Heaven that she was not prancing down Whitehall on a war-horse, not even sentencing a man to death" (119).

Stuart Clarke likewise argues that the trumpeters "are in effect representing the absent King" ("Lord Chief Justice" 12), whom Julia Briggs refers to as "the one figure notably missing from this pantheon of patriarchs" (325). The visual evidence provided by the photograph bolsters this reading, for the gold state coat and blue jockey cap worn by the trumpeters indicates a state occasion at which the monarch and/or members of the royal family would have, in fact, been present. Members of the Household Cavalry—"without whose gleaming breastplates and nodding plumes the King and Queen on state occasions would appear to their devoted subjects strange and forlorn indeed," as a 1936 *Time* magazine article notes—undoubtedly would have signified the monarchy for Woolf's readers in a powerful way ("Heroes Unhorsed" 20).

While true that "their function would have been to precede and prepare the way for the heralds' reading of a proclamation such as that proclaiming the coronation of a king," as Merry Pawlowski argues ("Veil" 731), it seems less conclusive that the occasion in question is the May 12, 1937 coronation of George VI, as she argues, given the spate of royal proclamations delivered throughout the 1935-37 period: this occasion just as easily might have been the proclamation of the accession of Edward VIII upon the death of George V (January 23, 1936), or that announcing the date of Edward VIII's impending coronation (May 29, 1936); or that announcing the accession of George VI upon the abdication of Edward VIII (December 14, 1936).[50] It seems possible, too, that the occasion might have been one related to George V's Silver Jubilee celebrations in 1935. Still, that coronations are never far

---

[50] Pawlowski postulates that Woolf intentionally mislabels the State Trumpeters as "heralds" in the book's List of Illustrations in order to form a "textual link" to an image that appears in vol. 2 of the Monks House scrapbooks, in which heralds can be seen announcing the proclamation of Edward VIII's coronation, an event that would never occur. Her view of the photograph as an ironic commentary on "the breakdown, even if momentary, of royal authority" ("Veil" 731-2) is consistent with that of other scholars who read the State Trumpeters as signifying this royal absence.

from Woolf's mind, interwoven as they are throughout the fabric of *Three Guineas*, adds further support to this argument. In one passage, she calls upon the daughters of educated men, for example, to absent themselves from scenes of "dictated, regimented, official pageantry, in which only one sex takes an active part—those ceremonies, for example, which depend upon the deaths of kings, or their coronations to inspire them" (134). Her reference to the exclusion of women from such pageantry is consistent with her twice-articulated complaint in that text that "[i]t was stated yesterday at the War Office that the Army Council have no intention of opening recruiting for any women's corps" (126, 210).

A second reference to coronations—"Let us think in offices; in omnibuses; while we are standing in the crowd watching Coronations and Lord Mayor's Shows; let as think as we pass the Cenotaph; and in Whitehall . . ." (77)—reveals something more than an isolated allusion to that event, however. While, at first glance, it may appear as if Woolf were haphazardly conflating distinctive ceremonies and geographical points, it becomes evident upon closer inspection that the common thread linking these items with one another is the very same Household Cavalry depicted in her photo. As active participants in both coronations and Lord Mayor's Shows, the Household Cavalry is also conjured by the two trail blazes that Woolf provides, "Whitehall" and "the Cenotaph," which position the reader in the immediate vicinity of Horse Guards and Horse Guards Parade, which is located on Whitehall, approximately one block from the Cenotaph. It is this military administrative and ceremonial site that can be seen in the background of the photographs of the State Trumpeters. Rather than simply signifying lack or royal instability, then, this photograph's clear rendering of members of the Household Cavalry and of Horse Guards compels us to consider the historical and cultural significance of these profoundly British institutions in order to understand what they would have signified for Woolf's readership.

The Household Cavalry is comprised of two regiments, the Life Guards and the Blues and Royals (the latter known during Woolf's lifetime as the Royal Horse Guards [The Blues]), the oldest and most senior ranking regiments in the British Army.[51] The Life Guards were formed from a group of royalists who had accompanied the exiled Charles II to France, Germany, and the Netherlands—many of whom had been members of a Horse and Foot guard protecting Charles I during the Civil Wars—and who would be raised officially in 1656 as Charles II's "private army" as a consequence of the King's military alliance with the King of Spain (Harwood 32; Watson 15). Six hundred Life Guards troops, including trumpeters and kettle-drummers, would accompany Charles on his ride back to London to restore the British monarchy. Subsequent negotiations with Parliament over "the raising of

---

[51] For the sake of clarity, the regiment known during Woolf's lifetime as the Royal Horse Guards (The Blues) will be called hereafter by its current name, the Blues and Royals.

a small protective force designed solely to protect the court" ensured that these Life Guards would be rewarded during the Restoration for their loyalty by becoming the foundation of the modern British Army (Harwood 36, 38). The history of the Blues and Royals is more complex. Originally a cavalry regiment in Cromwell's New Model Army, they were reformed in 1661 as the "Royal Regiment of Horse" and officially charged with serving the King as part of the Restoration government's efforts to disband the New Model Army and protect Charles II during this period of civil unrest (ibid.). Their numbers were made up of "private gentlemen," "men of 'good birth' and of some private means, obliged as they were to supply their own horses, swords, and pistols" (Watson 23).

Increased concerns for the King's safety as a result of the fictitious Popish Plot led to the formal assignation of bodyguards to the King in 1678, known as the Gold and Silver Sticks-in-Waiting. During the reign of Charles II, the Gold Stick-in-Waiting, a colonel of either regiment, was called to

> attend on the King's person on foot wheresoever he walks from his rising to his going to bed immediately next to the King's own person *before all others,* carrying in his hand an ebony staff or truncheon with a gold head engraved with his Majesty's cipher and crown . . . Near him also attends another principal commissioned officer with an ebony staff and silver head [the Silver Stick-in-Waiting], who is ready to relieve the Captain on all occasions. (qtd. in Watson 25; italics in original)

The Gold Stick, together with the Silver Stick-in-Waiting (generally the Lieutenant Colonel in Command of the Household Cavalry), occupy "those military appointments closest to the Sovereign" (Watson 16; Harwood 118). It is clearly the Silver Stick-in-Waiting to whom Woolf is referring in her reference to soldiers "in procession behind a man carrying a silver poker" (*TG* 24), a procession that might have been linked to the coronation, the Trooping of the Colour, or the State opening of Parliament, state ceremonial occasions at which the Silver Stick-in-Waiting can be seen, to this day, accompanying the monarch. Just as, in the photograph, the State Trumpeters might be said to gesture toward the absent King, in this passage, it is the Silver Stick-in-Waiting that indicates the physical presence (and textual absence) of the monarch.

That Woolf should include in *Three Guineas* a photograph of members of the Household Cavalry and refer to them throughout the text should come as no great surprise, given that the soldiers of this regiment were recognized within her lifetime, indeed well before it, as the very exemplars of "dictated, regimented, official pageantry" (*TG* 114), known as much for the precision of their movements and elaborate uniforms as for their rich history and proximity to the King. As historian J. N. P. Watson writes,

> What King and Parliament had in mind for England's first standing army was a resplendent force, based on the model of the French that would not only protect the King, his brother and the realm in general and present itself colourfully and in a well drilled fashion on State occasions, but also act as police and be ready to form a trained cadre for rapid expansion in war. (21, 22)

Among the most colorful and skilled members of the Household Cavalry are the musicians who form the Bands of the Life Guards and the Blues and Royals, who are called upon to parade both mounted and dismounted, both with their regiment and with the Massed Household Cavalry Band. As one history of the Household Cavalry suggests, mounted parades require special skill of its musicians, who are required to control their horses using only their feet ("Presenting"). The state dress uniform worn by members of the Massed Band, and by the State Trumpeters when in the presence of the monarch or members of the royal family, is the "oldest ceremonial uniform in the Army" (ibid.), dating back to the raising of the Life Guards. As John Childs writes, "Of all the little Army [of Charles II], the most gorgeously dressed were the three Troops of the Life Guard. Their trumpeters and kettle-drummers wore ceremonial uniforms which cost £58 3s 6d, their coats and cloaks covered in yards of lace and embroidery" (57).[52]

The primary annual events at which the Bands appear mounted are the Queen's Birthday Parade (Trooping the Colour); Beating Retreat; and the Lord Mayor's Show. As part of the regimental and Massed Band, State Trumpeters take part in these parades, performing a ceremonial function at all state functions, including the annual Garter Ceremony and the State Opening of Parliament (Watson 175). Dismounted fanfare teams such as the one seen in this photograph were regularly dispatched for the State Opening of Parliament, The Lord Mayor's banquet, and other banquets in honor of foreign dignitaries ("Presenting"). Incidentally, "Lord Mayor's banquets" are included by Woolf among those "obsolete ceremonies" to be banned by the Society of Outsiders (*TG* 141). Such state functions may be what Woolf has in mind when she explicitly directs the Outsider to "absent herself from military displays, tournaments, tattoos, prize-givings and all such ceremonies as

---

[52] The 2014 equivalent of this figure is calculated roughly as £5,818, or $9,163. The sartorial finery of trumpeters has been dictated historically by their association with the nobility, whose entrance into battle and tournaments they would announce. Although still maintaining a noncombatant role during the Restoration—a status indicated by the broken-off blades of their swords—trumpeters were "chosen for having an acceptable manner, the ability to carry messages and to parley with the enemy, and to act as special orderlies to Generals" ("Presenting"). Throughout British history, they have sounded orders for troops to charge, performing this function at battles including those of Dettingen (1743) and of Waterloo (1815).

encourage the desire to impose 'our' civilization or 'our' dominion upon other people" (129). There is, moreover, additional support to link such events with the State Trumpeters of the Household Cavalry, given her infantilizing allusion to them at the conclusion of this passage:

> [p]sychology would seem to show that it is far harder for human beings to take action when other people are indifferent and allow them complete freedom of action, than when their actions are made the centre of excited emotion. The small boy struts and trumpets outside the window: implore him to stop; he goes on; say nothing; he stops. (ibid.)

Additional uniform-specific clues embedded in the text of *Three Guineas* confirm that Woolf's specific interest is the King's Life Guards. "Who can say whether, as time goes on, we may not dress in military uniform," she inquires, "with gold lace on our breasts, swords at our sides, and something like the old family coal-scuttle on our heads, save that that venerable object was never decorated with plumes of white horsehair" (76). Her allusion here refers to the brass "Albert" helmet, with its white plume made of horsehair, worn by the Life Guards (and which looks very much like a Victorian coal-scuttle). One of the most memorable passages in *Three Guineas,* having to do precisely with the connection between soldiers' uniforms and war, is likewise fraught with references to the ceremonial uniforms of the Life Guards regiment of the Household Cavalry:

> The connection between dress and war is not far to seek; your finest clothes are those that you wear as soldiers. Since the red and the gold, the brass and the feathers are discarded upon active service, it is plain that their expensive and not, one might suppose, hygienic splendour is invented partly in order to impress the beholder with the majesty of the military office, partly in order through their vanity to induce young men to become soldiers. (26-7)

Her vivid rendering in this passage would have called immediately to the mind of Woolf's reader the Full Dress Mounted Review Order worn by Officers of the Life Guards, comprised of a red tunic stitched with "gold lace" detail at the cuffs, collar, and tail; a red cloak, trimmed with gold detail, worn during inclement weather; a gold belt and gold sling; a brass "Albert" helmet; a steel cuirass, plated with brass; and a ceremonial steel sword, its bowl decorated with brass regimental insignia.[53] It should be noted that the uniform Woolf describes here is quite

---

[53] The Household Cavalry website is exhaustive in its documentation of the division's history, customs, uniforms and functions: http://householdcavalry.info/uniforms.html.

different from that of the 13th Hussars worn by Lord Robert Baden-Powell in the *Three Guineas* photograph, whose distinctive features include a dark blue dolman jacket and ornamental busby ("The 13th Hussars").[54] Moreover, "Life Guards" are specifically indicated (alongside the "Heralds" whose images appear among the Monks House scrapbook clippings) among her list of "Admirals, Generals, Heralds, Life Guards, Peers, Beefeaters, etc.," to whose sartorial splendor she alludes in her rebuttal of Justice MacCardie's argument on fashion as feminine vice (*TG* 177). The specifically ceremonial nature of this uniform is implied by Woolf's reference to its being "discarded upon active service," a phrase that also signals her awareness that the function of these soldiers was not simply ceremonial, but operational as well.

Both Household Cavalry regiments have been engaged in active combat roles nearly continuously since their beginnings. The official British Army website identifies their involvement in the Third Dutch War of 1672, the Monmouth Rebellion of 1685, the Battle of the Boyne (1690), the War of Spanish Succession (1701-14), the Jacobite uprisings of 1715 and 1745, the War of Austrian Succession (1742-46), the Seven Years War (1756-63), the Peninsular War (1813), the 1815 Battle of Waterloo (where they formed the front charging line), the Crimean War (1853-56), the Boer War (1899-1902), and the Great War (1914-1918), where they were represented in major battles including Mons, the Marne, Ypres, Loos, Passchendaele, and Zandvoorde, where their losses were particularly heavy.[55] In addition to these battles, the three regiments comprising the Household Cavalry had a significant presence during the nineteenth century in Egypt, the Sudan, South Africa, India, and Palestine (Watson 135), thereby involving them directly in the administration of the rule of the British Empire in those countries. This context helps account for the postcard that Woolf sent to Clive Bell on June 5, 1930, one side bearing a photograph of the Royal House Guards in Whitehall, and the other Woolf's message, "This is just to remind you of the Empire" (*L4* 174).

That Woolf was keenly aware of the active war service supplied by these troops is suggested by her reference in *Orlando* to one's "prancing down Whitehall on a war-horse" (119). During her lifetime, the horses seen parading at Horse Guards, and the soldiers who rode them, might be destined for the front, or even recently returned from it.[56] As one historian explains,

[54] Additional images of Baden-Powell in full dress can be found at http://www.pinetreeweb.com/bp-hussars.htm
[55] For an overview of the Household Cavalry's involvement in these battles, see the official website of the British Army, http://www.army.mod.uk/armoured/regiments/28074.aspx.
[56] One such famous decorated war-horse, "Freddy of Paardeburg," resumed ceremonial duties following service during five different campaigns in the Second Boer War: "anyone attending guard mountings at Horse Guards after the South African War in 1901 cannot have failed to notice that one of the horses wore a campaign medal on its harness: this horse was 'Freddy'" (Harwood 118-120).

> By the time the Armistice brought the Great War to an end, in November 1918, the Household cavalry regiments had become machine-gunners, infantry and siege gunners. . . . The Household Cavalry provided a cavalry squadron and cyclist company for the Guards Division from its formation until June 1916, but generally the Household Cavalry served with cavalry divisions, as Army troops, or in the case of the 'Household Battalion', with the 4th Division. (Chappell 4-5)

The war service provided by the King's Life Guard was, in fact, the subject of public discussion during the Great War, as "contemporary comments about the Horse Guards sentries evading service abroad by choice were unequivocally rebutted at the time. A statement issued to the press revealed that the King's Life Guard 'was formed from men who had been invalided from the front, or who were re-enlisted men unable to serve abroad under the conscription terms'" (Harwood 120). In 1926, the Guards Memorial was erected adjacent to Horse Guards Parade, commemorating the King's Foot Guards regiments, as well as the regiments of the Household Cavalry, the Royal Regiment of Artillery Corps, and the Royal Medical Corps, among others, for their service in that war. Moreover, nearly all of the soldiers attached to the home units of the Household Cavalry were eligible for, and received, the Mons Star, also known as the "1914 Star," during its first issue in 1918.

The Mons Star was awarded to the Household Cavalry regiments on Horse Guards Parade, the same site where Queen Victoria had presented the regiments with war medals for their service in the Crimean War in 1855 (Harwood 12, 120). This location has deep historical and modern-day ties to the administration of military affairs, the protection of the sovereign, and the production of public spectacle. Given its proximity directly adjacent to the former Palace of Whitehall, it was an optimal location for the first emplacement of a formal guard unit to protect the king in 1640, and Oliver Cromwell would establish the first permanent guard unit on the site in 1649 to protect himself from the civil unrest that followed the execution of Charles I (Harwood 26, 30). It was on this site that Britain would issue a Proclamation declaring war with the Dutch in 1665, and where they would announce their victory in that conflict. From the early 1660s, the original structure, known as Old Horse Guards, served as "the earliest example of overall central military command"—effectively the first War Office, along with a duty barracks—where "the general military became used to their orders appearing on Horse Guards' door" (Harwood 50). The nascent War Office would continue to occupy "New Horse Guards" until the relocation of the bulk of its offices, first to Pall Mall in 1869-71, and then to the new War Office in Whitehall in 1907. The Household Cavalry's most senior administrative offices remain at New Horse Guards today, posts filled by senior-ranking military officers (of field grade and above) and their civilian equivalents (Harwood 116, 118).

Historically, Horse Guards Parade was a site for spectacles both ceremonial and punitive: from 1644 to 1827, the former site of King Henry VIII's palace Tiltyard housed what was known to spectators as the "wooden horse," described as "wooden boards on edge which offenders were required to 'ride,' often with leg weights attached, for the period of their sentence" (Harwood 45-6). That such punishments, lasting days on end, were meted out for "speaking mutinous and opprobrious words" (qtd. in Harwood 45) against a superior officer, and conducted simultaneously with the mounting of the Guard within view of passers-by, would have been of considerable interest to Woolf in light of her concerns about the risks of seditious speech in her own day. Upon the burning of the Palace of Whitehall in 1698, and King William's subsequent removal to St. James's Palace, Old Horse Guards became the sole official entrance to the Court and Palace of St. James, rendering the site increasingly associated with the courtiers, state processions, and royal family members who would pass through it (Harwood 64). A 1748 painting by the Italian painter Canaletto depicts the first-known Trooping of the Colour ceremony, while a diary entry of 1817 supplies the first-known reference to the Changing of the Guards ceremony at Horse Guards Parade (Harwood 76, 75).

The rich history evoked by these geographical sites and the Guards who protect them was the stuff of family lore, and thus immediately recognizable to Woolf and her contemporaries. Her reminiscences on the occasion of Edward VIII's abdication make this much clear. Encountering Ottoline Morrell opposite Horse Guards that evening, Woolf reflected on the sights of Whitehall:

> We looked up at the beautiful carved front of—what office? I don't know. That's the window out of which Charles the First stepped when he had his head cut off said Ottoline, pointing to the great lit up windows in their frame of white stone. So my mother always told me. (*D5* 42)

Whether the final line is a continuation of Woolf's parroting of Ottoline's historical narration, or confirmation on Woolf's own part of the veracity of that narration, this passage makes clear the interconnectedness of the public and the private, here made manifest in the permeable membrane conjoining national and family historical narratives.

Curiously, Ottoline's allusion to the Banqueting House—"that's the window out of which Charles the First stepped when he had his head cut off"—is repeated by Woolf in the early typescript version of *Between the Acts*, in a troubling passage that vivifies the rape of a young girl by Royal Horse Guards on April 27, 1938.[57] The typescript's reference to "the window in Whitehall from which Charles stepped

---

[57] See Stuart Clarke's "A Horse with a Green Tail" for a discussion of these events and their representation in the press.

to his execution" (Leaska 54-55)—a geographical marker that identifies the general vicinity of the scene of the crime—is replaced in the published version with increasingly specific details, naming both its perpetrator, the "guard at Whitehall," and its location, a barracks room from which the Arch at Whitehall can be seen—a room within historic Horse Guards itself. While it is clear that Woolf's decision to include the photograph of the State Trumpeters predates the rape incident, and thus could not have figured into her initial motivation for using it, that she did not remove or replace it (despite having known that it would signify this recent event for her readers) constitutes an implicit invitation to combat the romantic mythologizing of history with evidence drawn from "the daily paper, history in the raw" (*TG* 9).

Woolf's reminiscences on the abdication go on to suggest just how deeply entrenched such mythologies and romances can be, as the mere sight of the mounted Household Cavalry guards sends her into rapture:

> I felt I was walking in the 17th Century with one of the courtiers, & she [Ottoline] was lamenting not the abdication of Edward . . . but the execution of Charles. . . . Still he hadn't yet, so far as we knew, thrown it away. "It" seemed then, looking at the curved street, & at the red & silver guards drawn up in the court-yard with the Park & the white government buildings behind, very stately, very lovely, very much the noble & severe aristocratic Stuart England. (*D*5 42-43)

That Woolf's knowledge of history, along with her sense of romance and awe, were capable of having been triggered by a glimpse of the guards on duty at Horse Guards suggests something of the latent (and persistent) associations such images possessed for her and her British contemporaries. It may suggest, too, her endorsement of a particular way of reading such images, whether encountered in the text or on the street—one that sees the past superimposed upon the present image in order to reveal its fullest possible range of signification.

III Beating Retreat[58]

Woolf maintained that to eradicate war would require the concerted action of individuals; to that end, the text of *Three Guineas* is focused equally upon the methods of resistance available to the individual and the effects that these actions are

---

[58] According to the official website of the British Army, "Beating Retreat has its origins in the early years of organised warfare when the beating of drums and the parading of Post Guards heralded the closing of camp gates and the lowering of flags at the end of the day."

likely to have should they be undertaken by the requisite number of people.[59] What I would like to suggest in closing is that the work's photographs invite a similar way of apprehending the role of the individual and the collective in perpetuating war. While each photograph depicts a specific individual countenance, calling us to attend to the ways in which that figure is implicated indirectly in the perpetuation of war, each photograph also always exists as one of a series, each component of that series taking on additional meaning in relation to the others and thereby creating further links in each photograph's chains of signification. Our attention, like that of the members of a reviewing party before whom uniformed figures parade, is occupied alternately by the individual figure and the larger formation of which he is a part: not just the other men who are pictured, but that entire formation of educated men's sons who parade through the streets of *Three Guineas*' London. Woolf's own discourse likewise is divided between careful attention to isolated examples of women's systematic oppression, culled from biography and newspaper, and her skillful weaving together of those separate threads into an intricate tapestry in which the historic and ongoing oppression of British women is linked to Continental fascism and thereby to the perpetuation of war. The central tension of *Three Guineas* derives from this discursive toggling between the micro and the macro, the part and the whole.

The series of photographs under discussion here also always stands in relation to another set of photographs—those absent photographs of dead children and ruined houses. It is ironic that critics' preoccupation with Woolf's mysterious omission of this set of photographs has led them, in large part, to neglect the photographs that are present, given that the two can exist only in relation to one another, their relative absence and presence inscribed clearly into the text itself. While the presence of the photographs highlights the absence of these others, the opposite is true as well, and at least equally important for theorizing the work's visual dimensions. If absence ineluctably gestures toward its inverse, as is generally held to be true, then it can be argued that each iteration of dead bodies and ruined houses functions within the narrative as a pointing gesture that directs us toward the present photographs, as if to say that which dare not be spoken aloud, or written down, in 1938: "They did this."

---

[59] Interestingly, this number was one that changed repeatedly throughout Woolf's drafting of the work, vacillating between as few as ten and as many as two hundred and fifty people. See Wisor, "Versioning Virginia Woolf: Notes toward a Post-Eclectic Edition of *Three Guineas*."

Works Cited

Aldgate, Anthony and James C. Robertson. *Censorship in Theatre and Cinema.* Edinburgh: Edinburgh UP, 2005. Print.

Anderson, Gerald D. *Fascists, Communists, and the National Government: Civil Liberties in Great Britain, 1931-1937.* Columbia: U of Missouri P, 1983. Print.

"Authors and the Law of Libel, Plea for Reform." *The Times* 13 Mar. 1936: 10. Web. 12 Jul. 2014.

Baden-Powell, Sir Robert. *The Young Knights of the Empire.* 1917. Web. 11 Jul. 2014.

Baldwin, Stanley. "Freedom and Discipline." *This Torch of Freedom* 271-88. Print.

———. "Our Freedom Is Our Own." *This Torch of Freedom* 15-24. Print.

———. *This Torch of Freedom: Speeches and Addresses.* London: Hodder and Stoughton, 1935. Print.

———. "Unto Whomsoever Much Is Given." *This Torch of Freedom* 25-29. Print.

Barthes, Roland. *Camera Lucida—Reflections on Photography.* New York: Hill & Wang, 1981. Print.

Bell, Quentin. "*A Room of One's Own* and *Three Guineas.*" *Virginia Woolf and Fascism: Resisting the Dictators' Seduction.* Ed. Merry Pawlowski. New York: Palgrave, 2001. 13-20. Print.

Benjamin, Walter. "Theses on the Philosophy of History." *Illuminations: Essays and Reflections.* Ed. Hannah Arendt. Trans. Harry Zohn. New York: Schocken, 1968. 253-264. Print.

Berman, Jessica. *Modernist Commitments: Ethics, Politics, and Transnational Modernism.* New York: Columbia UP, 2011. Print.

Black, Naomi. Introduction. *Three Guineas.* By Virginia Woolf. Oxford: Blackwell, 2001. xiii-lxxv. Print.

———. "'Not a Novel, They Said': Editing Virginia Woolf's *Three Guineas.*" *Editing Women.* Ed. Ann M. Hutchison. Toronto: U of Toronto P, 1998. 27-54. Print.

———. *Virginia Woolf as Feminist.* Ithaca, New York: Cornell UP, 2004. Print.

Blom-Cooper, Louis and Terence Morris. *With Malice Aforethought: A Study of the Crime and Punishment for Homicide.* Portland, OR: Hart, 2004. Print.

Briggs, Julia. *Virginia Woolf: An Inner Life.* New York: Harcourt, 2005. Print.

The British Army. 2014. Web. 18 December 2014.

Burton, Diane. *An Aesthetic of Witness: The Interaction of Photographs and Nonfiction Prose in George Orwell's* The Road to Wigan Pier, *James Agee and Walker Evans's* Let Us Now Praise Famous Men, *and Virginia Woolf's* Three Guineas. Diss. University of Tulsa, 2003. Print.

Carpenter, Edward. *Cantuar: The Archbishops in Their Office.* Oxford: Mowbray, 1988. Print.

Chappell, Mike. *The Guards Division 1914-45.* London: Osprey, 1995. Print.

Childs, John. *Army of Charles II.* New York: Routledge, 2013. Print.

Clarke, Stuart N. "The Lord Chief Justice and the Woolfs." *Bulletin of the Virginia Woolf Society of Great Britain* 14 (Sept. 2003): 12-25. Print.

———. "The Horse with a Green Tail." *Virginia Woolf Miscellany* 34 (1990): 3-4. Print.

Coates, Kimberly Engdahl. "Photographing Violence: *Three Guineas* and Contemporary Feminist Responses to Images of War." *The Theme of Peace and War in Virginia Woolf's War Writing: Essays on Her Political Philosophy.* Ed. Jane Wood. Lewiston: The Edwin Mellen Press, 2010. 81-100. Print.

"Convocation of Canterbury, Loyal Tributes, Archbishop and 'A Very Dear Friend.'" *The Times* 23 Jan. 1936: 6.Web. 12 Jul. 2014.

Cooper, Duff. *Old Men Forget.* London: Rupert Hart-Davis, 1953. Print.

Dalgarno, Emily. *Virginia Woolf and the Visible World.* Cambridge: Cambridge UP, 2001. Print.

Daniels, Anthony. "The Man Who Made Scouting." *The New Criterion.* June 2004: 22-27. Print.

Department of the Army, Training Circular No. 3-21.5. 20 Jan. 2012. Web. 18 Dec. 2014.

Dickey, Colin. "Virginia Woolf and Photography." *The Edinburgh Companion to Virginia Woolf and the Arts.* Ed. Maggie Humm. Edinburgh: Edinburgh UP, 2010. 375-391. Print.

Duffy, Julia and Lloyd Davis. "Demythologizing Facts and Photographs in *Three Guineas.*" *Photo-Textualities: Reading Photographs and Literature.* Ed. Marsha Bryant. Newark, DE: U of Delaware P, 1996. 128-40. Print.

Eiland, Howard and Michael W. Jennings, eds. *Walter Benjamin: Selected Writings, Vol. 4: 1938-1940.* Cambridge, MA: Harvard UP, 2003. Print.

Enloe, Cynthia. *Bananas, Beaches & Bases: Making Feminist Sense of International Politics.* Berkeley: U of California P, 1990. Print.

Ewing, K. D. and C. A. Gearty. *The Struggle for Civil Liberties: Political Freedom and the Rule of Law in Britain, 1914-1945.* Oxford: Oxford UP, 2000. Print.

Gillis, John. *Youth and History: Tradition and Change in European Age Relations.* New York: Academic Press. 1974. Print.

Gillespie, Diane. "'Her Kodak Pointed at His Head': Virginia Woolf and Photography." *Virginia Woolf: Themes and Variations.* Ed. Vara Neverow-Turk and Mark Hussey. New York: Pace UP, 1993. 33-40. Print.

Goodheart, A. L. "*Thomas v. Sawkins*: A Constitutional Innovation." *Cambridge Law Journal* 6 (1936-38): 22-30. Print.

Gualtieri, Elena. "*Three Guineas* and the Photograph: The Art of Propaganda." *Women Writers of the 1930s: Gender, Politics and History.* Ed. Maroula Joannou. Edinburgh: Edinburgh UP, 1999. 165-78. Print.

Hartley, Jenny. "Clothes and Uniform in the Theatre of Fascism: Clemence Dane and Virginia Woolf." *Gender and Warfare in the Twentieth Century: Textual Representations.* Ed. Angela K. Smith. Manchester: Manchester UP, 2004. 96-110. Print.

Harwood, Brian. *Chivalry and Command: 500 Years of Horse Guards.* New York: Osprey, 2006. Print.

Hastings, Adrian. *A History of English Christianity 1920-1985.* London: Collins, 1986. Print.

"Heroes Unhorsed." *Time* 6 Jan. 1936: 20. Web. 17 Dec. 2014.

Heuston, R. F. V. *Lives of the Lord Chancellors 1885-1940.* Oxford: Clarendon, 1964. Print.

Hinnov, Emily. *Encountering Choran Community: Literary Modernism, Visual Culture, and Political Aesthetics in the Interwar Years.* Selinsgrove, PA: Susquehanna UP, 2009. Print.

Humm, Maggie. "Cinema and Photography." *Virginia Woolf in Context.* Ed. Bryony Randall and Jane Goldman. Cambridge: Cambridge UP, 2012. 291-301. Print.

———. *Modernist Women and Visual Cultures: Virginia Woolf, Vanessa Bell, Photography and Cinema.* New Brunswick, NJ: Rutgers UP, 2002. Print.

———. "Virginia Woolf and Visual Culture." *The Cambridge Companion to Virginia Woolf* 2nd ed. Ed. Susan Sellers. Cambridge: Cambridge UP, 2010. 214-230. Print.

"The 13th Hussars." http://www.pinetreeweb.com/bp-hussars.htm. Web. 17 Dec. 2014.

Hylson-Smith, Kenneth. *High Churchmanship in the Church of England.* Edinburgh: T & T Clark, 1993. Print.

Hynes, Samuel. *The Edwardian Turn of Mind.* Princeton, NJ: Princeton UP, 1968. Print.

Jackson, Robert. *The Chief: The Biography of Gordon Hewart, Lord Chief Justice of England, 1922-1940.* London: Harrap, 1959. Print.

Jeal, Tim. *The Boy-Man: The Life of Lord Baden-Powell.* New York: William Morrow, 1990. Print.

Johnston, John. *The Lord Chamberlain's Blue Pencil.* London: Hodder & Stoughton, 1990. Print.

Kidd, Ronald. *British Liberty in Danger: An Introduction to the Study of Civil Rights.* London: Lawrence & Wishart, 1940. Print.

Kirkpatrick, B. J. and Stuart N. Clarke. *A Bibliography of Virginia Woolf,* 4th ed. Oxford: Clarendon, 1997. Print.

Knowles, Nancy. "A Community of Women Looking at Men: The Photographs in Virginia Woolf's *Three Guineas*." *Virginia Woolf and Communities: Selected Papers from the Seventh Annual Conference on Virginia Woolf*. Ed. Jeanette McVicker and Laura Davis. New York: Pace UP, 1999. 91-96. Print.

Koppen, R. S. *Virginia Woolf, Fashion and Literary Modernity*. Edinburgh: Edinburgh UP, 2009. Print.

Leaska, Mitchell, ed. *Pointz Hall: The Earlier and Later Typescripts of* Between the Acts. NY: University Publications, 1983. Print.

Lee, Hermione. *Virginia Woolf*. London: Vintage, 1997. Print.

"'Lest We Run Too Far,' Aims of Scout and Guide Movements.'" *The Times* 30 Sep. 1937: 34. Web. 12 Jul. 2014.

Lilly, Amy M. "*Three Guineas,* Two Exhibits: Woolf's Politics of Display." *Woolf Studies Annual* 9 (2003): 29-54. Print.

Lockhart, J. G. *Cosmo Gordon Lang*. London: Hodder and Stoughton, 1949. Print.

"Lord Hewart: Tributes at the Law Courts." *Times* 7 May 1943: 8. Web. 12 Jul. 2014.

MacColl, James E. and W. T. Wells, "The Incitement to Disaffection Bill, 1934." *The Political Quarterly* 5.3 (July 1934): 352-64. Print.

MacDonald, Robert H. *Sons of the Empire: The Frontier and the Boy Scout Movement, 1890-1918*. Toronto: U of Toronto P, 1993. Print.

MacKenzie, John M. *Propaganda and Empire: The Manipulation of British Popular Opinion 1880-1960*. Manchester: Manchester UP, 1984. Print.

Marcus, Jane. Introduction. *Three Guineas*. By Virginia Woolf. New York: Harcourt Brace, 2006. Print.

———. "'No More Horses': Virginia Woolf on Art and Propaganda." *Women's Studies* 4 (1977): 265-290. Print.

———. "Thinking Back through Our Mothers." *New Feminist Essays on Virginia Woolf*. Ed. Jane Marcus. Lincoln: U of Nebraska P, 1981. 1-30. Print.

Marshik, Celia. *British Modernism and Censorship*. Cambridge: Cambridge UP, 2006. Print.

Middlemas, Keith and John Barnes, *Baldwin: A Biography*. London: Macmillan, 1969. Print.

Mills, Jean. "*Three Guineas:* The Movie?" *Virginia Woolf Miscellany* 74 (2008): 19.

Neverow, Vara. "Documenting Fascism in *Three Guineas* and *The Handmaid's Tale*: An Examination of Woolf's Textual Notes and Scrap Books and Atwood's 'Historical Notes'." *Virginia Woolf and the Common(wealth) Reader: Selected Papers from the Twenty-Third Annual International Conference on Virginia Woolf*. Ed. Helen Wussow and Mary Ann Gillies. Clemson, SC: Clemson U Digital P, 2014. 183-189. Print.

———. "Freudian Seduction and the Fallacies of Dictatorship." *Virginia Woolf and Fascism*. Ed. Merry Pawlowski. 56-72. Print.
"Newnham College, To the Editor of the *Times*." *Times* 6 Mar. 1936: 10. Web. 12 Jul. 2014.
"Newnham College, To the Editor of the *Times*. *Times* 8 Jan. 1937: 8. Web. 12 Jul. 2014.
O'Higgins, Paul. *Censorship in Britain*. London: Nelson, 1972. Print.
Ollard, S. L., Gordon Crosse, and Maurice F. Bond, eds. *A Dictionary of English Church History*. London: A. R. Mowbray, 1948. Print.
Pawlowski, Merry. "Virginia Woolf's Veil: The Feminist Intellectual and the Organization of Public Space." *Modern Fiction Studies* 53(2007): 722-51. Print.
———. "'Seule la culture désintéressée': Virginia Woolf, Gender, and Culture in Time of War." *War and Words: Horror and Heroism in the Literature of Warfare*. Ed. Sara Munson Deats, Lagretta Tallent Lenker, and Merry G. Perry. Lanham, MD: Lexington, 2004. 215-33. Print.
———. "The Virginia Woolf and Vera Douie Letters: Woolf's Connections to the Women's Service Library." *Woolf Studies Annual* 8 (2002): 3-62. Print.
———, ed. *Virginia Woolf and Fascism: Resisting the Dictators' Seduction*. New York: Palgrave, 2001. Print.
"Peace Aim of Scouting: No Politics or Militarism." *The Times* 13 Aug. 1937: 11. Web. 12 Jul. 2014.
"Peace and 'Pacifism.'" *The Times* 19 Jun. 1935: 15. Web. 12 Jul. 2014.
Petre, Jonathan. *By Sex Divided: The Church of England and Women Priests*. London: Harper Collins, 1994. Print.
Phillips, Kathy J. *Virginia Woolf against Empire*. Knoxville: U of Tennessee P, 1994. Print.
"Presenting the Household Cavalry Regiment." Web. 15 Dec. 2014.
Proctor, Tammy M. "'A Separate Path': Scouting and Guiding in Interwar South Africa." *Society for Comparative Study of Society and History* (2000): 605-31. Print.
Reed, Conor Tomas. "'Q. And babies? A. And babies': On Pacifism, Visual Trauma, and the Body Heap." *Interdisciplinary/Multidisciplinary Woolf: Selected Papers from the Twenty-Second Annual International Conference on Virginia Woolf*. Ed. Ann Martin and Kathryn Holland. Clemson, SC: Clemson U Digital P, 2013. 68-72. Print.
Rosenthal, Michael. *The Character Factory: Baden-Powell and the Origins of the Boy Scout Movement*. New York: Pantheon Books, 1984. Print.
Ross, Ellen. *Love and Toil: Motherhood in Outcast London*. New York: Oxford UP, 1993. Print.

"Sedition Bill, Criticism at Oxford." *The Times* 7 May 1934: 16. Web. 12 July 2014.

Sharpe, Emily Robins. "Pacifying Bloomsbury: Virginia Woolf, Julian Bell, and the Spanish Civil War." *The Theme of Peace and War in Virginia Woolf's Writings: Essays on Her Political Philosophy.* Ed. Jane Wood. Lewiston, NY: The Edwin Mellen Press, 2010. Print.

Shellard, Dominic and Steve Nicolson, with Miriam Handley. *The Lord Chamberlain Regrets . . . : A History of British Theatre Censorship.* London: The British Library, 2004. Print.

Snaith, Anna. "Wide Circles: The *Three Guineas* Letters." *Woolf Studies Annual* 6 (2000): 1-169. Print.

Springhall, John. "Baden-Powell and the Scout Movement Before 1920: Citizen Training or Soldiers of the Future?" *The English Historical Review* 102.405 (1987): 934-42. Print.

———. "The Boy Scouts, Class and Militarism in Relation to British Youth Movements, 1908-1930." *International Review of Social History* 16 (1971): 125-158. Print.

———. *Youth, Empire and Society: British Youth Movements, 1883-1940.* London: Croom Helm, 1977. Print.

Staveley, Alice. "Name That Face." *Virginia Woolf Miscellany* 51 (Spring 1998): 4-5. Print.

Street, Harry. *Freedom, the Individual, and the Law.* 4th ed. Middlesex, England: Penguin, 1977. Print.

Summers, Anne. "Militarism in Britain before the Great War." *History Workshop Journal* 2 (1976): 104-23. Print.

Tallents, Sir Stephen. *The Projection of England.* London: Faber & Faber, 1932. Print.

Taylor, Philip M. *The Projection of Britain: British Overseas Publicity and Propaganda, 1919-1939.* Cambridge: Cambridge UP, 1981. Print.

Wade, E. C. S. "Police Powers and Public Meetings." *Cambridge Law Journal* 6 (1936-38): 175-81. Print.

Wade, Eileen K. *The Piper of Pax: The Life Story of Sir Robert Baden-Powell.* London: C. Arthur Pearson, 1924. Print.

Warner, Marina. "Report to the Memoir Club: Scenes from a Colonial Childhood." *Contradictory Woolf: Selected Papers from the Twenty-First Annual International Conference on Virginia Woolf.* Ed. Derek Ryan and Stella Bolaki. Clemson, SC: Clemson U Digital P, 2012. 57-65. Print.

Warren, Allen. "Sir Robert Baden-Powell, the Scout Movement and Citizen Training in Great Britain, 1900-1920." *The English Historical Review* 101 (1986): 376-398. Print.

———. "Powell, Robert Stephenson Smyth Baden-." *Oxford Dictionary of National Biography.* Vol. 45. Ed. H. C. G. Matthew and Brian Harrison. Oxford: Oxford UP, 2004. 112-118. Print.

"Wateler Peace Prize for Lord Baden-Powell." *The Times* 9 Jul. 1937: 15. Web. 12 Jul. 2014.

Watson, J.N.P. *Through Fifteen Reigns: A Complete History of the Household Cavalry.* Staplehurst: Spellmount, 1997. Print.

Wilkinson, Alan. *Oxford Dictionary of National Biography.* Vol. 32. Ed. H. C. G. Matthew and Brian Harrison. Oxford: Oxford UP, 2004. 456-61. Print.

Williams, D. G. T. "Preventive Action and Public Order: The Principle of *Thomas v. Sawkins.*" *Cambrian Law Review* 16 (1985): 116-26. Print.

Williamson, Philip. "Baldwin's Reputation: Politics and History, 1937-1967." *The Historical Journal* 47.1 (2004): 127-168. Print.

———. *Stanley Baldwin: Conservative Leadership and National Values.* Cambridge: Cambridge UP, 1999. Print.

Winterhalter, Teresa. "'What Else Can I Do But Write?': Discursive Disruption and the Ethics of Style in Virginia Woolf's *Three Guineas.*" *Hypatia: A Journal of Feminist Philosophy* 18.4 (2003): 236-57. Print.

Wisor, Rebecca. "*My Country is the Whole World*": Three Guineas *and the Culture of Pacifist Dissent.* Diss. City University of New York, 2008. Print.

———. "Versioning Virginia Woolf: Notes toward a Post-eclectic Edition of *Three Guineas.*" *Modernism/modernity* 16.3 (2009): 497-535.

"Women at Cambridge, New Buildings for Girton." *The Times* 31 Oct. 1930: 10. Web. 12 Jul. 2014.

Wood, Alice. *Virginia Woolf's Late Cultural Criticism.* New York: Bloomsbury, 2013. Print.

Woolf, Leonard. *Downhill All the Way: An Autobiography of the Years 1919-1939.* New York: Harcourt Brace Jovanovich, 1967. Print.

Woolf, Virginia. *Orlando: A Biography.* New York: Harcourt Brace, 1928. Print.

———. *The Diary of Virginia Woolf.* 5 vols. Ed. Anne Olivier Bell and Andrew McNeillie. New York: Harcourt Brace Jovanovich, 1977-84. Print.

———. *The Essays of Virginia Woolf.* 6 vols. Ed. Andrew McNeillie. Vols. 1-4. New York: Harcourt Brace Jovanovich, 1987-2008. Ed. Stuart N. Clarke. Vols. 5-6. London: Hogarth, 2009-2011. Print.

———. *The Letters of Virginia Woolf.* 6 vols. Ed. Nigel Nicolson and Joanne Trautmann. New York: Harcourt Brace Jovanovich, 1975-1980. Print.

———. "'This is the House of Commons.'" *The London Scene: Six Essays on London Life.* New York: Ecco, 2006. 53-66. Print.

———. *Three Guineas.* Annot. and Intro. Jane Marcus. Orlando: Harcourt, 2006. Print.

Virginia Woolf's Reading Notes for *Three Guineas*: An Online Archive and Edition. Ed. Vara Neverow and Merry Pawlowski. woolf-center.southernct.edu. 2001. Web. 18 June 2014.

Wussow, Helen. "Virginia Woolf and the Problematic Nature of the Photographic Image." *Twentieth Century Literature* 40.1 (1994): 1-14. Print.

Melted Flesh and Tangled Threads: War Trauma and Modes of Healing in Virginia Woolf's *Mrs. Dalloway* and Leslie Marmon Silko's *Ceremony*

Kristin Czarnecki

Virginia Woolf's *Mrs. Dalloway* (1925) and Leslie Marmon Silko's *Ceremony* (1977) depict the trauma suffered by male veterans of war: Septimus Warren Smith, an English veteran of the First World War, and Tayo, a Laguna Pueblo man who fought in the Pacific Islands during World War Two. Both men are psychologically shattered by their war experience. Each has witnessed the death of a man he loved; each experiences flashbacks and hallucinations; each contends with guilt and self-accusations; and each meets with doctors incapable of administering proper treatment. Both characters also have disorienting urban experiences and sense a fraught connection with the natural world. Complicating matters is their inability, or refusal, to fulfill Western culture's proscribed gender roles. In Paula Gunn Allen's estimation, *Ceremony* is "a tale of two forces: the feminine life force of the universe and the mechanistic death force of the witchery" (119). The same might be said of *Mrs. Dalloway*, wherein the witchery—the Western worldview—insists that violence and warfare are natural and necessary and the female protagonist of which counters such ideology by embracing the multiplicity of human experience. Placing the novels alongside each other highlights the life-sustaining nature of feminine, matriarchal tenets and the patriarchal constructs that strive to undermine them.

While there exists an important and growing body of work on Woolf and multiethnic American women writers, there is to date very little scholarship on Woolf and Native American literature—yet such a discourse is proving to yield important new insights into the intersections of race, class, gender, feminism, and nation in women's writing.[1] Such is the case in analyses of Woolf and Zora Neale

---

[1] Justine Dymond finds Okanogan author Mourning Dove's 1927 novel, *Cogewea, the Half-Blood*, "troubl[ing] the formula of the Western romance" and "obtain[ing] a dimension of experimentation 'other' than, but tangential to, modernism's experiments in form" (298). In addition, the novel's "half-breed" female protagonist displays "the radical break Mourning Dove makes with modernity's ontology of the colonized, the 'primitive,' and the racialized other . . . allow[ing] us to reread canonical modernists such as Virginia Woolf and Gertrude Stein with an eye to the spatiality of race, subjectivity, and language that limits their experimentality" (309). In his postmodern reading of Ojibwe writer Louise Erdrich, Fabienne C. Quennet notes that like Woolf, Erdrich employs various narrative perspectives in her novels and stories (55). My own article examining Native American gender traditions in Woolf's *Orlando* and Erdrich's *The Last Report on the Miracles at Little No Horse* was recently published (Czarnecki, "Two-Spirits").

Hurston, Alice Walker, Paule Marshall, and Toni Morrison, among others, despite notable differences among them.[2] Reading Woolf's memoir, "A Sketch of the Past," together with Walker's *In Search of Our Mothers' Gardens*, for instance, Chella Courington states, "It is hard to imagine two writers more removed in their material circumstances than Walker and Woolf. Nevertheless, shared concerns may transcend racial, national, and generational differences" (245). I wish to suggest the potential of similar relational work regarding Woolf and Native American women writers.

While I find no evidence of Woolf directly influencing Silko, Woolfian poetics and Native American belief systems share similarities. As Allen explains in *The Sacred Hoop: Recovering the Feminine in American Indian Traditions*, American Indian cultures emphasize "complementarity rather than opposition" (19) and "egalitarian, gynecentric systems" as opposed to "hierarchical, patriarchal systems" (41). American Indians "view space as spherical and time as cyclical, whereas the non-Indian tends to view space as linear and time as sequential" (59). Tribespeople "acknowledge the essential harmony of all things and see all things as being of equal value in the scheme of things, denying the opposition, dualism, and isolation (separateness) that characterize non-Indian thought" (56). Therefore "tribal

---

[2] Jeannette McVicker finds "genuine affinities between [Woolf's and Hurston's] use of language, each providing pointed socio-political critique within narratives of skillful beauty" (279), yet she also places Woolf and Hurston in dialogue with each other to demonstrate the instability of traditional concepts of literary modernism. Anne E. Fernald and Laurie McMillan consider the feminist personal criticism of Woolf's *A Room of One's Own* and the essays in Walker's *In Search of Our Mothers' Gardens*. Writing of Walker's direct appeal to *Room* in creating her volume's eponymous essay, Fernald explores the question, "To what extent do we choose our models based on categories of identity politics, and to what extent on less categorizable qualities of mind?" (245). She cites "Woolf's and Walker's shared project of honoring and calling attention to women writers" while also revealing how such "similarities highlight the vast differences between Woolf and Walker's language and rhetoric" (246). Weighing the pros and cons of autobiographical criticism, McMillan states, "Both writers combine attention to socio-material conditions with performance and symbolism," yet "[a]t the same time, the change Walker is working towards becomes more pressing because the oppression she catalogues makes Woolf's concerns pale in comparison" (116). In terms of war trauma, the comparative work linking Woolf to African-American writers is well developed, but there is nothing linking Woolf to Native American texts in this respect. For example, Eileen Barrett examines shell shock in *Mrs. Dalloway* and Toni Morrison's second novel, *Sula*. Heeding Morrison's call in *Playing in the Dark: Whiteness and the Literary Imagination* for "new interpretations of literature" that "analyze the use of black images and the representation of black people" (Barrett 26), Barrett examines not only the manifestations of the veterans' trauma but also the responses to them of their respective communities. Addressing "not the communal but the militaristic spirit of London" in *Mrs. Dalloway* brings into even sharper focus how "Morrison rejects the masculine western tradition of war, its heroes and its madness" (27, 30). Lorie Watkins Fulton considers the "strikingly similar plots" of *Mrs. Dalloway* and *Sula* and how the latter overcomes the isolation and alienation she believes remain unresolved in the former (67).

people allow all animals, vegetables, and minerals (the entire biota, in short) the same or even greater privileges than humans" (57). These concepts reflect many of Woolf's tenets concerning life and literature as the nonlinearity, polyphonic narration, critique of patriarchy, rejection of false binaries, and emphasis on the natural world in her works attest.[3] Exploring war trauma in *Mrs. Dalloway* and *Ceremony* reveals many such commonalities while also "focus[ing] our attention on important differences between cultural perspectives on war" (Hussey 9).[4]

More specifically, the feminine characteristics and matriarchal nature of many Native American tribes, including the Laguna Pueblo, prove more conducive than patriarchal tenets to recovery from war trauma. Allen enumerates the prominent features of Native American gynocracies, such as "free and easy sexuality and wide latitude in personal style. This latitude means that a diversity of people, including gay males and lesbians, are not denied and are in fact likely to be accorded honor. Also likely to be prominent in such systems," Allen continues, "are nurturing, pacifist, and passive males (as defined by western minds) and self-defining, assertive, decisive women," characteristics to which young boys and girls, respectively, aspire (2). Dunn and Comfort similarly explain that for Native American women, "protecting and nurturing our families is a demonstration of female respect and honor, often greater in honor to that of men's roles within tribal society" (xv). In addition, matriarchal social structures emphasize community as opposed to patriarchy's emphasis on individuality. Of particular note in woman-centered cultures

---

[3] Toril Moi finds Woolf "reject[ing] the metaphysical essentialism underlying patriarchal ideology" (9), while Rachel Blau DuPlessis views Woolf's refutation of "gender polarization and the dichotomy of male and female, public and private spheres" as hallmarks of "female modernism" manifest in the "choral or group protagonist" of *The Years* and *Between the Acts* (162). Denise Delorey writes of the "unabashedly antimasculinist, pacifist ideological underpinnings" of Woolf's "feminist aesthetic" (93), along with her narrative techniques that deflate "the illusion" of "an overdetermined social structure" (105). Melba Cuddy-Keane finds Woolf "seek[ing] an alternative to the authorial / authoritative dominance of patriarchal discourse" (137) in her "object[ion] to monologic prose" (144), her "polyvocality" (151), and the "conversational turn" in her essays in particular—a strategy "enabling polyphonic thinking in the individual reader and challenging the monologic societal voice" (153). As Patricia Matson writes, "deconstructing patriarchal ideology and foregrounding woman's subjectivity are central to the textual politics at play in Woolf's fiction and essays" (162). In *Mrs. Dalloway*, she states, "The authority of the humanist subject and the authority of patriarchal value systems are challenged at every turn" (163), while Woolf's oeuvre overall "pose[s] a fundamental challenge" to dichotomies and dualism (163). Twenty-first-century Woolf scholarship has focused heavily on the natural world in Woolf's works. See Christina Alt, Bonnie Kime Scott, Czarnecki and Rohman, and #81 and #84 of the *Virginia Woolf Miscellany*, special topics issues on "Eco-Woolf" (edited by Diana Swanson) and "Woolf and Animals" (edited by Kristin Czarnecki and Vara Neverow), respectively.

[4] Hussey refers here to comparative studies of war in Woolf and Willa Cather, yet his words also express the value in exploring war trauma in Woolf and Silko.

"is the absence of punitiveness as a means of social control" (Allen 3). Rather, when someone has transgressed his or her tribe's cultural or ceremonial codes, the people hold themselves responsible for righting the imbalance and reintegrating the person into tribal life—in contrast to patriarchal modes of separating, isolating, and incarcerating those who break the law or engage in behaviors deemed contrary or dangerous to the social order. Before European contact, Native American matriarchies "were for the most part superbly healthy, simultaneously cooperative and autonomous, peace-centered, and ritual-oriented" (Allen 31).

When readers encounter the matriarchal nature of Laguna culture in *Ceremony*, they not only attain a greater understanding of Silko's themes and Native American traditions more broadly, but they can also view Western texts and literary criticism through a more discerning interpretive lens. Sandra Gilbert and Susan Gubar, for example, propose that English men's experiences of trench warfare resembled the lack of control and power endured by women in the nineteenth century. Conversely, women during the First World War experienced newfound freedoms in paid employment outside the home. Gilbert and Gubar believe both scenarios led to men's emasculation, which manifests itself in early twentieth-century Western literature. Yet equating entrapment and disempowerment with women, and linking women's independence with men's emasculation, proves inappropriate in a Native American context and fails to explain Native men's wartime and post-war trauma.[5] Gilbert and Gubar further state that during and after World War Two, gender divisions became even more pronounced.[6] Again, beginning from a place of gender division privileging males over females cannot account for Native American men's or women's experiences. Given the wartime sacrifices of Native men and their families, it becomes important to establish a cross-cultural dialogue allowing for defter readings of both Native and Western texts addressing personal and cultural recovery from trauma.

Such recovery proves elusive to Septimus Warren Smith in *Mrs. Dalloway*. On a June morning in 1923, Septimus sits in Regent's Park with his Italian wife, Rezia. We learn that he had eagerly enlisted in the army and now suffers from post-trau-

---

[5] "12,000 Indians—fully eighty-five percent of them volunteers—served in the First World War," Franco states. "During World War I, 600 Indian volunteers dominated the 36th Infantry Division," and "[n]umerous witnesses attested to the bravery of the American Indian in World War I" (60). In addition, A. LaVonne Brown Ruoff explains, "Because Indians volunteered, were wounded, and died in World War I far out of proportion to their numbers in the society, Congress awarded them citizenship [in 1924] out of gratitude for their service" (183).
[6] See Gilbert and Gubar's three-volume *No Man's Land: The Place of the Woman Writer in the Twentieth Century*, especially "Soldier's Heart: Literary Men, Literary Women, and the Great War," the seventh chapter in *Volume 2: Sexchanges* (258-323), and "Charred Skirts and Deathmask: World War II and the Blitz on Women," the fifth chapter in *Volume 3: Letters from the Front* (211-65).

matic stress disorder caused in part by witnessing the death of his commanding officer. Back in England, he is unable to summon what his doctors consider normal feelings, such as sexual desire towards his wife, yet his eyes well with tears when he sees "inexhaustible charity and laughing goodness one shape after another of unimaginable beauty" in the "smoke words" of the skywriting airplane he thinks is signaling him (*MD* 21). He feels with excruciating sensitivity that "leaves were alive; trees were alive. And the leaves [were] connected by millions of fibres with his own body" (*MD* 22). In addition, "The sparrows fluttering, rising, and falling in jagged fountains were part of the pattern" he perceives in all that surrounds him (*MD* 22), and he believes the sparrows sing to him in Greek that "there is no crime" (*MD* 24). Thus "two arguments, for the veteran and for the natural environment, are not exclusive in *Mrs. Dalloway*," writes Rachel Zlatkin. "Rather the two are inextricably bound in the character of Septimus Smith" (85)—as we will later see the veteran and the natural environment tightly bound in the character of Tayo in *Ceremony*. Septimus believes he carries "the greatest message in the world" (*MD* 81) and also that he has committed a grievous crime.[7]

Idealistic as he headed into the war to "save an England which consisted almost entirely of Shakespeare's plays" (*MD* 84), Septimus now sees the Bard as having sensed the depravity of humankind. "The war had changed Septimus's understanding of human nature," writes Karen DeMeester (657). "How Shakespeare loathed humanity—the putting on of clothes, the getting of children," Septimus thinks, "the sordidity of the mouth and the belly!" (*MD* 86). He sees "loathing, hatred, despair" in people, the "secret signal which one generation passes, under disguise, to the next" (*MD* 86), observing "Amelia What'shername, handing round cups of tea" at work, "a leering, sneering, obscene little harpy," and "the Toms and Berties in their starched shirt fronts oozing thick drops of vice" (*MD* 87-88). Worst of all are his threats of suicide and double-suicide as he implores his wife to join him. As Clarissa Dalloway runs errands in preparation for her party that night, Septimus and Rezia make their way to renowned psychiatrist Sir William Bradshaw when treatment from their regular practitioner, Dr. Holmes, proves fruitless.

Ceremony similarly begins several years after war has ended, in this case World War Two, with Tayo lying in bed sleepless, crying and vomiting. Having been on the Bataan Death March, in a prisoner of war camp, and in the mental ward of a Veteran's Administration hospital, Tayo has returned to his reservation in New Mexico only to grow increasingly ill. He hears a jumble of strange sounds along with the Laguna, English, and Japanese languages in his head, and as with Septimus, Tayo's tormented thoughts are closely related to bodily experience.

[7] "Back home," Christine Froula explains, "Septimus is fated to know 'everything,' to grasp 'the meaning of the world,' and to bear the burden of witnessing his civilization's unimaginable violence without being driven mad" (149).

Septimus ponders the "scientific explanation" for his sensations, concluding, "It was the heat wave presumably, operating upon a brain made sensitive by eons of evolution. Scientifically speaking, the flesh was melted off the world. His body was macerated until only the nerve fibres were left. It was spread like a veil upon a rock" (*MD* 66). Similarly, Tayo "could feel it inside his skull—the tension of little threads being pulled and how it was with tangled things, things tied together, and as he tried to pull them apart and rewind them into their places, they snagged and tangled even more" (*C* 6). As Jude Todd explains, "combat trauma [is] inscribed on [the] mind, emotions, and the body" (155).

Adding to Tayo's psychological and bodily anguish, conditions at home are grim. His cousin Rocky, with whom he had enlisted, has been killed in the war, his beloved Uncle Josiah is also dead, and drought plagues the land. While Septimus feels an affinity with the trees and birds around him, Tayo believes he has a ruinous connection with the natural world. In the Philippines, he had cursed the rain and prayed "for dry air, dry as a hundred years squeezed out of yellow sand, air to dry out the oozing wounds of Rocky's leg, to let the torn flesh and broken bones breathe, to clear the sweat that filled Rocky's eyes" (*C* 10)—and so he blames himself for the drought. Tayo's uncle and grandmother are quiet, concerned presences in the house, but his aunt has little patience or sympathy for Tayo, her sister Laura's half-breed child who she believes should be dead instead of her son, Rocky.

It becomes clear early on, then, that while Tayo's war experience plays a role in his trauma, previous aspects of his life also contribute to his suffering. His father is a white man he has never met, and his mother was a troubled young woman estranged from her family. As a young child living with her in makeshift shanties in Gallup, New Mexico, Tayo witnessed her and other women prostitute themselves for food and alcohol. He saw daily violence and degradation and scavenged the filthy floors of taverns for something to eat. Laura leaves Tayo with her sister's family when he is four years old, and she dies shortly thereafter. Throughout his life, Tayo struggles to recall her and fill the void of her absence. "At Laguna Pueblo in New Mexico, 'Who is your mother?' is an important question," Allen explains. "At Laguna, one of several of the ancient Keres gynocratic societies of the region, your mother's identity is the key to your own identity" (209). With no mother to guide him, Tayo feels ashamed of his biracial background, enduring taunts about it from other Indians and even from within his family.

Moreover, his years at an Indian boarding school impress upon him white society's vilification of the Laguna worldview. Tayo had trusted in his culture's stories, Silko writes, "until the teachers at Indian school taught him not to believe in that kind of 'nonsense'" (*C* 18), as his mother before him had been "[s]hamed by what they taught her in school about the deplorable ways of the Indian people" (*C* 63). Such colonizing tactics exist all around him and have been deeply imbibed by Auntie and Rocky. Auntie flaunts her Christianity, scoffs at tribal ways, and encourages Rocky's ambitions to leave the reservation. Like his mother, Rocky rejects Laguna beliefs, seen when he and Tayo hunt and kill a deer one day. As Rocky prepares to cut open the carcass, Tayo takes off his jacket and places it on the deer's head. Rocky asks Tayo why he does such a thing, and Tayo thinks, "they both knew why. The people said you should do that before you gutted the deer. Out of respect. But Rocky was funny about those things. He was an A-student and all-state in football and track. He had to win; he said he was always going to win" (47). For Rocky, winning means assimilating—converting to the white worldview. "So he listened to his teachers, and he listened to the coach. They were proud of him. They told him, 'Nothing can stop you now except one thing: don't let the people at home hold you back.' . . . Tayo saw how Rocky deliberately avoided the old-time ways" (47). Yet Tayo worships his cousin, which leaves him confused and bereft about his heritage and his place in the world. He is profoundly motherless, for Allen explains the Keres's expansive concept of mother:

> Of course, your mother is not only that woman whose womb formed and released you—the term refers in every individual case to an entire generation of women whose psychic, and consequently physical, 'shape' made the psychic existence of the following generation possible. But naming your own mother (or her equivalent) enables people to place you precisely within the universal web of your life, in each of its dimensions: cultural, spiritual, personal, and historical. . . . Failure to know your mother, that is, your position and its attendant traditions, history, and place in the scheme of things, is failure to remember your significance, your reality, your right relationship to earth and society. It is the same as being lost—isolated, abandoned, self-estranged, and alienated from your own life. (209-10)

While *Ceremony* demonstrates the effects upon Tayo of his lost mother and subsequent alienation, readers can only speculate about the roots of Septimus's trauma, which manifests about four years after the war, corresponding with the third of the "three clearly discernible life patterns for war neurotic ex-servicemen" outlined by Peter Leese (156):

> First were those affected by the war but able to recover relatively quickly, at the latest by the early 1920s. . . . Second were the veterans less able to shed their symptoms or reenter civilian life, and who either never recovered from the war or suffered a severe relapse some years afterwards. Third were cases of men who left the services apparently healthy, but whose mental condition later deteriorated. (156)

Outwardly, Septimus appeared to thrive in the war: "he developed manliness; he was promoted; he drew the attention, indeed the affection of his officer, Evans by name. It was a case of two dogs playing," Woolf writes, the younger playful and energetic, the elder "raising a paw, turning and growling good-temperedly" (*MD* 84), reflecting the bond often forged between men in wartime.[8] Septimus earned awards, which later earns the respect of his employer, Mr. Brewer, for before the war, Brewer had worried about Septimus's disinclination for sport and interest in poetry. Yet when Bradshaw questions him about his war experience, Septimus does not answer. Lest Bradshaw doubt his bravery, Rezia quickly assures him that her husband served with distinction.

Reminding Septimus of his promotions and medals only exacerbates his sense of guilt, which many critics attribute to his homosexual relationship with, or feelings for, Evans—feelings inadmissible in patriarchal culture. Suzette Henke notes Septimus's "frustrated homosexual desire" (15), and Karen S. McPherson states that his "vocabulary of crime and confession" includes the criminality, in his doctors' view, of "resisting heterosexual convention" (135). Mitchell A. Leaska considers the novel's "allusions to homosexuality too obvious to be ignored" in regard to Septimus and surmises that Septimus believes his feelings for Evans constitute "a transgression of society's moral code" (108). Similarly, Tonya Krouse believes "Septimus's emotional numbness leads to his ultimate inability to speak his grief, and this silencing of his emotions and of his voice directly relates to his society's prohibition against homosexuality" (15). Alternatively, DeMeester deems it "more likely that the crime [Septimus] refers to is the killing and, particularly, killing with indifference that he saw and more than likely participated in" during the war (654), noting, however, that "[d]uring combat, indifference is a survival tool that protects the psyche from being overwhelmed by the horror received through the senses" (658). Yet as *Mrs. Dalloway* makes clear, such indifference only heightens Septimus's anguish and confusion in later years.

Kathryn Van Wert goes back farther in Septimus's life to discover the source of his trauma. Examining Woolf's draft of *Mrs. Dalloway*, "The Hours," which devotes greater attention to Septimus's early years, she locates the source of his distress in the pedestrian, discordant aspects of home life. Van Wert acknowledges the difficulty of pinning down exactly what went awry for Septimus before the war, but even in *Mrs. Dalloway* we see him leaving home due to a mother who lied and a desire to be a poet—impossible, he believes, in his provincial hometown. Like Van Wert, Wyatt Bonikowski traces Septimus's post-war guilt and trauma to prewar experiences, namely his heterosexual, not homosexual, impulses. "Marriage, Septimus discovers, is not about love but about lies and seduction; his innocent

---

[8] "The bond between officer and man was usually good and often intense," states Leese, "and comparable to the relationship between husband and wife, or brother and brother" (28).

yearning for [his poetry teacher] Miss Isabel Pole contained within it an 'outrage'; and women who look on him see the mark of vice," he writes (53). "The 'crime,' in other words, had been within him and his relations with women all along, even before the war" (Bonikowski 53). Teasing out the precise cause of Septimus's distress is no easy task, yet the myriad theories proffered all point to the damage wrought upon him by heteronormative social codes.

Ceremony also explores young men's impulses to enlist, their wartime conduct, and their subsequent trauma—also related to Western norms regarding masculinity. At the post office one day, Rocky and Tayo approach an army recruiter, with Rocky telling Tayo it is their duty as Americans to enlist. In fact, "42% of the eligible adult Indian males served in the war . . . the highest ratio of service men of any ethnic minority or the white majority" (Abe 129). In *World War II and the American Indian*, Townsend writes:

> By November 1941, nearly forty-two thousand Native Americans, aged twenty-one to thirty-five, had fulfilled their registration requirement. This number represented almost two-thirds of all eligible Indian males. Not only did Indians comply with draft registration, many voluntarily enlisted in the armed forces rather than wait for induction orders. Of the 4,500 Indians in service one week before Pearl Harbor, more than sixty percent had enlisted. (61)

Many enlisted from "a sense of inclusion as Americans" in their response to Hitler's domination. "A war in which a minority race was to be exterminated carried very real and vivid images and emotions among American Indians," Townsend explains (76). Indians also wished to fight for the land. "In contrast to the temporal and linear underpinnings of Christian religion and its fundamental premise that God's Word is universal, Indian spirituality was (and is) spatial. All life, knowledge, and truth are derived from the land, as is tribal identity" (Townsend 77). Native Americans were also attracted by military pay and the opportunity to learn skills that would be, they were led to believe, of practical use to them after the war.

In *Ceremony*, however, Rocky enlists without regard for tribal concerns. Throughout his life, he repudiates his Laguna heritage and resolves to join the white world. Tayo, in turn, resists enlisting because he promised to help Josiah care for a herd of Mexican spotted cattle. Contrary to Septimus, Rocky, and the millions of young men who heeded the injunction to go to war abroad, Tayo feels compelled to stay on his own land. Pressured by Rocky and overwhelmed with emotion when Rocky tells the recruiter that he and Tayo are brothers, however, he succumbs, and unlike the benumbed Septimus, he goes on to feel intense emotion during his service. He sobs uncontrollably at the carnage around him, including the death of Rocky at the hands of a Japanese soldier. Later he tries to muffle the pain with alcohol and occasional bursts of violence, including a drunken assault on a fellow veteran at a bar one night. Allen explains the individual and communal post-war sickness experienced by characters in *Ceremony*:

> Tayo's illness is a function of disordered thinking—his own, that of those around him and that of the forces that propelled them all into the tragic circumstances of World War II. The witchery put this disordered thinking into motion long ago and distorted human beings' perceptions so that they believed that other creatures—insects and beasts and half-breeds and whites and Indians and Japanese—were enemies, rather than part of the one being we all share, and thus should be destroyed. (125)

Tayo's fellow veterans believe in the witchery, replacing traditional Laguna rituals with post-war barroom rituals of their own: "[T]hey repeated the stories . . . like long medicine chants," Silko writes, "the beer bottles pounding on the counter tops like drums" (*C* 39). Tayo declines to join them in their gloating over the killing of Japanese soldiers, for he does not hate the Japanese and never did.

During the war, Tayo notes that the skin of the Japanese resembles his and even sees his uncle Josiah's face in one of theirs. Unlike Septimus's "killing with indifference," Tayo refuses to engage in combat and begins to cry when the man he believes to be Josiah is killed. Although "Rocky made him look at the corpse and said, 'Tayo, this is a *Jap*!'" (*C* 7), Tayo screams, convinced it is Josiah who lies dead at his feet. Later, army doctors tell him "it was all superstition, seeing Josiah" (*C* 181). However, John Peacock explains, the "Navajo medicine-man named Betonie, to whom Tayo goes for a curing ceremony, takes it as a profound insight into the facial identity of Native Americans who crossed the Bering Strait from Asia thirty thousand years ago" (302): "It isn't surprising you saw [Josiah] with [the Japanese]," Betonie says. "You saw who they were. Thirty thousand years ago they were not strangers" (*C* 114-15).[9] Tayo will grow increasingly aware of the significance of his vision when he reintegrates into his Pueblo community. "[H]e

---

[9] The Bering Strait theory is a disputed hypothesis. F. David Peat states that some, the Early Arrivalists, "place the first human beings in the Americas at between 30,000 years ago and as many as 250,000 years ago" (103). Some of their evidence has been dated "as being many tens of thousands of years old. . . . If these dates are correct, then it means that the Americas were occupied long before the first hypothetical hunter-gatherer group could have marched across the Bering Strait" (103). Vine Deloria, Jr., is among those asserting that "the insistence on seeing American Indians as recent arrivals on the continent has as much to do with an ideological investment in denying them rights to the land as it does with hard evidence" (Murray 329).

will realize that in a crucial sense the executed man actually was Josiah," writes Louis Owens, "that all men and women are one and all phenomena inextricably interrelated. What is dismissed as a form of insanity is, Silko ultimately argues in the novel, the only sane view of the world. The alternative is universal death" (98). Additionally, a Japanese soldier reminds Tayo of a friend from Albuquerque Indian School; amidst the chaos, Tayo addresses this man as "Willie" (*C* 40).

Listening to his fellow veterans try to recapture their wartime glory, Tayo tells them that any notoriety they received during the war, particularly sexual attention from white women, was due only to their uniform, "voic[ing] Euramerican dismissal of Indians as well as Indian anger over it," states David Rice (123). Tayo listens impassively as the men recount their sexual exploits in vulgar detail, egging each other on and repeating the misogynist stories they have told dozens of times.[10] One occurrence in particular shows how the men had to hide their Indian identity from white women if not from their white fellow soldiers. Emo tells of a night when he decides to sleep with a woman he sees at a bar. His drinking buddy encourages him with, "Go get 'em, Chief," and in mapping out his strategy, Emo decides, "I'm Italian tonight" (*C* 53). Townsend states:

> Cultural differences typically dimmed once in training. Those differences that persisted generally received light-hearted attention. Often, Indian soldiers were called "chief" or "Geronimo" by white comrades, but the conveyance of a racial slur was normally not intended or inferred. In fact, Indian soldiers widely expressed a certain approval for the names given them. (140)

On the contrary, Jere' Bishop Franco finds that "some World War II participants, out of respect for a ranking officer, never used the appellation" (134). She cites a veteran who had a Native American sergeant "that the troops never dared address . . . as 'Chief.' 'We never called him that,' remarked [the veteran], 'because we wanted to respect him'" (134).

---

[10] Townsend explains the aimlessness and hopelessness of World War II Indian veterans such as those in *Ceremony*, stating, "returning Indians found . . . limited choices. Reservation services and economies deteriorated during the war . . . . Wartime necessities stripped tribal communities of most federal services. Schools and medical facilities had either closed entirely or suffered from shortages in personnel and supplies, land remained uncultivated, and irrigation projects had fallen victim to appropriations cuts. . . . Native American veterans themselves compounded the social pressures that pervaded Indian communities in late 1945 and in 1946. The war left its mark on thousands of men. Physical dismemberment, alcoholism, and memories of the war's brutality affected many of them, and the ever-present sight of orphans, widows, and parents who had lost sons proved a constant and grim reminder of the war" (217).

We see the disrespect intended in *Ceremony* when a white man uses the name "Geronimo" as a slur. Out drinking one night, the veterans Pinkie, Leroy, and Harley ask Emo to "tell the one about the time that guy told on you" (55). As Emo becomes uncharacteristically quiet, the others tell of a night he was having sex with a woman when "the Irishman knocked on the door and yelled, 'Hey, Geronimo!'" (55). The white woman with Emo hears this but does not realize what it means, asking Emo who Geronimo is. "She says, 'That's an Indian, isn't it?' She yells back at him, 'This guy's an Indian?' He says, 'Yeah—his name is Geronimo.' She starts screaming and faints. Passes out" (55). Humiliated again, Emo deflects attention away from himself by taunting Tayo. A moment later, he takes out his prized wartime souvenir, a small bag full of Japanese teeth, and pours them onto the table, revealing the intersections between warfare, misogyny, racism, and internalized racism as he crows over his killing of Japanese officers, curses the barren land, and desires the trappings of white success, including white women.

Unlike those around them, Septimus and Tayo reject war rhetoric. Although Septimus initially believed it, as did Tayo's cousin Rocky, five years after the Armistice, he embodies the horrors of war the English refuse to acknowledge as they ignore or scorn the veterans among them and focus instead on raising monuments to those who have died. Septimus is left to sit idly in Regent's Park and meander through London, his despondent wife at his side. He mutters, jots things down, looks furtively around, and notes "revelations on the backs of envelopes" (*MD* 24). The sound of a car backfiring sends him into a paroxysm of paranoia and fear, while other Londoners enjoy imagining who might be inside the sleek sedan. If *Mrs. Dalloway* is "a full-scale Modernist onslaught on the official version of World War I" (Poole 81), Septimus's palpable anguish serves as its most potent weapon. He harbors a truth no one will hear and defies in body and mind English war and post-war rhetoric in all of its "heroic visions and masculinist fantasies" (Showalter 169).

During World War Two, the American military developed its own rhetoric rooted in stereotypes of Native Americans to showcase the aforementioned high Indian enlistment numbers and loyalty to American military interests. Such rhetoric depicted American Indian men at war as killing machines with "natural fighting abilities" (Townsend 133). In a Congressional Report published in the *Washington Star*, Major Lee Gilstrap says of the Indians he observed at an army training post:

> "The sense perception of many Indians is so acute that they can spot a snake by sound or smell before they can see it. They have an uncanny faculty at weaseling over any kind of terrain at night, and there is a saying that 'the only Indian who can't find his way back to his own lines is a dead Indian.'" Physically, "their long, sleek muscles are built for endurance.

> . . . I never saw an Indian who lacked rhythm, timing, coordination." (qtd. in Townsend 133-34)

It is not only Tayo's revulsion at violence and killing that belies such rhetoric but also his tribe's attitude toward war:

> War is so distasteful to [the Keres] that they long ago devised ritual institutions to deal with antagonism between persons and groups such as medicine societies. They also developed rituals that would purify those who had participated in warfare. If a person had actually killed someone, the ritual purification was doubly imperative, for without it a sickness would come among the people and would infect the land and the animals and prevent the rainfall. (Allen 21)

Such are the precise conditions depicted in *Ceremony*.

Attendant with their rejection of jingoism is Septimus's and Tayo's inability, or refusal, to fulfill further aspects of Western culture's proscribed role for men. Septimus marries Rezia in a panic at his inability to feel—his wartime indifference spilling over into his post-war life—and perhaps to mask his homosexuality. His wife and doctors dwell on the couple's lack of children, and Bradshaw asks him outright about his sexual impulses—a tactic also deployed by British propaganda posters suggesting the sexual impotence of non-enlisters,[11] while after the war, impotence was a widespread symptom of shell shock.[12] Despite his disinclinations, Septimus's rare moments of happiness and lucidity stem from being with Rezia. "Miracles, revelations, agonies, loneliness, falling through the sea, down, down into the flames, all were burnt out, for he had a sense, as he watched Rezia trimming the straw hat for Mrs. Peters, of a coverlet of flowers" (*MD* 139). Relaxing, he begins to joke with her and help her with the hat, for "When she sewed, he thought, she made a sound like a kettle on the hob; bubbling, murmuring" (*MD* 140)—the soothing sounds of the maternal *chora*, theorized by Julia Kristeva as the warm, safe space of the womb where structured language, subjectivity, and threats to subjectivity do not yet exist.

Jesse Wolfe views such moments as problematic, however, stating that while "his metaphorically feminine qualities speak well to his compassion and gentleness: his Christ-like suffering, his concern for the trees, his participation with Rezia in making hats . . . it is during his states of most severe distraction—bordering on disintegration—that these feminine qualities emerge most intensely" (41). While Wolfe sees Virginia Woolf imbuing Septimus's androgyny with "suggestions of arrested development or maladjustment" (41), I see Woolf critiquing a society that

---

[11] Freedman 17-18.
[12] Showalter 172.

deems certain characteristics essentially female and strives to eradicate them in men. Septimus believes his crime lies in not feeling, yet as Elaine Showalter observes, "Septimus's problem is that he feels too much for a man" (193). McPherson concurs, stating, "In the novel it is clearly *feeling too much* that transgresses acceptable and normal behavior" (136). Septimus is plagued by thoughts of suicide and cries in terror over "faces laughing at him, calling him horrible disgusting names" (*MD* 65). Rezia recalls him "arguing, laughing, crying, getting very excited and making her write things down . . . about death; about Miss Isabel Pole" (*MD* 65). In Regent's Park, his feelings vacillate between agony, fear, bewilderment, and peace as he imagines himself privy to divine messages, believes himself joined to the earth with flowers growing through his flesh, and envisions Evans coming toward him through the shrubs.[13]

Just as an array of images elicits strong emotion in Septimus, Tayo's tears flow often and urgently after the war at memories of Rocky and Josiah and from helplessly watching his family's starving animals during the drought. In her article on gender in *Ceremony*, Kristin Herzog calls attention to "male figures [in Native American literature] who are sensitive instead of ruthless, gentle instead of heroic, community-conscious instead of individualistic" (25). She identifies Tayo as one such "feeling man" with a "thinking woman" in the background: a Laguna "female divinity" (25), Thought-Woman, whom Silko presents on the first page of *Ceremony* as the originator of the story to come and creator of the world: "Thought-Woman, the spider, / named things and / as she named them / they appeared" (*C* 1). As Judith A. Antell observes, Tayo's healing ceremony involves embracing "the power and importance of the feminine principle," one that "acknowledges and supports the ancient power of Indian women in tribal life, a power which has been sustained to the present" (213). Growing up in colonized spaces and engaging in warfare, however, effects a rupture between Tayo and the woman-centered nature of his tribe. Healing this rupture becomes vital to his ceremony.

Woolf and Silko depict the different modes of treating these damaged young men: the conversion tactics of Septimus's doctors and the healing rituals of Tayo's community. DeMeester views modern literature as "a literature of trauma" depicting characters' psychological damage along with their "need . . . to give meaning to their suffering in order to recover from the trauma. Septimus's death," she writes, "is the result of his inability to communicate his experiences to others and thereby give those experiences meaning and purpose" (649). No one except Rezia will listen to Septimus, and even she struggles to do so, try as he might to transmit his messages on torn up scraps of paper. As McFarlane and van der Kolk find, "many [post-traumatic stress disorder] victims suffer from an impaired capacity to translate their intense emotions and perceptions related to the trauma into communicable

---

[13] See *MD* 66, 67, and 68.

language" (27). Those who should be furnishing Septimus with a fruitful means of relaying his anguish, such as Holmes and Bradshaw, are instead among those determined to deny or ignore war's impact on its former soldiers.

As Christine Froula states, "*Mrs. Dalloway*'s postwar world of multifarious and contested realities pits Septimus's reality against that of his doctors to frame 'madness' as censored truth" (110). Holmes insists there is nothing wrong with Septimus that a little heavy food, fresh air, and exercise cannot cure.[14] "'So you're in a funk,' he said agreeably . . . He had actually talked of killing himself to his wife, quite a girl, a foreigner, wasn't she? Didn't that give her a very odd idea of English husbands? Didn't one owe perhaps a duty to one's wife?'" (*MD* 89-90). His words echo those of an English nerve specialist to a shell-shocked soldier in 1917: "You are a young man with a wife and child at home; you owe it to them if not to yourself to make every effort to restore yourself. You appear to me to be very indifferent, but that will not do in such times as these. . . . You must recover your speech at once" (qtd. in Showalter 176). Both doctors believe in belittling their patients' suffering and goading them into recovery. This "lack of validation and support," state McFarlane and van der Kolk, generally prolongs the damaging effects of traumatic memories upon PTSD victims (25).[15]

While McFarlane and van der Kolk find that providing and restoring social support are widely accepted means of treating PTSD (24), complications arise when "the psychological needs of victims and the needs of their social network" clash (25), particularly "when the meaning of the trauma is secret, forbidden, or unacceptable (as in intrafamilial abuse or government-sanctioned violence)," such as war (25). Unlike Holmes, Sir William senses immediately the gravity of Septimus's condition but proposes to treat him by shutting him away in an asylum. "Woolf's portrait of shell shock shows close attention to the public debates of the early 1920s," Leese writes, and Bradshaw's "treatment is a composite of Woolf's

---

[14] Showalter notes that in the latter part of the nineteenth century, nerve specialists "were conspicuously and aggressively masculine in their interests, attitudes, and goals. . . . They were athletic rather than literary; sportsmen and clubmen rather than stay-at-home fathers of a lunatic *famille nombreuse*. Maudsley won ten gold medals in sports at the university; John Charles Bucknill was an ardent sportsman, proficient in fishing, hunting, sailing, coursing, and riflery; G. Fielding Blandford developed his taste for sports at Rugby; Lyttleton Winslow was a fanatical cricketer; George Savage was a passionate golfer, fisherman, and Alpine climber. . . . In their practice too, healthy physical exercise, in the form of 'manly sport and games,' was fervently recommended as an antidote to idleness and morbid introspection" (117).

[15] This lack of validation affects more than the PTSD victim alone: "Failure to deal with the plight of victims can be disastrous for a society," write McFarlane and van der Kolk. "For example, in the aftermath of World War I, the inability to face its effects on the capacity of the veterans to function effectively in society, and the social intolerance of their 'weakness,' may have substantially contributed to the subsequent rise of Fascism and militarism" (34).

experiences with Dr George Savage and Sir Maurice Craig, both of whom were in some way involved in the treatment of traumatic neurosis during the war" (166). Holmes is the more bumbling of the two doctors yet possesses a threatening brute strength, while Sir William, wielding greater influence, is the more insidious as the novel's remarkable passage on Proportion and Conversion indicates. Proportion, Sir William's goddess, constitutes a way of life, Woolf writes, a patriarchal, machine-like society—Silko calls it the witchery—exerting subtle yet relentless pressure on its citizens to conform. Proportion taken to extremes becomes Conversion, "less smiling, more formidable a Goddess" (*MD* 97), eradicating people's individuality as Lady Bradshaw, for instance, experiences the "slow sinking, water-logged, of her will into" her husband's (*MD* 98). Conversion operates not only in England but also in the colonization of "the heat and sands of India, the mud and swamp of Africa" (*MD* 97).

Conversion has been decimating American Indian cultures for nearly 500 years when *Ceremony* opens. The denigration of Indian ways Tayo experiences as a schoolboy had caused his identity to disintegrate years before he went to war. In a mental hospital in Los Angeles afterwards, drugged by doctors, he determines to vanish altogether. He metaphorizes himself as "white smoke" in which he loses consciousness of himself, believes he is invisible, and speaks of himself in the third person. The doctors call Tayo's condition "battle fatigue" and tell his aunt and uncle that "the cause . . . was a mystery, even to them" (*C* 28). The treatment for it has changed somewhat since the First World War, for "by the mid-1940s, and in the midst of a major military conflict, in popular imagination shell shock was acknowledged and tolerated as a part of modern combat" (Leese 160). While Holmes advises Rezia to distract Septimus from thinking about himself, hence her continual injunctions to him to "Look" when he grows distracted, Tayo's white doctors yell at him "that he had to think only of himself, and not about the others, that he would never get well as long as he used words like 'we' and 'us'" (*C* 116). And, they admonish, "No Indian medicine" (*C* 31). Disconnecting psychologically from his community, however, causes Tayo to dissociate from his own psyche. At his lowest moments, he longs to be white smoke again, for "the smoke had been dense; visions and memories of the past did not penetrate there" (*C* 14). After he has been discharged and gone home, he grows worse until his family calls in old Ku'oosh, a Laguna priest. Ku'oosh proves ineffective, however, for he relies solely on traditional medicine, finding the white world and its inhumanity—genocide, atomic weapons—beyond his comprehension, as is the notion that Tayo might have killed someone in the war and not know it.[16] Weeks later, Tayo's uncle tells

---

[16] Discussing Silko's writing of *Ceremony*, Chavkin says, "she recalled that after World War II ended, frequently the Pueblo and the Navajo performed traditional purification rituals for returning veterans. Unfortunately, the effectiveness of these rituals for some of the soldiers

him that Ku'oosh stopped by and "told your grandma what some of the old men are thinking. They think you better get help pretty soon" (*C* 98).

It is in terms of the two men's treatment and the results thereof that the novels most sharply diverge as *Ceremony* depicts a matriarchal culture that heals the wounded, and *Mrs. Dalloway* critiques a patriarchy that will not. Septimus's fate is sealed by his doctors' insistence on proportion, for he understands as Holmes barges into his home that conversion in the form of confinement is near at hand. Although he loves life at this particular moment, feeling at ease creating hats with Rezia, he jumps out the window onto the railings below in order to preserve, as Clarissa sees it upon hearing of his death, "the thing there was that mattered" (*MD* 180)—the honesty and integrity forfeited by so many throughout their lives. DeMeester states that "modernist forms are . . . well-suited for depicting the traumatized mind but ill-suited for depicting recovery" as "the task of giving individual and cultural meaning to the suffering falls to later generations of artists" (649, 652). In fact *Mrs. Dalloway* does lend meaning to Septimus's suffering, proffering an alternative to patriarchy in his symbiotic if unsettling relationship with nature; his revelations about time, the body, war, and death; and his transmission of his insights onto paper—in short, his accessing "the power of art, thought, and imagination to grapple with reality and console for loss" (Froula 112). Entrapped in a society denying such strategies to men, Septimus loses his life.

Imbued with Laguna history, myth, symbolism, poetry, ritual prayers, and elements of the oral tradition, it is the language of *Ceremony* that constitutes recovery, starting with Tayo's name. "'Tayo' is the name of a Laguna folk hero," Todd explains. "Spider Woman gave this legendary Tayo gifts, which he took back to help his people. Readers familiar with this story suspect that Silko's Tayo will perform similar feats" (161). Paul Beekman Taylor points out the difference between names in Euramerican and Native American cultures. "Even names for whites are but banal indicators of people with little or no secret signifying power," he writes, "whereas an Indian's names—in both their native and European forms—are hidden texts of being. . . . the Indian carefully guards the story force in names, which can be marshaled at an appropriate moment" (46-47). Such symbolism contrasts starkly with the naming of Septimus: "London has swallowed up many millions of young men called Smith," Woolf writes, "thought nothing of fantastic Christian names like Septimus with which their parents have thought to distinguish them" (*MD* 82). Ariela Freedman refers to Septimus as "nameless" (3), and Showalter notes that in post-war England, "there was a theory that 'strange first names' were symptomatic of latent family degeneracy" (179).[17]

was inadequate, which some people interpreted as evidence of the inadequacy of American Indian beliefs. Silko suggests, however, that because these rituals were not devised with modern warfare in mind, they must be modified if they are to be effective" (6).

[17] I wish to thank Anne E. Fernald for pointing out that the name Septimus does carry al-

Along with his name, other factors save Tayo's life. Above all, healing him becomes a communal endeavor. A group of elders gathers to weigh their options, leading Tayo's uncle Robert to bring him to the Navajo medicine man, Betonie, who teaches Tayo important lessons, listens to what he needs to say, and allows him periods of silent reflection, unlike Septimus's doctors. Tayo doubts Betonie at first, unsettled by the proximity of his hogan to the squalid city below. Looking down at the "broken glass, blinding reflections off the mirrors and chrome of the wrecked cars in the dump below," he "felt the old nausea rising up in his stomach" (*C* 108). Nevertheless he senses "something familiar about the old man" as he looks into his eyes (*C* 109). "They were hazel like his own. The medicine man nodded. 'My grandmother was a remarkable Mexican with green eyes,' he said" (*C* 109).[18] Although Tayo has been tormented by his biracial heritage, Betonie sees wholeness and strength in hybridity—like that of the spotted cattle, missing since Josiah's death, a mixed breed able to survive drought.

Once inside the hogan, Tayo again has misgivings about Betonie when he sees a seemingly haphazard jumble of Native and Western items: "bouquets of dried sage and the brown leaves of mountain tobacco," newspapers, telephone books, and Woolworth bags, "shrunken skin pouches and black leather purses trimmed with hammered silver buttons," and "[l]ayers of old calendars, the sequences of years confused and lost" (*C* 110, 110, 111). Betonie acknowledges that many Indians distrust him because of where he lives and for his mixing of Native and Western ways. "They think the ceremonies must be performed exactly as they have always been done," he says, but points out that they began to change long ago, "if only in the aging of the yellow gourd rattle or the shrinking of the skin around the eagle's claw, if only in the different voices from generation to generation, singing the chants" (*C* 116). He explains that in the past, the ceremonies were well suited to achieving balance and harmony within Native American cultures. After European contact, however, "it became necessary to create new ceremonies. I have made changes in the rituals. The people mistrust this greatly, but only this growth keeps the ceremonies strong" (*C* 116), an idea that "challenges Euramerican stereotypes of Native American ritual as codified and stagnant and thus unable to survive the change of Euramerican encroachment and expansion" (Rice 127). Betonie surmounts false binaries by merging traditions of the past with contemporary conditions in an ongoing process of transition. "But don't be so quick to call something good or bad," he tells Tayo. "There are balances and harmonies always shifting, always necessary to maintain. . . . It is a matter of transitions, you see; the chang-

---

legorical weight. If Septimus is the seventh son, as his name suggests, then according to lore, he is imbued with special powers; so many siblings would also account for his family's poverty, perhaps another reason he flees his hometown and later enlists. In addition, Dante designated the seventh circle of hell for suicides.

[18] Septimus also has hazel eyes (*MD* 14).

ing, the becoming must be cared for closely" (*C* 120). Transition, not conversion, proves key to strength and survival.

Conversely, during and after the First World War, England sought to reaffirm polarities. By 1916, "with the nation's fighting strength being drained away by the death toll at the front," writes Cate Haste, "fears built up that its moral strength was being undermined at home" (39, 50). The pre-war sense of liberation and change for women gave way to "countervailing social pressures . . . to curtail women's economic independence, revive their 'femininity' and dependence, and send women back to the home and keep them as nurturers of the future" (Haste 63). After the war, such pressures only increased. "[M]en were feared to have been brutalised by the War," states Jessica Meyer, "a concern that influenced the desire to re-establish pre-war gender norms in order to control the effects of such brutalisation. On the other hand . . . men were understood to have been emasculated by war, especially through their experience of neurasthenia" (119). Both theories led to a reification of gender dichotomy in England. Meyer goes on to note "that in the case of neurasthenic pensioners, isolation from the family could be a deliberate part of the treatment" (125), for it was believed that the sympathy of relatives, particularly females, would exacerbate the patient's symptoms and delay or even prevent his recuperation.

Thus while doctors in *Mrs. Dalloway* resolve to separate Septimus from his wife, in *Ceremony*, Tayo's experiences with women are essential to his recovery. Shortly before the war, his intimacy with Josiah's mistress, a Mexican woman called Night Swan, initiates an understanding of his world that he will later call upon throughout his healing journey. Several years before the war, he brings a message to Night Swan from Josiah, and the blue of her room along with the cotton ball filling a hole in her screen represent her link to nature—to the sky, clouds, and rain that finally arrives after the years-long pre-war drought. Night Swan strengthens Tayo's communion with the rhythms of the natural world, and before he leaves her, she mentions the color of his eyes. "I always wished I had dark eyes like other people," Tayo responds, believing his hazel eyes evoke his mother's shame (*C* 92). As Betonie will later reiterate, Night Swan tells him that the people fear his biracial status. "Indians or Mexicans or whites—most people are afraid of change," she says. "They think that if their children have the same color of skin, the same color of eyes, that nothing is changing. . . . They are fools. They blame us, the ones who look different. That way they don't have to think about what has happened inside themselves" (*C* 92)—as the English fail to look inward to acknowledge their own culpability in patriarchal atrocities. As Tayo leaves, Night Swan tells him that while he might not immediately understand their encounter, he "will recognize it later. You are part of it now" (*C* 92)—part of the ceremony he will continue to live out. "Through Night Swan," Owens explains, "Silko lays out her rationale for the power of the mixed blood to introduce a new vitality into the Indian world" (105).

A woman foreseen by Betonie plays an even more integral role in the ceremony. "Remember these stars," Betonie says to Tayo after conducting the sandpainting ceremony. "I've seen them and I've seen the spotted cattle; I've seen a mountain and I've seen a woman" (*C* 141). After heading out to search for the cattle, Tayo follows the constellations that lead him to the home of a woman named Ts'eh, whose name incorporates part of the name of "the sacred mountain, Tse-pi'na, 'the woman veiled in clouds.' Tse-pi'na (Mount Taylor on modern maps) is blue in the distance, the color associated by Keres people with west, the direction of rain" (Owens 103-4). Ts'eh invites Tayo in, feeds him, talks with him, and after they make love, he dreams of the cattle. With her and in sight of the mountain, he begins to feel whole again, for "there was no sign the white people had ever come . . . they had no existence then, except as he remembered them" (*C* 171). As Tayo sets out from Ts'eh's home to renew his search for the cattle, "Betonie's vision was a story he could feel happening—from the stars and the woman, the mountain and the cattle would come" (*C* 173), and indeed they do. Tayo finds Ts'eh again during a snowstorm that ends when she folds her "black storm-pattern blanket" (*C* 193-4)—one of several indications that she is a "supernatural being, a Holy Person" (Owens 109), and, like Night Swan, an avatar of Thought Woman. Tayo goes to Ts'eh once more the following summer, when she teaches him about "the roots and plants she had gathered" to cultivate and transplant in order to bring forth light, warmth, and rain (*C* 208). Ts'eh is a "mysterious woman who is also—on the mythological level—a goddess or mountain spirit," Herzog writes. "She is so important in his gradual recovery that Paula Gunn Allen speaks of Tayo's 'initiation into motherhood' through Ts'eh, because she taught him to care for all living beings, to be a nurturer, to create new life" (29).

The importance of feminine principles to Tayo's healing occasions another look at Septimus's post-war views on humanity, particularly women. Commonly understood as a means of resisting social pressure, Septimus's refusal to have sex and start a family with Rezia may indicate his misogyny—a further effect upon him of Western social mores. Rather than recognize, let alone cherish, the interconnectedness of all life forms, Septimus sees himself at a remove from others. He considers sexual intimacy with a woman defiling and procreation a disgusting, merely biological act. In Native America, conversely, "maternity is a concept reaching far beyond biological reproduction" (Allen 255). Even Auntie, despite her problematic posture towards Tayo, grasps this truth. "An old sensitivity had descended in her, surviving thousands of years from the oldest times," Silko writes (*C* 62):

> When Little Sister had started drinking wine and riding in cars with white men and Mexicans, the people could not define their feeling about her. The Catholic priest shook his finger at the drunkenness and lust, but the

> people felt something deeper: they were losing her, they were losing part of themselves. The older sister had to act; she had to act for the people, to get this young girl back. . . . Her older sister must bring her back. For the people, it was that simple, and when they failed, the humiliation fell on all of them; what happened to the girl did not happen to her alone, it happened to all of them. (*C* 63)

Lacking such a concept of communal responsibility, a concept integral to "Native American oral tradition and worldview" (Owens 107), the English feel no compulsion to draw Septimus or other suffering veterans back into the fold.

Septimus's isolation is therefore not of his own making, of course, nor is his aversion to intimacy with women given the prevalence of misogyny throughout his society, including military culture as the veterans' experiences with women in *Ceremony* also indicate.[19] "Thus," write Gilbert and Gubar, "where the liberating sisterhood experienced by women [during the First World War] was mostly untainted by hostility to men . . . the combatants' comradeship . . . was as often energized by a disgust with the feminine as it was by a desire for the masculine" (*No Man's Land v. 2* 302). When considered alongside the Laguna worldview, Western culture's derogatory stance toward women, writ large in Septimus's post-war frame of mind, can only lead to, in Owens's words, universal death.

Nevertheless *Mrs. Dalloway* concludes with a woman experiencing a renewed appreciation for life due, I would argue, to a worldview not unlike that of Native Americans. As a young woman, Clarissa grasps the relatedness of all things and the circular, cyclical contours of human experience. "She was all that," she realizes one day surveying the bustling city and people around her. "So that to know her, or any one, one must seek out the people who completed them; even the places. Odd affinities she had with people she had never spoken to . . . It ended in a transcendental theory" that there are seen and unseen parts of us, and "the unseen might survive, be recovered somehow attached to this person or that, or even haunting certain places after death" (*MD* 149). Such an understanding allows Clarissa to survive within social constructs fostering divisiveness.

---

[19] Paul Delany's keynote address at the 2013 Annual Conference on Virginia Woolf, published in the subsequent book of conference proceedings, raises the specter of Septimus's misogyny. In "'The Death of a Beautiful Man': Rupert Brooke in Memory and Imagination," Delany notes that Septimus may have been modeled on Rupert Brooke. "Woolf was told everything about Brooke's 1913 breakdown by Ka Cox," Delany writes, "whose flirtation with Henry Lamb had set off the crisis. For the first half of 1913 Ka tried to make amends in every way possible, as an uneasy combination of mistress and psychiatric nurse. She had a private income, and the time and disposition to nurture the more fragile of her friends. By August Rupert had cast her off brutally in a torrent of misogynistic abuse; something of this may appear in Septimus's sexual rejection of his wife" (53).

In the same vein, Clarissa welcomes key moments from the past into her consciousness. As she embraces both joyous and painful memories while walking in London or in the solitude of her attic room, she exemplifies the importance of linking the past with the present—of continually transitioning from one to the other rather than allocating past and present to irreconcilable categories. It is in retrospect, for example, after experiencing sexual disappointment with her husband and reliving her days at Bourton, that Clarissa appreciates the magnitude of her earlier relationship with Sally Seton. Having extinguished that relationship upon her marriage, Clarissa rekindles it repeatedly in her mind and gains a deeper understanding of its significance. When they arrive at her party, Peter Walsh and Sally construe her breezy affection toward them as the superficial put-on of a hostess. On the contrary, Clarissa is sincere, for by rehearsing the past earlier that day, she has reaffirmed and revived her selfhood. By the time her party is in full swing, she has acknowledged the past, released it, and prepared herself for what may come, a process that repeats itself each day, if this particular day in June is any indication. Her rich inner life defies her society's resolve to deny the past.

Clarissa also remains open to the vagaries of the present. Upon overhearing Bradshaw tell her husband about Septimus's suicide, her displeasure at having such a matter mentioned at her party turns to more meaningful introspection as she walks into a quiet room to contemplate the event. As she envisions what must have occurred, details emerge that are absent from the abrupt suicide scene itself. "He had thrown himself from a window," she thinks. "Up had flashed the ground; through him, blundering, bruising, went the rusty spikes. There he lay with a thud, thud, thud in his brain, and then a suffocation of blackness. So she saw it" (*MD* 179). Clarissa is unafraid to acknowledge the tragedy, to arrest the procession of events that night and consider the ramifications on her of the life and death of another human being, even one she has never met. Septimus's sacrifice "made her feel the beauty; made her feel the fun" of a life often filled with terror (*MD* 182). "This is why death comes to Clarissa's party, of all the parties in London," Froula writes: "because she can admit it; because she lets it in" (102).[20]

The beggar woman outside the Tube station in *Mrs. Dalloway* also evokes a world in opposition to the alienating modern city and the machinery of warfare.

---

[20] DeMeester, conversely, believes Clarissa "silences Septimus and robs his death of meaning by refusing to change in response to his message" (663). Moreover, she finds Clarissa complicit in the conversion enforced by Holmes and Bradshaw: "Clarissa and the members of her social class do not abolish evil; they merely domesticate it," DeMeester states. "They veil it with social convention and protocol, but the evil is evident in England's perpetuation of its empire and its sacrifice of a generation to war" (665). Clearly, there is a great deal more to be said about Clarissa's response to Septimus's death along with her thoughts regarding her life experience, the function of her parties, and the state of her relationships, yet I wish in this article to maintain the focus on Septimus, Tayo, and war trauma.

Peter is the first to hear the battered woman singing in "a voice bubbling up without direction, vigour, beginning or end, running weakly and shrilly and with an absence of all human meaning into ee um fah um so / foo swee too eem oo—the voice of no age or sex, the voice of an ancient spring spouting from the earth" (*MD* 78-9)—the voice, once again, of the maternal *chora*. The battered woman suggests a primordial past that unsettles other characters and subverts an imperialist, racist, and misogynist status quo. Kate Sedon sees in the battered woman Woolf's revision of the youthful, fertile Mother Nature archetype, drawing attention to society's "social retrogressions and psychological devaluations of aging women" (163). In light of Native American matriarchy, we see that it is Western society that devalues aging women. Peter puts money into the battered woman's outstretched hand, a common means of assuaging a pang of guilt when faced with society's have-nots and also indicative of Peter's cavalier stance toward women altogether.

Rezia wonders what brought the woman to this point and where she sleeps at night, revealing her own unhappiness and worries about her fate should Septimus not recover. But the battered woman is without shame or guile: "'And if someone should see,' her song seems to say, 'what matter they?'" (*MD* 81)—a resounding counterpoint to Rezia's terror that someone might see Septimus acting strangely and to his doctors' determination to hide him away in a sanitarium. The woman's haunting song "made [Rezia] suddenly quite sure that everything was going to be right" (*MD* 81). Yet everything goes wrong as Septimus's doctors easily outmaneuver any potentially influential female, particularly a poor and aged one.

Tayo's alternative to patriarchy lies in embracing his tribe's prevailing feminine precepts. In doing so, he recognizes the folly of believing the lie of white hegemony. "The liars had fooled everyone," he thinks, "white people and Indians alike; as long as people believed the lies, they would never be able to see what had been done to them or what they were doing to each other" (*C* 177). Ts'eh had also warned him about the lies told by "the ones who would insist upon the Indian as victim, those who insist upon the 'vanishing American' image of the Indian as incapable of change and invariably defeated" (Owens 111). Rejecting the lies, Tayo returns to his people with the truth. Significantly, Ku'oosh and the other elders have been awaiting him. They invite him into the kiva to learn from his experience of healing and cultural understanding. "It took a long time to tell them the story," Silko writes; "they stopped him frequently with questions about the location and the time of day; they asked about the direction [Ts'eh] had come from and the color of her eyes" (*C* 238). As he shares his stories and engages in dialogue with the elders, he becomes a "culture hero" (Swan 229), whereas Septimus's doctors consider him a threat to be shut away and silenced.

In light of such imposed silences, I concur with Bonikowski that the implications of the effect of Septimus's death on Clarissa could help foster better relations between the sexes and lead to positive cultural change. The connection forged between them upon his death "suggests the possibility of a new relation between a man and a woman," Bonikowski states, "one not subject to the cultural and social requirements that Septimus finds repulsive and that many of the novel's characters, including Clarissa, find unfulfilling" (167-8). Of course, it is too late for Septimus to benefit from any such new relation; he gains no relief through Clarissa's empathy with his isolation. In the same vein, Froula considers the possibility that "Clarissa's elegy for Septimus [may be] inadequate to arraign the world before the truths it brands madness" (118). Although Tayo returns to his tribe with renewed spiritual and mental health, thereby strengthening the Laguna people overall, *Ceremony* resembles *Mrs. Dalloway* in its equivocal ending. The novel illustrates the life-affirming, life-sustaining nature of certain cultural and social injunctions when situated in a matriarchal rather than a patriarchal context, yet, we are told in the end, the witchery is "dead for now," not forever (*C* 243). Just as Tayo's journey to recovery does not follow a straight trajectory, we see that his and his people's struggle will perhaps never be truly over.

The novels' conclusions also resemble each other in offering hopefulness, for Froula goes on to state, "*Mrs. Dalloway* captures [Septimus's] message within its fictional bounds for the actual world beyond them. Not Clarissa but we readers receive (or not) the message of Septimus's death" (118). The novel harbors numerous tragedies—the suffering and dying war veteran, the denigration of women in patriarchy—but "Woolf's elegiac art battles alongside them on the side of Love for a future that history had not, in 1925, foreclosed," Froula writes (125), citing, for example, Peter Walsh's sense of "an exhilarating forward motion in postwar civilization" (126). Similarly, Tayo realizes that the world has "no boundaries, only transitions through all distances and time" (*C* 219), that "Josiah and Rocky were not far away. They were close; they had always been close. And he loved them then as he had always loved them . . . nothing was ever lost as long as the love remained" (*C* 204). When he returns to his reservation after the war and reintegrates into his woman-centered tribe, the promise of a new beginning holds forth in the simple verse that encircles the novel: "Sunrise" at the story's opening (*C* 5), and "Sunrise, / accept this offering, / Sunrise" at the end (*C* 244).[21] As Clarissa's party continues, as Tayo's community nurtures him, and as he in turn becomes a nurturer, feminine principles keep the witchery at bay and offer a path forward.

---

[21] Woolf's *The Waves* (1931) similarly links character and narrative to the natural world's cycles.

Works Cited

Abe, Juri. "Fighting a White Man's War: Participation and Representation of the Native American During WWII." *Rikkyo American Studies* 33 (2011): 129-45. Print.

Allen, Paula Gunn. *The Sacred Hoop: Recovering the Feminine in American Indian Traditions*. 1986. Boston: Beacon Press, 1992. Print.

Alt, Christina. *Virginia Woolf and the Study of Nature*. Cambridge: Cambridge UP, 2010. Print.

Antell, Judith A. "Momaday, Welch, and Silko: Expressing the Feminine Principle Through Male Alienation." *American Indian Quarterly* 12.3 (1988): 213-20. Print.

Barrett, Eileen. "Septimus and Shadrack: Woolf and Morrison Envision the Madness of War." Hussey and Neverow 26-32. Print.

Bonikowski, Wyatt. *Shell Shock and the Modernist Imagination: The Death Drive in Post-World War I British Fiction*. Burlington, VT: Ashgate, 2013. Print.

Chavkin. Allen, ed. Introduction. *Leslie Marmon Silko's* Ceremony*: A Casebook*. Oxford: Oxford UP, 2002. 3-16. Print.

Courington, Chella. "Virginia Woolf and Alice Walker: Family as Metaphor in the Personal Essay." Hussey and Neverow 239-45. Print.

Cuddy-Keane, Melba. "The Rhetoric of Feminist Conversation: Virginia Woolf and the Trope of the Twist." Mezei 137-61. Print.

Czarnecki, Kristin. "Two-Spirits and Gender Variance in Virginia Woolf's *Orlando* and Louise Erdrich's *The Last Report on the Miracles at Little No Horse*." *Virginia Woolf: Twenty-First-Century Approaches*. Ed. Dubino et al. Edinburgh: Edinburgh UP, 2014. 205-22. Print.

Czarnecki, Kristin, and Carrie Rohman, eds. *Virginia Woolf and the Natural World: Selected Papers from the Twentieth Annual International Conference on Virginia Woolf*. Clemson: Clemson U Digital P, 2011. Print.

———, and Vara Neverow, eds. *Virginia Woolf Miscellany* 84 (2013). Print.

Delany, Paul. "'The Death of a Beautiful Man': Rupert Brooke in Memory and Imagination." *Virginia Woolf and the Common(wealth) Reader: Selected Papers of the Twenty-Third Annual International Conference on Virginia Woolf*. Ed. Helen Wussow and Mary Ann Gillies. Clemson: Clemson U Digital P, 2014. 50-58. Print.

Delorey, Denise. "Parsing the Female Sentence: The Paradox of Containment in Virginia Woolf's Narratives." Mezei 93-108. Print.

DeMeester, Karen. "Trauma and Recovery in Virginia Woolf's *Mrs. Dalloway*." *Modern Fiction Studies* 44.3 (1998): 649-73. Print.

Dunn, Carolyn, and Carol Comfort. *Through the Eye of the Deer: An Anthology of Native American Women Writers*. San Francisco: Aunt Lute Books, 1999. Print.

DuPlessis, Rachel Blau. *Writing Beyond the Ending: Narrative Strategies of Twentieth-Century Women Writers*. Bloomington: Indiana UP, 1985. Print.

Dymond, Justine. "Modernism(s) Inside Out: History, Space, and Modern American Subjectivity in *Cogewea, the Half-Blood*." *Geomodernisms: Race, Modernism, Modernity*. Ed. Laura Doyle and Laura Winkiel. Bloomington: Indiana UP, 2005. 297-312. Print.

Fernald, Anne E. "A Room, A Child, A Mind of One's Own: Virginia Woolf, Alice Walker, and Feminist Personal Criticism." Hussey and Neverow 245-51. Print.

Franco, Jere' Bishop. *Crossing the Pond: The Native American Effort in World War II*. Denton, TX: U of North Texas P, 1999. Print.

Freedman, Ariela. *Death, Men, and Modernism: Trauma and Narrative in British Fiction from Hardy to Woolf*. New York and London: Routledge, 2003. Print.

Froula, Christine. *Virginia Woolf and the Bloomsbury Avant-Garde: War, Civilization, Modernity*. New York: Columbia UP, 2005. Print.

Fulton, Lorie Watkins. "'A direction of one's own': Alienation in *Mrs. Dalloway* and *Sula*." *African American Review* 40.1 (2006): 67-77. Print.

Gilbert, Sandra, and Susan Gubar. *No Man's Land: The Place of the Woman Writer in the Twentieth Century*, 3 Vols. New Haven and London: Yale UP, 1988, 1989, 1994. Print.

Haste, Cate. *Rules of Desire: Sex in Britain: World War I to the Present*. London: Chatto & Windus, 1992. Print.

Henke, Suzette A. "Virginia Woolf's Septimus Smith: An Analysis of 'Paraphrenia' and the Schizophrenic Use of Language." *Literature and Psychology* 31.4 (1981): 13-23. Print.

Herzog, Kristin. "Thinking Woman and Feeling Man: Gender in Silko's *Ceremony*." *MELUS* 12.1 (1985): 25-36. Print.

Hussey, Mark, ed. "Living in a War Zone: An Introduction to Virginia Woolf as a War Novelist." *Virginia Woolf and War: Fiction, Reality, and Myth*. Syracuse: Syracuse UP, 1991. 1-13. Print.

———, and Vara Neverow, eds. *Virginia Woolf: Emerging Perspectives: Selected Papers from the Third Annual Conference on Virginia Woolf*. New York: Pace UP, 1994. Print.

Krouse, Tonya. "Sexual Deviancy in *Mrs. Dalloway*: The Case of Septimus Smith." *Virginia Woolf Miscellany* 70 (2006): 15-16. Print.

Leaska, Mitchell A. *The Novels of Virginia Woolf: From Beginning to End*. New York: John Jay Press, 1977. Print.

Leese, Peter. *Shell Shock: Traumatic Neurosis and the British Soldiers of the First World War*. New York: Palgrave Macmillan, 2002. Print.

Matson, Patricia. "The Terror and the Ecstasy: The Textual Politics of Virginia Woolf's *Mrs. Dalloway*." Mezei 162-86. Print.

McFarlane, Alexander C., and Bessel A. van Der Kolk. "Trauma and its Challenge to Society." *Traumatic Stress: The Effects of Overwhelming Experience on Mind, Body, and Society*. Ed. Bessel A. van der Kolk, Alexander C. McFarlane, and Lars Weisaeth. New York and London: Guilford Press, 1996. 24-46. Print.

Mezei, Kathy, ed. *Ambiguous Discourse: Feminist Narratology and British Women Writers*. Chapel Hill and London: U of North Carolina P, 1996. Print.

McMillan, Laurie. "Telling a Critical Story: Alice Walker's 'In Search of Our Mothers' Gardens.'" *Journal of Modern Literature* 28.1 (2004): 107-23. Print.

McPherson, Karen S. *Incriminations: Guilty Women/Telling Stories*. Princeton: Princeton UP, 1994. Print.

McVicker, Jeannette. "Modernism, Power, and the Elite: Teaching Woolf and Hurston Together." *Re: Reading, Re: Writing, Re: Teaching Virginia Woolf: Selected Papers from the Fourth Annual Conference on Virginia Woolf*. Ed. Eileen Barrett and Patricia Cramer. New York: Pace UP, 1995. 279-85. Print.

Meyer, Jessica. "'Not Septimus Now': Wives of Disabled Veterans and Cultural Memory of the First World War in Britain." *Women's History Review* 13.1 (2004): 117-37. Print.

Moi, Toril. *Sexual/Textual Politics: Feminist Literary Theory*. London and New York: Routledge, 1985. Print.

Murray, David. "Sovereignty and the Struggle for Representation in American Indian Nonfiction." *The Columbia Guide to American Indian Literatures of the United States Since 1945*. Ed. Eric Cheyfitz. New York: Columbia UP, 2006. 319-56. Print.

Owens, Louis. "'The Very Essence of Our Lives': Leslie Silko's Webs of Identity." Chavkin 91-116. Print.

Peacock, John. "Unwriting Empire by Writing Oral Tradition: Leslie Marmon Silko's *Ceremony*." *(Un)Writing Empire*. Ed. Theo D'haen. Amsterdam and Atlanta: Rodopi, 1994. 295-308. Print.

Peat, F. David. *Blackfoot Physics*. Newburyport, MA: Weiser Books, 2005. Print.

Poole, Roger. "'We all put up with you Virginia': Irreceivable Wisdom about War." Hussey 79-100. Print.

Quennet, Fabienne C. *Where "Indians" Fear to Tread?: A Postmodern Reading of Louise Erdrich's North Dakota Quartet*. Hamburg: LIT Verlag, 2001. Print.

Rice, David A. "Witchery, Indigenous Resistance, and Urban Space in Leslie Marmon Silko's *Ceremony*." *Studies in American Indian Literatures* 17.2 (2005): 114-43. Print.

Ruoff, A. LaVonne Brown. "Introduction to American Indian Literatures." *Background Readings for Teachers of American Literature*. Ed. Venetria K. Patton. Boston: Bedford/St. Martin's, 2006. 180-98. Print.

Scott, Bonnie Kime. *In the Hollow of the Wave: Virginia Woolf and Modernist Uses of Nature*. Charlottesville: U of Virginia P, 2012. Print.

Sedon, Kate. "Moments of Aging: Revising Mother Nature in Virginia Woolf's *Mrs. Dalloway*." Czarnecki and Rohman 163-8. Print.

Showalter, Elaine. *The Female Malady: Women, Madness, and English Culture, 1830-1980*. New York: Pantheon Books, 1985. Print.

Silko, Leslie Marmon. *Ceremony*. 1977. New York: Penguin, 2006. Print.

Swan, Edith. "Laguna Symbolic Geography and Silko's *Ceremony*." *American Indian Quarterly* 12.3 (1988): 229-49. Print.

Swanson, Diana, ed. *Virginia Woolf Miscellany* 81 (2012). Print.

Taylor, Paul Beekman. "Silko's Reappropriation of Secrecy." *Leslie Marmon Silko: A Collection of Critical Essays*. Ed. Louise K. Barnett and James L. Thorson. Albuquerque: U of New Mexico P, 1999. 23-62. Print.

Todd, Jude. "Knotted Bellies and Fragile Webs: Untangling and Re-Spinning in Tayo's Healing Journey." *American Indian Quarterly* 19.2 (1995): 155-70. Print.

Townsend, Kenneth William. *World War II and the American Indian*. Albuquerque: U of New Mexico P, 2000. Print.

Van Wert, Kathryn. "The Early Life of Septimus Smith." *Journal of Modern Literature* 36.1 (2012): 71-89. Print.

Wolfe, Jesse. "The Sane Woman in the Attic: Sexuality and Self-Authorship in *Mrs. Dalloway*." *Modern Fiction Studies* 51.1 (2005): 34-59. Print.

Woolf, Virginia. *Mrs. Dalloway*. 1925. Annotated and with an introduction by Bonnie Kime Scott. New York: Harcourt, 2005. Print.

Zlatkin, Rachel. "The Flesh of Citizenship: Red Flowers Grew." Czarnecki and Rohman 84-9. Print.

The "Supreme Portrait Artist" and the "Mistress of the Phrase": Contesting Oppositional Portrayals of Woolf and Bell, Life and Art, in Susan Sellers's *Vanessa and Virginia*

Bethany Layne

> I was the carnal sister, you were the intellectual, so the story runs. The truth is rather different. (Sellers 76)

I

Among the latest in a series of novels about Woolf, Susan Sellers's *Vanessa and Virginia* (2008) falls into the generic category of biofiction, a form which has enjoyed a noticeable increase in popularity over the last ten-to-fifteen years. A hybrid genre, biofiction enables novelists to tell the same kinds of stories as biographers and literary critics, while making use of modes of representation unique to fiction, namely "the novel's techniques for representing subjectivity, rather than the objective, evidence-based discourse of biography" (Lodge 8). Described by practitioner Michael Cunningham as the result of a collective decision that "we have the right to enter the minds, hearts, and souls of people who actually lived" (94), the emergence of biofiction has been attributed to two developments in contemporary literature. The first of these, as outlined by Michael Lackey in the introduction to his *Conversations with American Biographical Novelists*, was "an expanded understanding of the inner complexity of the human" (99). This prompted a shift in emphasis away from the "superficial and untrustworthy" external world of the realist and towards the "more fundamental and primary" inner world of the subconscious (14). Our understanding of the unconscious, although originating in mid-nineteenth-century discourses including psychical research (Johnson), became more fully established in the Modernist period with the advent of Freud. This helps to explain the attractiveness of Modernist writers as the subjects of biofiction, namely Woolf, Conrad, Eliot, and Freud himself.[1] As articulated by Cunningham in relation to his biofiction *The Hours*, fiction proved an ideal vehicle for the exploration of the subconscious: whereas "a biographer is restricted to what the subject is able to tell him or her," a novelist "can go all the way into [their] characters, down to their very hearts and souls" (93). Biofiction's ability to plumb the hidden depths of the subject is confirmed by critic Monica Latham in her survey of biographical novels about Woolf: "they can delve into her imaginary world, construct an 'as if,' bring the reader into her psyche" (356).

---

[1] See, for instance, Edwin M. Yoder Jr.'s *Lions at Lamb House* and Carol de Chellis Hill's *Henry James's Midnight Song*, both about Freud and James, Cynthia Ozick's "Dictation," about Conrad and James, and Martha Cooley's *The Archivist*, about Eliot.

The other half of the equation which produced biofiction was "the collapse of the distinction between fact and fiction," a phenomenon that had been the subject of considerable vacillation on Woolf's part (Lackey 99). In "The New Biography" (1927), she praised Harold Nicolson's success in combining "truth of fact and truth of fiction," perhaps with an eye to her own work-in-progress, the genre-bending *Orlando* (154). Yet the essay concluded, with a logic that is not entirely transparent, that the truths were "incompatible," "antagonistic: let them meet and they destroy each other" (155). The fact-fiction dichotomy was then laid to rest in "The Art of Biography" (1939), Woolf's final word on the subject: "no one, the conclusion seems to be, can make the best of both worlds; you must choose, and you must abide by your choice" (124). Yet the effect of postmodernity's "incredulity towards metanarratives" was to subvert Woolf's prognosis, levelling the hierarchies between biographical and fictional narratives by querying the former's claim to superior "truthfulness" (Lackey 12). Whereas Woolf espoused the incompatibility of fact and fiction, postmodernism revealed that "fact is fiction" by emphasizing the biographer and the novelist's "use of the same rhetorical devices, strategies and techniques" (2).

The undermining of biography's fundamental "claim to be non-fictional" questions Sellers's definition of the biographer's art as analogous with the photographer's (2). Both, she states, "aim for a true likeness," whereas biofiction, like portraiture, offers "an individual view." Yet the proliferating biographical versions of Woolf across the latter half of the twentieth century query this distinction, lending weight to the growing understanding that "all biography is ultimately fiction" (Parini 252). While the thesis-driven biographies of the 1970s and 1980s may have striven for "a true likeness," for "the real Virginia Woolf," they collectively produced versions of the subject that were both plural and partial (Stanley 11). There was "Woolf the incest survivor, Woolf the repressed lesbian" (Cunningham 97-98), Woolf "the victim of repressive attitudes towards mental illness" (Lee, "Biomythographers"177-78), each version requiring the denial of others in order to substantiate its "individual view." The multiplication of these biographical subjects confirmed, as Jay Parini writes in a different context, that "no single biography is ever definitive" but is instead "a particular story from perhaps dozens of stories one could tell" (252). Or, as Woolf put it in *Orlando*, an ostensibly "complete" biography accounts for but three or four selves, "whereas a person may well have as many thousand" (273).

As a genre, biofiction finds its authority in this growing understanding that "biographies are really novels in disguise," an idea which it celebrates and extends (Parini 252). It exploits the greater license offered by its demarcation as fiction to "play with […] even invert […] the historical material" (Middeke 3), to "invent stories that never happened in order to answer perplexing questions" (Lackey 8), and to renounce claims to truth and authority in the service of "a larger effort to create a richer, more varied portrait" (Cunningham 94). Thus Sellers "plays with" Woolf's and Bell's memoirs to suggest continuities in their experience, Claire Morgan invents a pregnancy-and-adoption narrative "to answer perplexing questions" about Woolf's sexuality, and Sigrid Nunez juxtaposes multiple versions of the subject in order to render Woolf's popular representation "richer, more varied." This generic freedom and open-endedness is the defining feature of biofiction, enabling the subject to be reimagined without the need to "say […] that they were this or were that" (*MD* 6).

Sellers's *Vanessa and Virginia* is perhaps the most ambitious of these novels, tracing its subjects' lives across a period of time unrivalled by previous works. Whereas Nunez's *Mitz: The Marmoset of Bloomsbury* restricts itself to the four-year period in which animal and author's lives intersect, and while Cunningham's *The Hours* famously confines itself to a single day, *Vanessa and Virginia* adopts a panoramic range, taking the form of an extended letter from elder sister to younger written in the wake of Virginia's suicide. Moments from the sisters' childhood and adult lives are interleaved with reflective passages from the mature Vanessa in an episodic structure, creating the effect of uninterrupted speech. Such narrative continuity recalls Bell's later letters to Woolf, in which she "dispenses with conventional openings and simply begins, as if speaking to someone seated beside her, or opening a vein that runs continually between two people" (Marler in Vanessa Bell, *Letters* 443). As Woolf wrote, "we are too intimate for letter writing; style dissolves as though in a furnace; all the blood and bones come through" (*L*1 343).

Drawing on both an implicit and an explicit critical apparatus, *Vanessa and Virginia* heralds new possibilities for biofiction about Woolf, possibilities which have, thus far, received startlingly little attention. The novel is situated at the intersection of fiction, biography, and Bloomsbury art theory, and enters into creative dialogue with more conventional forms of scholarship. Sellers is, of course, herself a prominent critic and Woolf expert: the editor of *The Cambridge Companion to Virginia Woolf* and co-editor, with Jane Goldman, of the new Cambridge Edition of Woolf's novels. In her contribution to the Making Sense colloquium at the University of Cambridge, she described how her "sense" of Woolf and Bell was "derived in part from years of reading and viewing all of the available extant materials" (133). The novel is "proof of this intimate knowledge of the Woolf corpus" (Latham 367), drawing on a wealth of intertexts including Woolf's "Reminiscences" (1907-8), "22 Hyde Park Gate" (1920), "Old Bloomsbury" (1920), and "A Sketch of the Past" (1939-40), and Bell's "Notes on Virginia's Childhood" (1949) and "Life at Hyde Park Gate after 1897" (c.1950). Sellers's handling of these sources is threefold: she rewrites events to produce different outcomes, creates new versions, or collates descriptions gleaned from multiple sources. One example of a collated image is an account of George Duckworth on the eve of Vanessa's first ball: "he raises his eyeglass and appraises me. There is no difference between this gesture and his scrutiny of the Arab mare he has bought for my daily rides" (22). This blends Bell's reference to "a lovely grey Arab mare" in "Life at Hyde Park Gate after 1897" with Woolf's description of Duckworth's gaze in "Sketch of the Past": "he looked me up and down for a moment as if I were a horse brought into the show ring" (153). Readers familiar with Woolf's memoir thus experience the uncanny effect of Vanessa viewing the world through the veil of her sister's perceptions. This upholds Woolf's belief that the sisters had "the same pair of eyes, only different spectacles" (*L6* 158), allowing Vanessa, as Bell put it, to "borrow your green eyes in my old age" (*Letters* 29).

Sellers's novel positions itself, significantly, as a lost document, and ends with the narration of its own destruction: "I untie my parcel and dip the first sheet in the water. The words blur. When the last one has been released I make my dedication. This story is for you" (181). By staging Vanessa drowning her book, Sellers imbues her novel with the intrigue of a "rediscovered lost manuscript," to borrow a phrase used by Cora Kaplan to describe the allure of the Henry James biofictions (63). As well as engaging with "the available extant materials," she thus invokes the specter of Bell's missing papers, and locates the impetus for the novel in precisely this "'sense' of ellipses in the surviving record" (Sellers and Wright 133). The lost documents include a memoir of George Duckworth which, Woolf wrote, "so flooded me with horror that I cant [*sic*] be pure minded on the subject" (*L5* 299), and the autobiographical "jumble of all the people and incidents I can remember up to the age of 14" that inspired "Reminiscences" (Bell, *Letters* 57). By framing her novel as a recovered text, Sellers is able to address the "unanswered but crucial questions" created by these fissures in Bell's literary remains (Sellers and Wright 133). "Allowing interpretations—without foreclosure or distortion of 'known' facts," the form thus affords her a licence to speculate that conventional biography and literary criticism withholds (134). Yet given Sellers's scholarly expertise and status, the line between biofiction and these sister-genres becomes increasingly difficult to define, and the resultant ambiguity of status is given full acknowledgement by the narrator. In the end, Vanessa insists, hers is not only "a work of fiction" but also "an attempt to discern the truth" (31).

As indicated by my epigraph, these "truth[s]," once revealed, are used to discredit the "story" that has sprung up around the sisters, with a particular emphasis on contesting the oppositions that underpin their legacies. By refocusing attention on their similarities rather than their differences, Sellers proposes revisions to narrow, reified constructions of Bell and Woolf as the 'proper' versus the 'inauthentic' woman respectively. Diane Gillespie notes the convenience of these biographical and critical shorthands:

> It serves the purposes of Virginia Woolf and Vanessa Bell, or their later biographers and critics, to think of the virginal, barren woman versus the sensual, maternal one; the domestically inept versus the practical and competent; the dependent versus the independent; the conversationalist versus the silent listener; the mentally unstable versus the sane. (5)

One such dualism is challenged by Sellers: that Vanessa "was the carnal sister" and Virginia "the intellectual," a mode of representation already apparent in Henry James's opposition of the "crushed strawberry glow of Vanessa's beauty" to "the promise of Virginia's printed wit" (374). Sellers reveals that Vanessa, like Virginia, endured long periods of celibacy, while the fact of the novel attests to her considerable literary gifts. The author's fictional re-negotiation of the relationship between her subjects is, she acknowledges, informed by "four extraordinary biographies: Frances Spalding's *Vanessa Bell*, Angelica Garnett's *Deceived with Kindness*, Jane Dunn's *Virginia Woolf and Vanessa Bell: A Very Close Conspiracy* and Hermione Lee's *Virginia Woolf*" (Acknowledgements, n.pag.). Dunn's popular biography warrants further attention at this juncture because of the way in which she, like Sellers, explicitly foregrounds the relationship between the sisters. Her thesis is that "the sense of never being loved enough, especially by a mother who had prematurely abandoned them, united the sisters in an emotional symbiosis, that to Virginia particularly was central to her life" (115). Thus despite the "polarities in their characters," which led them to "divide […] the worlds of art and experience into two," there cohered a bond which "could be both inhibiting and inspiring" (1-4). Dunn provides a template for Sellers's resistance to oppositional portrayals of the sisters, asserting that "the simple equation that Vanessa had chosen life at the expense of her art and Virginia had chosen art at the expense of life […] was only one construction in the intimate interlacing of their lives" (217). Instead, Dunn perceives their relationship as one of "complementary intimacy," asking, in the words of *Flush*, "could it be that each completed what was dormant in the other?" (5).

Dunn's further suggestion that "each [sister] had a distinctive influence on the art of the other" is redolent of the argument of Diane Gillepsie's *The Sisters' Arts: The Writing and Painting of Virginia Woolf and Vanessa Bell* (5). Gillespie suggests that Woolf and Bell "identified with each other as artistic rebels and experimenters," often finding themselves "stimulated by each other's work or capable of creating parallel works" (8-10). Indeed, she argues that "the amount of potential each did fulfil was due in large part to the professional example of the other" (7). A reference point for Dunn and an implicit one for Sellers, Gillespie's monograph has three main objectives: "to shift the emphasis in the ongoing discussion of Virginia Woolf and the visual arts from Roger Fry to Vanessa Bell; to shift the emphasis from the psychological to the professional and aesthetic and, in these contexts, to define and reveal more fully the pervasive role of the visual arts in Woolf's writing" (2). Like Dunn, Gillespie focuses attention on the relationship between the sisters, but her predominant accent is critical rather than biographical. Feeling that "the psychological tugs of war and intimacies between the sisters" had been emphasized "at the expense of their relationship as professional artists," Gillespie redirects attention away from "sexuality, domesticity, sociability, [and] pathology," and towards "artistic productivity" (4-5). She does, however, add the caveat that "a recognition of the family relationships between these two women as artists and between their art forms calls into question some of the other dualities as well" (5).

Whereas Gillespie excavates the professional and aesthetic relationship between the sisters, and indicates the ways in which her findings may be used to trouble their biographical creation as contrasting figures, Sellers approaches the problem from the opposite angle. If, for Gillespie, the sisters were "artists who were also women" (11), for Sellers they were women who were also artists; the biographical provides a gateway into the critical rather than a distraction from it. Furthermore, while Gillespie acknowledges that "aspects of Vanessa Bell's creativity inevitably emerge" from her study, her primary focus is "Virginia Woolf's writing" (7). Sellers, conversely, is more even-handed, using her title and choice of narrator to redistribute interest traditionally directed towards Woolf. As will be demonstrated in the first half of this article, she uses fiction to challenge and re-negotiate oppositional portrayals of Woolf and Bell, posing an intriguing intervention into narratives of life and of the body. She then goes on to foreground the interplay between the sisters' arts in terms of their structural dynamics. I shall demonstrate this by engaging her nuanced, synthesized narrative of their lives with a different kind of criticism: the art theory of Roger Fry and Clive Bell.

At this juncture, it is sufficient to state broadly that both Fry's and Bell's theories are characterized by a hostility towards representation for its own sake, a prioritization of formal design, and a belief in the need to "disentangle our reaction to pure form from our reaction to its implied associated ideas."[2] Yet Sellers's use of ekphrasis, unaccompanied by artistic plates, precludes a reaction to "pure form" on the part of the reader. Expressing the vision of a painter in "the words of a writer" (Latham 367), she instead *describes* form in such as way as to maximize its

---

[2] Both Fry and Bell added caveats with regard to representation, namely when such representation was placed at the service of form and aesthetic emotion. Fry wrote that "We may, then, dispense once for all with the idea of likeness to nature, of correctness or incorrectness as a test, and consider only whether the emotional elements inherent in true form are adequately discovered, unless, indeed, the emotional idea depends at any point upon likeness, or completeness of representation" (27). Similarly, Bell wrote "Let no one imagine that representation is bad in itself; a realistic form may be as significant, in its part of the design, as an abstract. But if a representative form has value, it is as form, not as representation" (25).

associations. For instance, three flowers in Vanessa's painting *The Tub* (1917), two of which "stand in close proximity" while "the other stands estranged and aloof," are suggestive of the relationship between Clive Bell, his lover Mary Hutchinson, and Vanessa (111). Such associations conflict with Fry and Bell's assumption that "'literary,' in the sense of depending upon outside elements […] rather than on formal elements within the picture itself, is a pejorative term" (Gillespie 5). As shall be seen, Sellers reengages the formal design of a work of art with its associative or "literary" connotations to produce a broader framework for interpretation. This dialogue constitutes an implicit challenge to Fry and Bell's preoccupation with the "universal aspects" of form (207). Instead, Sellers illuminates those moments wherein formal interest coexists with, even arises from, biographical elements, thereby championing the aesthetic potential inherent in women's lives.

In so doing, she inserts her novel into a recent body of scholarship that is attentive to the artistic interplay between Woolf and Bell, and sensitive to the points of departure between their aesthetics and those of Clive Bell and Fry. This develops prevalent work on the intersections between Woolf's writing and Fry's formalism by Allen McLaurin, Marianna Torgovnick, and Ann Banfield. Taking her cue from Woolf's assertion that "many of [Fry's] theories held good for both arts" (249), Banfield frames Woolf's Granite and Rainbow and Fry's Vision and Design as related concepts, both concerned with "the discovery of intellectual form in chaotic sense-data" (274). Although Banfield's approach reveals fascinating parallels between modernist fiction and Post-Impressionism, her primary interest is in the "philosophical framework for an aesthetic," rather than the implementation and adaptation of that aesthetic on canvas (260). She thus underemphasizes a potent area of overlap between Modernist literature and art: the dialogues between Woolf's novels and her sister's paintings.

While Banfield subscribes to the idea, noted wryly by Gillespie, that "you'll find a man at the bottom of it" (3), critics taking their cue from Gillespie herself have indicated a contrasting, at times conflicting, dynamic of influence at play between Woolf and Bell. Jane Goldman's landmark study *The Feminist Aesthetics of Virginia Woolf* finds in Bell's "development as a colourist" (130) and refusal to "subordinate content to […] formal aspects of her work" (145) a parallel with Woolf's own "love of colour" and "fascination with literary analogy" (138), and positions both sisters at odds with Fry and Clive Bell's move "away from colour towards significant form" (137). A related stance is adopted by Lisa Tickner in her analysis of *Studland Beach*, which notes the coherence of "a certain psychological intensity" in the composition's "simplified forms" (64). She finds in this co-existence of form and content evidence for a different conceptualization of Significant Form on Vanessa Bell's part, one that is concerned with "the distillation—rather than the rejection or transcendence—of social experience" (64-5).

Turning from painting to "the marginalia of the margins," Maggie Humm has interpreted the sisters' "private obsession with photography" as suggesting a wish "to explore forms of representation outside the objectifications of masculine modernism" (5). Accordingly, she reads both *To the Lighthouse* and the narrative organization of Woolf's photograph albums as contesting "Fry's emphasis on pure artistic plasticity" (17). More recently, Justyna Kostkowska, while reasserting the continuities between the sisters' arts and the "Post-Impressionist method[s]" espoused by Fry and Clive Bell, has furthered understanding of the mutual influence between her subjects, reading *Jacob's Room* as "a literary rendering of [Vanessa Bell's] experiments" from 1911-1913 (82). While by no means comprehensive, this survey provides compelling evidence for *Vanessa and Virginia*'s contribution to an active field of criticism. Sellers, as shall be seen, realizes the democratic potential of biofiction to include "the common reader" in these ongoing academic conversations.

II

In emphasizing the similarities between the sisters and their arts, Sellers breaks with a mode of characterization prevalent in fictional representations of Woolf since Leonard Woolf's *The Wise Virgins* (1914). Alone among the novels under consideration, *The Wise Virgins* conceals its characters' identities under pseudonyms, and, as such, should be classified as *roman à clef* rather than biofiction proper. Whereas contemporary writers' use of Woolf's name is the product of an age in which "the biographical novel is partly legitimised" (Lackey 10), *The Wise Virgins*' attempt to preserve the anonymity of its subjects is in keeping with early-twentieth-century literary convention, and maintains a level of respect appropriate to Woolf's close acquaintance with the persons described. To the contemporary reader, however, the subterfuge of *The Wise Virgins* is shattered by its author's status as Virginia Woolf's husband and literary executor. It does not, today, require an interpretative lockpicker to deduce that "Katharine" is Leonard Woolf's sister-in-law and "Camilla" his wife. While evading some of the restrictions of biofiction by changing his characters' names, Woolf's *roman à clef* nevertheless shares certain integral characteristics with contemporary biofictional representations of his subjects.

In *The Wise Virgins*, the Vanessa figure, Katharine, is described as "flesh and blood, [...] flush[ing] the fair skin red and the full lips," a stark contrast to her sister, Camilla, "so white and fair," "not a woman, but a fine lady in a dream or a play" (119). Though Leonard Woolf's novel attends only to the sisters' pre-marital lives, the opposition noted by Gillespie between "the virginal, barren woman" and "the sensual, maternal one" is nevertheless apparent (5). Katharine's face "was already like that of a mother's," whereas Camilla's "would always retain something of the virgin's" (94). Gillian Freeman's novel *But* Nobody *Lives in* Bloomsbury, published almost a century later, demonstrates the enduring appeal of the contrast. Freeman employs similar descriptors to contrast "Virginia Stephen [...] beautiful, slender, intense, with a high forehead and green eyes," with Vanessa, "equally beautiful, but with a more sensual appearance, an oval face, grey-green eyes and full, sensitive mouth" (2). Physical characteristics are used to distinguish "the intellectual" from "the carnal sister": Virginia, with her high forehead, is quite literally a highbrow, while Vanessa has a "more sensual appearance," a rounder face and the "full" lips described by Leonard Woolf. As in *The Wise Virgins*, the sisters' respective futures as virginal or sensual are indexed to their facial features.

Michael Cunningham is as easily tempted to reproduce the popular division. In *The Hours*, Virginia "has the austere, parched beauty of a Giotto fresco," whereas Vanessa "is more like a figure sculpted in rosy marble by a skilled but minor artist of the late Baroque," "a distinctly earthy and even decorative figure, all billows and scrolls" (144). Vanessa's lavish "abundance" is suggestive of voluptuousness and a fully realized sexuality, while Virginia's austerity carries connotations of virginity, even asceticism. Significantly, Virginia is linked to the named artist, the Giotto, while Vanessa's creator is anonymous, "skilled but minor," a purveyor of merely decorative art. In contrast to Leonard Woolf and Freeman, Cunningham reads the sisters' physiognomies not only for clues regarding their future, but also for indications of the relative values of their work.

While Leonard Woolf, Freeman, and Cunningham's narrators are anxious that women be one thing or another, Sigrid Nunez's Vanessa is a boundary-breaker who has both "her art *and* her children" (35). In *Mitz*, the comparison of the sisters is focalized through Virginia, who notes "how she looked to herself: very plain and dull beside Vanessa—a goddess in Virginia's eyes, a radiant Madonna, a complete woman, impossible not to envy. Vanessa had what people insisted could not be had" (35). Like Sylvia Plath half a century later, who envisaged a future comprised of "Books & Babies & Beef stews," Vanessa achieves the seemingly impossible in combining artistic pursuits with domesticity (269). However, Virginia's childlessness remains the unspoken corollary to Vanessa's ability to 'have it all'. If, in short, one must have art *and* children to be "a complete woman," Virginia is, implicitly, incomplete in having 'only' her art. Indeed, Woolf herself suggested as much in noting that Vita Sackville-West's "maturity and full-breastedness" and "motherhood" made her "(what I have never been) a real woman" (*D*3 62).

Virginia's childlessness is redressed in Claire Morgan's *A Book for All and None*, an academic quest narrative detailing two scholars' search for the intersections between Woolf and Nietzsche. Morgan emphasizes the rude health of the mountaineer's daughter frequently seen "striding along with a stick in one hand," and asserts that "that life in her, the energy, the force of it," is "only a hair's breadth [...] from sexuality" (203). Whereas Cunningham, Freeman, and Leonard Woolf reinforced the opposition of Bell's carnality to Woolf's intellect, Morgan's character Raymond Mortimer asserts that "art and sex" are "two sides of the same coin" (228). The author's reclamation of a sexualized Woolf culminates in the revelation that Virginia secretly gave birth to, and relinquished, a child. While, as Catherine Taylor noted in *The Guardian*, Morgan's "final revelation defies credibility," her insistence that Woolf had the potential to be sensual and maternal as well as intellectual suggestively allies her project with Sellers's. Unlike the other writers under consideration, Morgan and Sellers present their subjects less as extremes on a continuum than as variations on a theme. For Sellers, they are "inexact replicas of each other, as if the painter were trying to capture the same person from different angles" (4). As shall be seen, this mode of representation enables her ultimate emphasis on the interplay between her subjects' arts.

In thus countering the prevalent direction of biofiction about Woolf, Sellers challenges a pervasive mythology that can be traced back to the sisters themselves. Loosely summarized, this opposes Woolf's supposed frigidity to Bell's sensuality, Woolf's mental instability to Bell's tranquillity, and Woolf's skill with words to Bell's painterly silence. Since such myths, as Hermione Lee asserts, have "powerfully affected" Woolf's "posthumous life," *Vanessa and Virginia*'s resistance to dualisms represents a significant intervention into popular representations (*Woolf*, 119). The stubborn characterization of Woolf as "a chaste, chill, sexually inhibited maiden—Virginia the virgin" may have originated in a letter from Bell to her husband following her sister's marriage (Lee, *Woolf* 244). Bell wrote that the couple

> seemed very happy, but are evidently both a little exercised in their minds on the subject of the Goat's coldness. I think I perhaps annoyed her but may have consoled him by saying that I thought she had never understood or sympathised with sexual passion in men. Apparently she still gets no pleasure at all from the act, which I think is curious. They were very anxious to know when I first had an orgasm. I couldn't remember. Do you? But no doubt I sympathised with such things even if I didn't have them from the time I was 2. (132)

Bell's letter implicitly opposes "the Goat's coldness," ironic in context given the animal's stereotypically sexual associations, with her own, far more sensual nature. "I couldn't remember. Do you?" is suggestively ambiguous; is Bell asking her husband when *he* first had an orgasm or, rather, when *she* did? The suggestiveness is intensified by Bell's repeated use of the word "sympathised," a word that carries connotations of simultaneous climax.[3] "The Goat's coldness"

---

[3] See, for instance, John Dowland's "Come Again": "Come again! Sweet love doth now invite / Thy graces that refrain / To do me due delight, / To see, to hear, to touch, to kiss, to die / With thee again, in sweetest sympathy."

forms a seeming precursor to Bell's own erotic overtures; by highlighting the unresponsiveness of her husband's former love interest, she shores up her self-image as a sexual woman.

Lee asserts that along with *The Wise Virgins*, "the version of their marital sex-life put about by Vanessa and Clive […] perpetuated the legend of Virginia's frigidity" (*Woolf* 244). Dunn similarly credits the Bells with the formation of "a pervasive attitude towards Virginia and sexuality, one which [Woolf] did little to counter, and on which the whole suggestion of her sexual frigidity was based" (186). The enduring impact of the letter is demonstrated by its (mis)quotation some ninety years later in *But* Nobody *Lives in* Bloomsbury. Clive accuses Virginia of being "a sexual coward," to which Vanessa responds, "if only she was like me. Orgasms since I was two!" The contrast is reiterated with the narratorial interpolation "she looked ready to have another" (52). In *Vanessa and Virginia*, the revelation that Virginia "appeared to find lovemaking unappealing" occurs in an exchange of letters between Leonard and Vanessa from which their spouses are excluded entirely (79). Vanessa states that she "told him you had always been physically unresponsive, especially with men. I told him I did not think he could change you" (79-80). Sellers's decision to render this conversation as a written, rather than a verbal exchange indicates the lasting implications of Bell's rejection of her sister's sexuality. As Dunn writes, "so much of received opinion about Virginia's character, even her art, rests on certain assumptions of her sexual, or asexual, nature" (187). Sellers forces Vanessa to acknowledge her own complicity in the formation of these assumptions: "Fate was to punish me for this" (80).

Yet Sellers also acknowledges that Vanessa's sensuality, rather than being the foundation of truth upon which the "virgin Virginia" legend was founded, was itself a constructed image. Turning to her current work-in-progress, a self-portrait, immediately after writing to Leonard, Vanessa notes that "it seemed to me my face had regained its bloom" (80). Yet she immediately reveals that "the rose flush on my face, the look of dreamy contentment, were a lie. I had not told Leonard everything" (80). The nature of the concealed material is boldly stated by Louise DeSalvo: "although the image persists of Vanessa's sexuality as a kind of voluptuous abandon, nonetheless both she and Virginia lived the greater part of their lives in a condition of celibacy" (87). The subject's "look of dreamy contentment" thus belies the fact that her marriage was, by the time of the portrait's composition in 1912, in name only, and that her affair with Roger Fry was to end the following year when she "transferred her affections to Duncan Grant"("Archive Journeys"). Sellers suggests that Vanessa destroyed the portrait "the day Duncan confessed he could never be my lover again" (80), reminding us of the irony noted by Lee: "that Vanessa, whom Virginia had envied all her life for her sensuality and maternal calmness, should from her late forties onwards be living in a sexually thwarted and emotionally unreciprocated relationship" (*Woolf* 540). Building on the work of Lee and DeSalvo, Sellers starts to bridge the gap established by the sisters' myth-making by situating them at the same extreme of the sexual continuum. This begins to frame them as allied, rather than opposing figures, highlighting the novel's capacity to intervene in the popular representation of its subjects.

Sellers's gradual revelation that while Virginia may have had the "sexless marriage," Vanessa endured the greater isolation culminates in a striking moment of union between the sisters (80). This takes the form of Vanessa's attempt to drown herself, the "anaesthetising chill of the water" a panacea for "Duncan's declaration […] that he could never make love to me again" (147). As well as anticipating Virginia's eventual death by drowning, this event recalls the watery imagery used to evoke the adolescents' quasi-sexual bond. Attempting to console Virginia in the aftermath of her first breakdown, Vanessa "reach[es] up and unfasten[s] my dress and your baby mouth suckles my breast. I am your dolphin mother once more, glistening and sticky from your kisses. I will take you deep into the ocean where no-one can harm us" (42). Such textual patterning allows for a secondary interpretation of Vanessa's suicide attempt, as an attempt to return to the primordial attachment she previously shared with Virginia. Just as Sellers's representation of the sisters' mutual celibacy queries their oppositional representation as frigid and sensual, this implication of queer attachment confirms, albeit in a different way, the similarities in their sexualities. It implies that Virginia responded differently to her sister than to her husband, and that Vanessa's letter to Leonard overemphasized Virginia's frigidity in a jealous attempt to preserve their sexual bond.

Sellers's hint that Virginia's "frigidity" was confined to heterosexual encounters reflects the growing understanding of "the centrality of lesbian relationships to Woolf's life and literary work" (Swanson 190). Grounded in feminist criticism and drawing on the newly published letters and diaries, late-twentieth-century lesbian readings of Woolf recast her as "a passionate and vibrant woman who loved other women physically and emotionally" (185). These approaches destabilized the popular representation of Woolf as frigid, instigated in Vanessa and Clive Bell's epistolary discussion of "the Goat's coldness" and propagated in their son's biographical representation of a "sexless Sappho" (Barrett 6). Thus while readers of Quentin Bell's biography were encouraged to view Woolf as "disconcertingly ethereal," "both in her personality and in her art" (Quentin Bell, *Virginia* 6), forty years later Diana Swanson observed that the fact of Woolf's lesbianism "seems to be largely accepted" (190). While Sellers's dominant emphasis is on the sisters' shared celibacy, the insinuation of a lesbian attraction enables her to acknowledge this "building consensus" (199), and to further complicate simplistic popular representations of the subjects.

By suggesting that Vanessa tried to take her own life, Sellers also queries a further aspect of the sisters' legacy: the opposition of "the mentally unstable" and "the sane" (Gillespie 5). Indeed, the description of the incident borrows its particulars not from Bell's own life, but from Woolf's possible suicide attempt of March 18, 1941. As described by Dunn, Woolf

> had returned to Monk's House from one of her walks, wet through and shaken, having fallen in a dyke, she said. Two days later Vanessa came to tea and, concerned by her sister's state of mind but not expecting such a rapid deterioration, wrote that evening what was to be her last letter to Virginia. (299)

Sellers inverts the sisters' respective roles, having Virginia arrive for tea at Charleston to find Vanessa "soaking wet. And covered in blood" (148). Just as Woolf claimed to have "fallen in a dyke," Virginia asks Vanessa, "[h]ave you had an accident? Did you fall in the river?" (148). Virginia's realization of the reality of the situation prompts a dramatic shift in her perceptions: "I thought that I was the only one who contemplated ending it all. I always picture you happy—in the centre of things" (148). This echoes Woolf's recorded shock at "hearing Nessa say she was often melancholy & often envied me—a statement I found incredible" (*D3* 242-3).

Sellers's audacious intervention is supported by Leonard Woolf, who asserted that Bell's "tranquillity was to some extent superficial" and concealed "a nervous tension which had some resemblance to the mental instability of Virginia" (*Growing* 14). This suggestion is in turn corroborated by Angelica Garnett, who viewed her mother's "intermittent but crippling bouts of lethargy" as evidence for "a severe depression, different in effect but not perhaps unrelated to Virginia's instability" (32). Sellers grounds Vanessa's suicide attempt in such "crippling" periods of depression, which are shown to recur at intervals throughout her life. For instance, the miscarriage Vanessa suffers immediately after becoming Roger Fry's lover prompts a delirium in which she "think[s] constantly of water. […] Only water can obliterate what I have done. Only drowning will thwart the monsters I might still create" (70). By invoking Woolf's means of suicide, such imagery reminds us that the waves threatened to submerge both sisters at different points in their lives, and that "as one of us surrenders, the other must fight" (171). This forms a stark contrast to Freeman's text, in which Virginia alone is governed by death, "the pounding waves growing louder and louder in her head," and eventually kills herself "in a frenzy" after hearing the birds singing in Greek (84; 165-6). By insisting that both of the sisters' lives contained moments of hopelessness, Sellers frames breakdown and attempted suicide as responses to an extremity of circumstance rather than manifestations of a pre-existing tendency. Her depiction of Vanessa's emotional makeup thus allows her to contest the pathologizing of Woolf, and the concurrent fetishizing of Bell's "maternal calmness" (Lee, *Woolf* 541).

The novel's potential to thus renegotiate the popular representation of its subjects is reiterated in the paratextual material, which promises "a dramatic new interpretation of one of the most famous and iconic events in twentieth-century literature—Woolf's suicide by drowning" (n.p.). While this most obviously refers to Sellers's creation of a parallel suicide attempt for Vanessa, it also evokes her representation of Virginia's suicide as a paradoxically life-affirming act. Vanessa visits Virginia on the day of her death to tell her that "I—can't go on any longer," and Sellers strongly implies that Virginia's suicide prevented a second attempt on her sister's part (176). Describing Virginia's death several years later, Vanessa experiences a moment of catharsis: "The water is in my mouth, my lungs, as the river drags us under. This time I cannot escape" (177). Virginia's death is thus permitted to serve for both sisters, allowing Vanessa to turn again towards life. This is symbolized by her decision, in the novel's final lines, to paint "a blaze of daffodils under the apple trees" instead of the cut flowers on her desk: "I gaze at the yellow, vivid and tangible in the sunlight. You are right. What matters is that we do not stop creating" (181). Vanessa's belief in the sustaining power of creativity paraphrases Woolf's conclusion in an earlier draft of "Anon": "only when we put two and two together—two pencil strokes, two written words, two bricks [...] do we overcome dissolution and set up some stake against oblivion" (Silver 403).

Sellers's contestation of oppositional representations of Woolf and Bell culminates in a challenge to corresponding restrictions in the discussion of their work. She insists that their chosen disciplines were not hermeneutically sealed, but were instead characterized by mutual engagement, a suggestion that finds ample support in Woolf's own writing. While Woolf's assertion that "a story-telling picture is as pathetic and ludicrous as a trick played by a dog" echoes Fry and Clive Bell's hostility towards "literary" art ("Pictures" 142), her essay "Walter Sickert: A Conversation" (1934) argues, instead, that "painting and writing have much to tell each other" (241), and enumerates with interest those artists who "are always making raids into the lands of others" (243).[4] The artists include Sickert and Vanessa Bell, and the territory in question is, significantly, Woolf's own. "What a poet you are in colour" (*L6* 381), she writes to Bell, whom she describes elsewhere as "a satirist, a conveyer of impressions about human life: a short story writer of great wit" (*L2* 498). Thus while "Pictures" and Woolf's introductions "suppl[y] the orthodox creed" that in painting, "no stories are told," Woolf privately champions

---

[4] Anthony Uhlman reads "Walter Sickert" as illuminating "a difference between Fry and Woolf"; for Woolf "the literary painter is not worse than the pure painter: rather, he or she is a different type of painter, one who thinks in a different way, and who, therefore, is capable of different things" (60).

the co-existence of the "literary" with the visual in her sister's oeuvre (Goldman 156). She also counts herself among "the hybrids, the raiders" on occasion when writing about her own work ("Walter Sickert" 243). One of the most notable examples concerns her attempts to write about her sister in *Roger Fry*: "it's rather as if you had to paint a picture using dozens of snapshots in the paint" (*L6* 285). It is apparent from these extracts that Woolf and Bell's commitment to the formal completeness of a work of art was not incompatible with perceived excursions into the other's chosen form.

In *Vanessa and Virginia*, it is possible to trace the evolution of the sisters' working relationship from a combative to a complementary one, as their adolescent struggles to prove that "mine is the more difficult art" are succeeded by a mature appreciation of the interconnections between their disciplines (28). Their growing recognition of the influence of each other's art culminates in an act of collaboration, as Vanessa, admiring the woodcuts carved by Dora Carrington for the newly founded Hogarth Press, becomes fascinated by the idea that such images may be used not simply "on the dust-jacket" but "alongside the words" (115). Reading a copy of "Kew Gardens" later that evening, her

> mind races with ideas. I find paper and charcoal. I sketch flowers, stems, leaves, around your words. I sketch the two women talking in the garden, hats tilted at an angle as they exchange confidences. I work quickly, excitedly. Soon I have covered your words with my pictures. (115)

While Vanessa is ultimately dissatisfied with Leonard's arrangement of the woodcuts, their design is radical in terms of the abolition of boundaries. Significantly, her images do not provide a decorative supplement for the front cover, but surround, and are inspired by, Virginia's prose. The suggestion that Vanessa "covered your words with my pictures," while perhaps indicating a residual competitiveness, provides a vivid illustration of the cross-fertilization between fiction and visual art.

As previously suggested, such illumination of Woolf and Bell's mutual engagement enables a targeted interrogation of the restrictive assumptions of Clive Bell and Roger Fry. In the above passage, Vanessa's sketch of "the two women talking in the garden" is an illustration of lines in Virginia's prose. It thus falls into Clive Bell's category of "Descriptive Painting," in which "forms are used not as objects of emotion, but as means of suggesting emotion or conveying information" (16-17). Along with portraiture, "topographical works," and "pictures that tell stories," he suggested that illustrations "leave untouched our aesthetic emotions" (17). This was because they lacked "the essential quality in a work of art[:] significant form" (100), the phenomena wherein "lines and colours combined in a particular way, certain forms and relations of forms, stir our aesthetic emotions" by conveying "a sense of ultimate reality" (8; 54).

Fry was similarly critical of what is variously referred to as description, representation, or the creation of illusion in art. Like Bell, he prized "The Movement" of Post-Impressionist painters after Cézanne for a perceived return to Primitive art's "ideas of formal design which had almost been lost in the fervid pursuit of naturalistic representation" (203). As defined in "The French Post-Impressionists," "these artists [...] do not seek to imitate form, but to create form; not to imitate life but to find an equivalent for life" (167). Fry coined the term "Structural Design" to describe this approach, and added that "the logical extreme of such a method would undoubtedly be the attempt to give up all resemblance to natural form, and to create a purely abstract language of form—a visual music" (167). Both critics' prioritization of form over representation demanded one essential quality on the part of the artist: detachment. The artist's sole concern must be with "the relation of forms and colours to one another, as they cohere within the object," necessitating, for Fry, "the most complete detachment from any of the meanings and associations of appearances" (33-8), for Bell, "the most absolute abstraction from the affairs of life" (266).

For the purposes of my argument, that the sisters' arts were mutually engaged and open to biographical as well as structural readings, Fry and Bell's ideas have two significant implications. Firstly, their emphasis on formal unity, and their associated hostility towards descriptive or representative qualities, are precepts which may be applied to literary as well as visual art. As indicated by Gillespie, a novelist "taking cues from modern painting [...] can render the self elusive through multiple and partial points of view; she can place her individuals in larger patterns, and subordinate them to the overall form of her own work of art" (17). Similarly, Banfield finds in Woolf's "elimination of the first person and representation of a third person privacy" a parallel to Fry's "reduction of the ego to the perspective" (293). Gillsepie and Banfield thus extrapolate from Fry and Bell a 'way of looking' at Woolf's fiction that prizes impersonality, formal coherence and structural unity. Such an approach would reject the accumulation of autobiographical details, as these would prevent a work being contemplated "as a whole" and instead require the viewer to "pass outside it to other things necessary to complete its unity" (Fry 22). This attitude is intrinsically at odds with the approach to the sisters' arts prioritized by Sellers. To frame Virginia's writing and Vanessa's painting as reciprocally engaged is to emphasize the outward-facing qualities of both, and to contest Fry and Bell's emphasis on a self-contained formal unity.

Secondly, Fry and Bell's insistence on the necessity of detachment has implications for the viewer as well as the artist. Fry states that in order "to appreciate a work of art we need bring with us nothing from life, no knowledge of its ideas and affairs, no familiarity with its emotions"; we require only "that clear disinterested contemplation which is a characteristic of the aesthetic attitude" (25; 21). This attitude is again at odds with the generic features of biofiction in general, and with Sellers's technique in particular. For while Clive Bell asserted that "for the purposes of aesthetics we have no right [...] to pry behind the object into the state of mind of him who made it," Sellers's representation of artistic objects as moments of ekphrasis within a biographical narrative encourages the reader to do precisely that (11). And whereas Fry praised Clive Bell's efforts to "isolate the purely aesthetic feeling from the whole complex of feelings which may and generally do accompany the aesthetic feeling when we regard a work of art," Sellers champions the biographical "complex of feelings" as legitimate criteria for interpretation (207). This approach is supported by Vanessa Bell herself, who, while seeming to validate her husband's belief in "a language simply of form and colour," acknowledged that "the form and colour nearly always do represent life and I suppose any allusions may creep in" (406). It is corroborated by Quentin Bell, who remained unconvinced by his mother's denials, towards the end of her career, "that the story of a picture had any importance whatsoever," and found her work "replete with psychological interest" (*Bloomsbury* 84).

A prototypical example of the coexistence of formal and biographical interest in *Vanessa and Virginia* is the passage detailing the creation of Bell's 1912 portrait of Woolf:

> I think of Mother in her deck chair in the garden at St Ives, her eyes closed as she allowed herself a few minutes' peace after lunch. My brush restores the caress of hands, the longed-for shelter of loving arms. I fill out the brim of your hat, the band of hair framing your face. I form the arch of your nose, the bow of your mouth. When the features of your face are done I stop and examine the effect. I have failed. I pick a knife and scrape the paint clear. I gaze at your closed eyelids, the back of your head resting against the chair. I wash the entire oval of your face in a flesh tone. I look again. This time your expression is a blank. I set my brush aside. I have painted what you are to me. (108)

By foregrounding the resonance between Virginia's pose and that of Julia Stephen, reclining "in her deck chair in the garden," Vanessa situates the objects in her composition as "means": her deck chair is "a means to physical well-being, [...] an object associated with the intimate life of a family, [...] a place where someone sat saying things unforgettable" (Clive Bell 52). This runs counter to the ideal artistic vision described by Clive Bell, in which the artist feels emotion "for objects seen as pure forms—that is, as ends in themselves" (52). For Fry, "the disadvantage of such an art of associated ideas is that its effect really depends on what we bring with us: it adds no entirely new factor to our experience" (169). He opposed this to "classic" art, synonymous with that of the Post-Impressionists, which "records a positive and disinterestedly passionate state of mind," and conveys "a new and otherwise unattainable experience" (169). Yet a careful reading of Sellers's passage reveals an implicit challenge to Fry and Bell's dualisms. Vanessa's painstaking attempts to reproduce "the arch of your nose," "the bow of your mouth" are succeeded by the decision to "wash the entire oval of your face in a flesh tone"; in Fry's terms, she ceases to "imitate life" and instead "find[s] an equivalent for life" (167). By suggesting that Vanessa's elimination of facial detail was a spontaneous strategy to render the impenetrability of her subject, Sellers allows "an art of associated ideas" to give rise to an incidence of "pure form" (Clive Bell 169; Fry 92). She thus challenges the restrictive assumptions of Fry and Bell by permitting the reader to consider the biographical resonances of the portrait in conjunction with its structural relations.

Sellers reads *To the Lighthouse* as similarly balancing associative elements with formal significance, even while appearing to prioritize biographical inspiration. Vanessa describes a "recurring dream" that emphasizes Bell's usefulness to Woolf as a template for Mrs. Ramsay:

> I am sitting by a window, looking out over a garden. I am wearing mother's green shawl and there is a boy by my side. He is cutting shapes from a magazine, frowning as he concentrates on his task. You are in the garden, reclining in a deckchair, your notebook open on your knee. I watch your hand moving implacably across your page. Suddenly I become aware of a presence in the doorway. I look up and glimpse a man's outline, but the brilliance of the light prevents me from making out his features. I suspect it is Duncan, though I cannot be sure. He comes over to me and lays his hand on my shoulder. I feel the child stir beside me, restive and jealous. I sense that I am needed, though part of me longs to go on sitting quietly by the window, my child by my side. (127)

The tableau described by Sellers mirrors that of "The Window": Vanessa takes the place of Mrs. Ramsay, the child at her side represents James, and Duncan Grant is Mr. Ramsay, interrupting the mother and the resentful child with his demands for sympathy. Superficially, it is suggested that Virginia, her "notebook open on [her] knee," transcribes the scene directly into her novel. However, the observation that Vanessa is "wearing Mother's green shawl" frustrates attempts to find specific analogues for the work in the life, instead suggesting that Mrs. Ramsay was a composite of both Vanessa and Julia Stephen. This is supported by a letter from Woolf to Bell in which she admitted to blending elements of her sister's character with those of their mother's: "probably there is a great deal of you in Mrs. Ramsay; though, in fact, I think you and mother are very different in my mind" (*L*3 383). Even when foregrounding the use of biographical inspiration, Sellers thus emphasizes that *To the Lighthouse* was not an imitation of life but a work of art that collated and blended detail in order to *create* life. Despite invoking the real-world associations of its characters, the novel thus maintains the artistic autonomy prized in the work of the Post-Impressionists.

Attention to the biographical resonances of *To the Lighthouse* is then juxtaposed with overt emphasis on its aesthetics, represented via the interplay between the novel and an image designed by Bell in 1930 for a tile fireplace at Monk's House. The image as described by Gillespie features "a lighthouse on a rocky island" which "provides a line down the centre, and unites the two masses" (157). It thus recalls Lily Briscoe's painting in *To the Lighthouse*, in which "a line there, in the centre" represents the culmination of her "vision" (281), the tree of her pre-war composition having been simplified into Significant Form (Goldman 171). Yet in *Vanessa and Virginia*, the tile is painted shortly after Vanessa's move to Charleston in 1916, inverting the dynamics of sisterly influence:

> You gesture towards one of the tiles. 'Is this meant to be the sea?'
> [...]
> 'I suppose I was thinking about the sea, though of course it was the colour and pattern I had most clearly in mind.'
> You consider my answer.
> 'So if you weren't thinking about a particular seascape, what did you intend this mark to be here?' You draw your finger along a straight black line down the centre of the tile. 'I had assumed it was a lighthouse.'
> I look at the line. I remember painting it, sensing that the swirls of blue required an anchoring point.
> 'I'm not sure I meant anything in particular by it, though of course I've no objection to you seeing it as a lighthouse.'
> [...]
> 'But if it isn't a lighthouse—or anything specific—why is it there?'
> [...]
> 'The blue needed it, the pattern needed it. It gives the eye something to rest on.' (106)

The exchange is underpinned by the arguments of Fry and Clive Bell, which Virginia interrogates and Vanessa symbolically defends. Virginia seeks in the "anchoring point" amid the "swirls of blue" what Fry called a "resemblance to natural form," implicitly the lighthouse of the sisters' childhood summers at

St. Ives (167). Like Bell's biographer, Frances Spalding, Virginia thus analyzes Vanessa's "simple geometric shapes" for signs of "a deeper significance" (xiv). This resonates amusingly with Clive Bell's assertion that "the majority of [...] charming and intelligent people [...] appreciate visual art impurely" and that "the appreciation of almost all great writers has been impure" (35).

Conversely, Vanessa's prioritizing of color and pattern over the accurate depiction of "a particular seascape" recalls Clive Bell's suggestion that any representative element in art "must do double duty; as well as giving information, it must create aesthetic emotion by being simplified into significant form" (225). Vanessa insists of the lighthouse that "the blue needed it, the pattern needed it. It gives the eye something to rest on." This attests to a concern with the "aesthetic," rather than the "cognitive" value of representative forms, a desire to "treat them as though they were not representative of anything" (Clive Bell 225). Thus while the image has "cognitive" interest as a lighthouse amid the waves, Vanessa, like Lily Briscoe, is primarily concerned with what Fry called "the balancing of the attractions to the eye about the central line," which gives the image its essential "unity" (22). Significantly, her acknowledgment that "I'm not sure I meant anything in particular by [the line in the center]" is suggestive of Woolf's own use of "terms suggestive of significant form" in a letter to Fry (Goldman 167): "I meant *nothing* by The Lighthouse. One has to have a central line down the middle of the book to hold the design together" (*L3* 385). Along with Vanessa's earlier description of her painterly quest for "a single joining line" that has no bearing on "the world at large" (91), this resonance allows Vanessa symbolically to convert her sister to "the Bloomsbury belief that art only achieves unity and completeness if it is detached" (Spalding xiv).

However, Goldman has noted how Woolf "does not dismiss altogether the possibility of meaning" even while "appealing to Fry's aesthetics" (167); she accepted, in short, that "the central line down the middle of the book" would be turned by readers into "the deposit for their own emotions" (*L3* 385). Sellers's description of the finished novel resolves this tension between form and meaning, defending the "unity and completeness" of a work of art that reunites aesthetics with "associated ideas" (Fry 206; 169). Upon reading *To the Lighthouse*, Vanessa marvels at how Leslie and Julia Stephen become "archetypal as well as vivid, instructional as well as real" (76). For Vanessa, the affective power of the novel lies in the way in which it manages to achieve aesthetic unity while simultaneously reaching back into the sisters' shared past, "bridg[ing] the gap between biography and art" (75). She notes how she "began to see equivalent hurdles and prospects in my own work," that "what you had achieved was so momentous it advanced us both" (76). Her subsequent attempts to capture Julia Stephen are initially hampered by comparison with "the portrait of Mother you drew in your novel," the visual analogy echoing Woolf's assertion, in "Sketch of the Past," that "to give a sense of my mother's personality one would have to be an artist." For Vanessa, *To the Lighthouse* represents her sister's discovery of "a language with the powers of Cézanne's painting" (Banfield 296); the "portrait" is

> so convincing that I heard her voice, saw the perpendicular of her back, as I read. I gaze at my picture. The emptiness remains. I paint a random figure, hurriedly, haphazardly, to fill the space, then take the canvas down. It is only years later when I look at the picture again I realise the figure is my daughter. (134)

Like the novel itself, the portrait of Angelica inspired by *To the Lighthouse* reunites pure form with associative or biographical qualities. The subject is "a random figure," painted in an attempt "to fill the space," echoing the way in which, for Clive Bell, "the subject [...] is of no consequence in itself. It is merely one of the artist's means of expression or creativity" (68). In accordance with the dictates of Bell and Fry, the portrait aims not to represent life, but to satisfy the composition's need for "certain forms and relations of forms" (Clive Bell 68). Yet upon subsequent inspection, the figure is revealed to have a deep personal significance for the artist, demonstrating how "form and content may cohere in a painting without making it imitative or 'descriptive'" (Goldman 146-47). Sellers thus represents *To the Lighthouse* and Vanessa's painting of Angelica as mutually-inspiring works that reengage narrative elements with aesthetics, enabling an abolition of the boundaries raised by Fry and Clive Bell.

    Sellers's attribution of personal significance to abstracted forms in Vanessa's painting enables a new reading of *To the Lighthouse* itself. The suggested reading combines two dominant critical approaches, the biographical and the symbolic, by demonstrating how Lily Briscoe's painting exerts a transformative influence over real-life figures, affording them an emblematic meaning. This reading accords with the popular interpretation of the painting as "an analogue for the novel itself" (Hussey 312), in which Lily, like her creator, "bridged the gap between biography and art" (Sellers 76). Even in Part One of *To the Lighthouse*, Lily's longing for intimacy with the Ramsays is starting to evolve into a perception of them as fading Victorian symbols. As she looks at Mr. and Mrs. Ramsay "standing close together watching the children throwing catches," "suddenly the meaning [...] came upon them, and made them in the dusk standing, looking, the symbols of marriage, husband and wife" (99). This shift in perception ultimately allows Lily to move past her fascination with Mrs. Ramsay's physical beauty towards an artistic understanding of the couple's potential as aesthetic symbols, enabling the Ramsays to leave "the private world of memory" and enter "a shared world of art" (Hussey 316). Such a reading accords the painting inventive as well as commemorative potential; it is, in the words of Banfield, "no pale reflex" of Mrs. Ramsay but "a transformation of the vision of which she was part" (289).

Resuming work on her abandoned painting in the aftermath of the First World War, Lily is newly sensitive to the importance of formal perspective to her artistic design, recognizing that "so much depends on whether people are near us or far from us" (99). She realizes that her "feeling for Mr Ramsay changed as he sailed further and further across the bay," and "seemed to become more and more remote" (99). Finally, "'He has landed,' she said aloud. 'It is finished'" (280). It is the knowledge that Mr. Ramsay has alighted on the island, has attained the furthest geographical distance from the bay, that enables Lily to finish her painting. The juxtaposition indicates her need to distance herself from the familiar associations of the Ramsays in order for them to assume their place in her composition as abstracted forms. But the Ramsays are not abandoned or left behind; they are instead transformed into symbols. In short, the "form and colour" in Lily's painting "do represent life," while at the same time having aesthetic significance as abstract shapes (Vanessa Bell, *Letters*, 406). In this reading, enabled in part by Sellers, Lily's painting represents, in microcosm, *To the Lighthouse*'s successful reunion of biographical elements with formal aesthetics.

Sellers's emphasis on the mutual engagement between her subjects' art forms culminates in the interplay suggested between *The Waves* and Bell's lost painting, *The Nursery*. Bell's letter to Woolf from Cassis describing moths "flying madly in circles round me and the lamp" provided inspiration for the novel that was to become *The Waves* (314), and with it, one of Woolf's most explicit corroborations of the reciprocal inspiration between her sister and herself: "perhaps you stimulate the literary sense in me as you say I do your painting sense" (*L*3 372). Sellers reconstructs the scene described in Bell's letter, transporting Virginia to Cassis to witness the moth at first hand. Virginia then elucidates the symbolic meaning of the scene through conversation with Vanessa, telling her that

> 'You hold the light. Then there are lonely moths like me circling the lamp, searching for a way in.'
> 'I knew you'd make a scene out of it! So what about all the other people sitting round the table tonight? How do they feature in your sketch?'
> You lean back and gaze at me steadily.
> 'They personify the different voices—emblematised by the moth.'
> 'Sounds like the start for one of your novels.' (143)

By locating the roots of one of Woolf's most abstract, formally experimental works in a familial, domestic scene, this exchange once again emphasizes the potential for aesthetic and biographical qualities to co-exist and complement each other.

This is a significant departure from the representation of Virginia's earlier work, in which a dependence on outside elements was perceived to hamper formal unity. Whereas *The Voyage Out* was dismissed as "mere journalism" and therefore "not literature," the attempt to reproduce lived experience is instead seen to catalyse the formal radicalism of this later work (75). From the clash of voices at a family dinner emerges the experimental polyphony of *The Waves*, in much the same way as Vanessa's elimination of facial detail evolved from a piece of associative art.

Gillespie writes that *The Waves*, once completed, heralded "a new phase in [Bell's] response to Virginia's writing," namely "an attempt to see in her sister's work a creative struggle similar to her own" (159). Writing to Woolf after her first reading of the novel, Bell ventured a tentative comparison to her current work-in-progress, suggesting, as Kostkowska has written in a different context, "not just general affinities between [the sisters'] aesthetics but also a possibility of specific influence" (90):

> Will it seem to you absurd and conceited or will you understand at all what I mean if I tell you that I've been working hard lately at an absurd great picture I've been painting on and off for the last 2 years—and if only I could do what I want to—but I can't—it seems to me it would have some sort of analogous meaning to what you've done. How can one explain, but to me painting a floor covered with toys and keeping them all in relation to each other and the figures and the space of the floor and the light on it means something of the same sort that you seem to mean. (367-68)

Bell's letter significantly informs an understanding of her attitude to "literary" or interdisciplinary qualities in art. It emphasizes her quest for an internal formal unity in *The Nursery*, a unity comprised of what Clive Bell called "pure forms in certain relations to each other," in this case the toys, the figures, the space, and the light (51). Yet while preserving this sense of formal unity, Bell is able to reach out to Woolf's parallel project, *The Waves*, detecting "a common sense of intersubjectivity" between painting and novel (Goldman 150). Bell's suggestion that the two works "mean something of the same sort" is indicative of a different conceptualization of "literary" art to that of Fry and Clive Bell, who used the term to denigrate an incomplete work that is dependent on external associations for its effect. Instead, we see how the term might characterize a self-contained work, which, when viewed in relation to a work of literature, has an "analogous meaning." This new interpretation of "literary" art enables Woolf and Bell's works to be experienced in dialogue, without diminishing the achievement of either.

Bell's acknowledgment of mutual influence between herself and Woolf is corroborated in *Vanessa and Virginia*, where Sellers incorporates what can be seen as an ekphrastic description of *The Nursery* into a scene in Vanessa's life:

> You gesture towards the hearth, the ripe peaches and apricots I have worked round it. Your hand finds the pattern in the stems and leaves, connecting the fruit, weaving the chaos of my decoration into shape. I hear Julian and Quentin playing happily again in the garden. Soon Duncan will appear, and I will go into the kitchen and see to lunch. Gradually the scraps of my life—the debris from the party, the children's discarded clothes, my half-finished fireplace—coalesce into a whole. You have made a painting. (96-97)

As with her aforementioned description of Vanessa's portrait of Virginia, Sellers emphasizes Vanessa's perception of the objects in her composition as "means" rather than as "pure forms" or "ends in themselves" (Clive Bell 52). Whereas Fry observed that "the greatest art seems to concern itself most with the universal aspects of natural form, to be the least preoccupied with particulars" (207), Vanessa is sensitive to the "unaesthetic matter" or "associations" of her chosen forms (Clive Bell 55), the particularity of her own "half-finished fireplace" and her "children's discarded clothes." Sellers's description suggests that had *The Nursery* survived, its formal significance would have arisen, in part, from these associative elements; the "scraps" of the artist's life would, together, have "made a painting." This is supported by Tickner, for whom Bell's enlisting of "domestic subject matter" for "radical experiments in style and technique" is suggestive of a Woolfian "consciousness of everyday life as something to be caught and held in new forms of expression" (75). Both novelist and critic thus challenge Fry's preoccupation with the "universal aspects" of form, asserting the innate aesthetic potential of domestic female lives (207).

The mutual resonances that Bell perceived between *The Nursery* and *The Waves* are also represented, symbolized by Virginia having a "hand" in Vanessa's art. By "connecting the fruit, weaving the chaos of my decoration into shape," Virginia reveals *The Nursery*'s "design," defined by Clive Bell as the means by which "every form in a work of art [is] made a part of a significant whole" (228). Rather than the formal unity of the work of art being hindered by the engagement between painter and author, it is the hand of the writer that enables the forms to "coalesce into a whole." This passage is therefore symptomatic of Sellers's overall approach, challenging the controlling assumptions of the Bloomsbury critics by revealing how formal significance can coexist with, even arise from, associative or "literary" qualities in art.

III

To conclude, *Vanessa and Virginia* has a hitherto unexplored potential to intervene in the popular representation of its subjects. Creating in the gaps and silences of Woolf's and Bell's letters, diaries, and memoirs, Sellers uses biographical scholarship to inform her fictional portrait, troubling the oppositional portrayals that haunt the sisters' posthumous reputations. As reproduced in other works of biofiction, these include the contrasting of Woolf's supposed sexual timidity and her periods of mental illness to Bell's fecundity and apparent ease of mind. Through a layering of historical and invented detail, Sellers bridges the dichotomy between "the virginal, barren woman [and] the sensual, maternal one," "the mentally unstable" and "the sane" (Gillespie 5). In doing so, she reveals how narrowly reifying are the taxonomies between the "real" and the "incomplete" woman, instead producing a more nuanced, synthesized, understanding of the interconnections between the sisters' lives. This process of fictional re-negotiation culminates in her revelation of the sustained interplay between their arts. Whereas, for instance, Cunningham's reference to "the children and paints and lovers, the brilliantly cluttered house" presents Bell's art as an incidental spillover from her life, Sellers's use of ekphrasis enables sustained analysis of her artistic process, and foregrounds Woolf's developing engagement with her sister's work (169). Sellers thereby advances Gillespie's acknowledged aims: to "shift the emphasis in the ongoing discussion of Virginia Woolf and the visual arts from Roger Fry to Vanessa Bell" and to "reveal more fully the role of the visual arts in Woolf's writing" (2). *Vanessa and Virginia* offers a companion achievement to *The Sisters' Arts*, redistributing attention in the discussion of Vanessa Bell and the *literary* arts from Roger Fry to Virginia Woolf, and using ekphrasis to suggest the influence of literature on Bell's painting.

By embroidering these moments of ekphrasis into a biographical narrative, Sellers suggests that appreciation of the formal elements of a work, be it visual or literary, is enhanced rather than diminished by "outside associations of character and story" (Gillespie 2). This represents a significant challenge to the scholarly tendency, noted by Spalding and Gillespie, to "*cherchez l'homme*" (Gillespie 3) and to assume that the sisters' arts adhered uncritically to Fry and Clive Bell's opposition of "pure form" and "unaesthetic matter" (Fry 92; Bell 55). Sellers instead illuminates moments in Virginia's writing and Vanessa's painting wherein attention to their subjects' real-life associations gave rise to formal significance, and insists that art may have biographical resonances without sacrificing its structural unity. As demonstrated by my analysis of Lily Briscoe's painting in *To the Lighthouse*, such reunion of an "art of associated ideas" with Structural Design and Significant Form has the potential to generate new and intriguing readings of the interrelation between narrative and aesthetic elements in Woolf's and Bell's works (Fry 169). Thus blending fiction with "critical hypothesizing" (Gilbert 3), the novel provides a unique insight into the work of Woolf, "the supreme (portrait) artist," and Bell, the "mistress of the phrase" (Bell 316; Woolf *L3* 340).

Works Cited

"Archive Journeys: Bloomsbury: Roger Fry." Tate Online. http://www2.tate.org.uk/archivejourneys/bloomsburyhtml/bio_fry.html Web. 9 Apr. 2014.

Banfield, Ann. *The Phantom Table: Woolf, Fry, Russell, and the Epistemology of Modernism*. Cambridge: Cambridge UP, 2000. Print.

Barrett, Eileen. "Introduction." *Virginia Woolf: Lesbian Readings*. Ed. Eileen Barrett and Patricia Cramer. New York: New York UP, 1997. 3-9. Print.

Bell, Clive. *Art*. London: Chatto and Windus, 1914. Print.

Bell, Quentin. *Bloomsbury*. London: Weidenfeld and Nicolson, 1968. Print.

———. *Virginia Woolf: A Biography*. 2 vols. London: Hogarth, 1972-73. Print.

Bell, Vanessa. *Selected Letters of Vanessa Bell*. Ed. Regina Marler. London: Bloomsbury, 1993. Print.

———. "Life at Hyde Park Gate After 1897." *Sketches in Pen and Ink*. Ed. Lia Giachero. London: Pimlico, 1998. Print.

———. "Notes on Virginia's Childhood." *Sketches in Pen and Ink*. Ed. Lia Giachero. Print.

Cooley, Martha. *The Archivist*. Preston: Abacus, 1999. Print.

Cunningham, Michael. *The Hours*. London: Fourth Estate, 2003. Print.

DeSalvo, Louise. *Virginia Woolf: The Impact of Childhood Sexual Abuse on her Life and Work*. London: The Women's Press, 1989. Print.

Dunn, Jane. *Virginia Woolf and Vanessa Bell: A Very Close Conspiracy*. London: Pimlico, 1996. Print.

Freeman, Gillian. *But Nobody Lives in Bloomsbury*. London: Arcadia, 2006. Print.

Fry, Roger. *Vision and Design*. London: Chatto and Windus, 1920. Print.

Garnett, Angelica. *Deceived With Kindness: A Bloomsbury Childhood*. London: Chatto and Windus, 1984. Print.

Gilbert, Sandra. "Dead Poet's Society." *The Women's Review of Books* 20 (2003): 1 + 3-4. Print.

Gillespie, Diane. *The Sisters' Arts: The Writing and Painting of Virginia Woolf and Vanessa Bell*. New York: Syracuse UP, 1988. Print.

Goldman, Jane. *The Feminist Aesthetics of Virginia Woolf*. Cambridge: Cambridge UP, 1998. Print.

Hill, Carol de Chellis. *Henry James's Midnight Song*. New York: W.W. Norton and Company, 1995. Print.

Humm, Maggie. *Modernist Women and Visual Cultures: Virginia Woolf, Vanessa Bell, Photography and Cinema*. Edinburgh: Edinburgh UP, 1992. Print.
Hussey, Mark. *Virginia Woolf A to Z: A Comprehensive Reference for Students, Teachers and Common Readers to Her Life, Work and Critical Reception*. London: Cecil Woolf, 2011.
James, Henry. *Selected Letters*. Ed. Leon Edel. London: Hart Davis, 1956. Print.
Johnson, George M. *Dynamic Psychology in Modern British Fiction*. Basingstoke: Palgrave Macmillan, 2005. Print.
Kaplan, Cora. *Victoriana: Histories, Fictions, Criticism*. Edinburgh: Edinburgh UP, 2007. Print.
Kostkowska, Justyna. "*Studland Beach* and *Jacob's Room*: Vanessa Bell's and Virginia Woolf's Experiments in Portrait Making 1910-1933." *Partial Answers: Journal of Literature and the History of Ideas* 9 (2011): 79-93. Print.
Lackey, Michael. *Truthful Fictions: Conversations with American Biographical Novelists*. New York and London: Bloomsbury, 2014. Print.
Latham, Monica. "Serv[ing] Under Two Masters: Virginia Woolf's Afterlives in Contemporary Biofictions." *a/b: Auto-Biography Studies* 27 (2012): 354-373. Print.
Lee, Hermione. "Biomythographers: Rewriting the Lives of Virginia Woolf." *Essays in Criticism* 46 (1996): 95-114. Print.
———. *Virginia Woolf*. London: Vintage, 1997. Print.
Lodge, David. *The Year of Henry James: The Story of a Novel*. London: Penguin, 2007. Print.
McLaurin, Allen. *Virginia Woolf: The Echoes Enslaved*. Cambridge: Cambridge UP, 1973. Print.
Middeke, Martin. "Introduction." *Biofictions: The Rewriting of Romantic Lives in Contemporary Fiction and Drama*. Ed. Martin Middeke and Werner Huber. Suffolk: Camden House, 1999. 1-26. Print.
Morgan, Claire. *A Book for All and None*. London: Weidenfeld and Nicolson, 2012. Print.
Nunez, Sigrid. *Mitz: The Marmoset of Bloomsbury*. Brooklyn, NY: Soft Skull, 2007. Print.
Ozick, Cynthia, "Dictation." *Dictation: A Quartet*. Boston and New York: Mariner Books, 2009. 1-50. Print.
Parini, Jay. *Some Necessary Angels*. New York: Columbia UP, 1997. Print.
Plath, Sylvia. *The Journals of Sylvia Plath: Transcribed from the Original Manuscripts at Smith College*. Ed. Karen V. Kukil. London: Faber, 2000. Print.
Sellers, Susan. *Vanessa and Virginia*. Ross-shire: Two Ravens, 2008. Print.

———, ed. *The Cambridge Companion to Virginia Woolf*. Cambridge: Cambridge UP, 2010. Print.
Sellers, Susan, and Elizabeth Wright. "Painting in Prose: Performing the Artist in Susan Sellers's *Vanessa and Virginia*." *Making Sense: For an Effective Aesthetics*. Eds. Lorna Collins and Elizabeth Rush. Oxford: Peter Lang, 2011. 133-40. Print.
Silver, Brenda. "'Anon' and 'The Reader': Virginia Woolf's Last Essays." *Twentieth Century Literature* 25 (1979): 356-441. Print.
Spalding, Frances. *Vanessa Bell*. London: Weidenfeld and Nicolson, 1983. Print.
Stanley, Liz. *The Auto/Biographical I: The Theory and Practice of Feminist Auto/Biography*. Manchester: Manchester UP, 1992. Print.
Swanson, Diana L. "Lesbian Approaches." *Palgrave Advances in Virginia Woolf Studies*. Ed. Anna Snaith. Basingstoke: Macmillan, 2007. 184-208. Print.
Taylor, Catherine. "Catherine Taylor's first novel choice – reviews." *Guardian* 1 July 2011. http://www.theguardian.com/books/2011/jul/01/first-novels-roundup-review Web. 9 Apr. 2013.
Tickner, Lisa. "Vanessa Bell: Studland Beach, Domesticity, and 'Significant Form'." *Representations* 65 (1999): 63-92. Print.
Torgovnick, Marianna. *The Visual Arts, Pictorialism, and the Novel: James, Lawrence, and Woolf*. New Jersey: Princeton UP, 1985. Print.
Uhlmann, Anthony. "Virginia Woolf and Bloomsbury Aesthetics." *The Edinburgh Companion to Virginia Woolf and the Visual Arts*. Ed. Maggie Humm. Edinburgh: Edinburgh UP, 2010. 58-73. Print.
Woolf, Leonard. *The Wise Virgins*. London: Persephone, 2003. Print.
———. *Growing: An Autobiography of the Years 1904-1911*. London: Hogarth, 1961. Print.
Woolf, Virginia. "22 Hyde Park Gate." *Moments of Being*. Ed. Jeanne Schulkind. London: Pimlico, 2002. 31-42. Print.
———. "The Art of Biography." *The Death of the Moth and Other Essays*. London: Hogarth, 1943. 119-26. Print.
———. *The Diary of Virginia Woolf*. Ed. Anne Olivier Bell and Andrew McNeillie. 5 vols. London: Hogarth, 1977-84. Print.
———. *Flush: A Biography*. Ed. Kate Flint. Oxford: Oxford UP, 2002. Print.
———. *The Letters of Virginia Woolf*. Ed. Nigel Nicolson and Joanne Trautmann. 6 vols. London: Hogarth, 1975-80. Print.
———. "The New Biography." *Granite and Rainbow*. London: Hogarth, 1960. 49-55. Print.
———. "Old Bloomsbury." *Moments of Being*. Ed. Schulkind. 43-61. Print.
———. *Orlando*. London: Penguin, 2006. Print.
———. "Pictures." *The Moment, and Other Essays*. London: Hogarth, 1947. 140-44. Print.

———. "Reminiscences." *Moments of Being*. Ed. Schulkind. 1-30. Print.
———. *Roger Fry*. London: Vintage, 2003. Print.
———. "A Sketch of the Past." *Moments of Being*. Ed. Schulkind. 78-160. Print.
———. *The Voyage Out*. Ed. Lorna Sage. Oxford: Oxford UP, 2001. Print.
———. *To the Lighthouse*. Ed. Margaret Drabble. Oxford: Oxford UP, 2000. Print.
———. "Walter Sickert: A Conversation." *Collected Essays.* Ed. Leonard Woolf. 4 vols. London: Hogarth, 1966-67, II (1966). 233-44. Print.
———. *The Waves*. Ed. Gillian Beer. Oxford: Oxford UP, 1998. Print.
Yoder, Edwin M. Jr. *Lions at Lamb House*. New York: Europa Editions, 2007. Print.

Guide to Library Special Collections

If an archive has submitted revisions since 2014 they are reflected below; however, you should consult the relevant websites for the most current information.

Name of Collection: The Beinecke Rare Book and Manuscript Library

Contact: Kevin Repp, Curator of Modern Books and Manuscripts
Nancy Kuhl, Curator of American Literature

Address: Yale University Library
P.O. Box 208240
New Haven, CT 06520-8240

URL: http://beinecke.library.yale.edu/

Access Requirements: Registration required at first visit.

Holdings Relevant To Woolf: General Collection includes autograph manuscript of "Notes on Oliver Goldsmith." Comments on Edward Gibbon, William Beckford Collection. Letters from Virginia Woolf in the Bryher Papers, the Louise Morgan and Otto Theis Papers, and the Rebecca West Papers. Related material: 41 letters from Vita Sackville-West to Violet Trefusis; files relating to Robert Manson Myers's *From Beowulf to Virginia Woolf* in the Edmond Pauker Papers.

Yale Collection of American Literature includes typewritten manuscripts of "The Art of Walter Sickert," "Augustine Birrell," "Aurora Leigh," "How Should One Read a Book?" "Letter to a Young Poet," "The Novels of Turgenev," "Street Haunting." Dial/Scofield Thayer Papers: manuscripts of "The Lives of the Obscure," "Miss Ormerod," and "Mrs. Dalloway in Bond Street." Letters from Virginia Woolf in the William Rose Benet Papers, the Benet Family Correspondence, Henry Seidel Canby Papers, the Seward Collins Papers, the Dial/Scofield Thayer Papers, and the

Yale Review archive. Material relating to translations of Woolf in the Thornton Wilder papers. Related material: Clive Bell, "Virginia Woolf" (Dial/ Scofield Thayer Papers); 43 letters from Leonard Woolf to Helen McAfee (*Yale Review*); 11 letters from Leonard Woolf to Gertrude Stein.

Name of Collection: The Henry W. and Albert A. Berg Collection of English and American Literature

Contact: berg@nypl.org for access procedures
Isaac Gewirtz, Curator
isaacgewirtz@nypl.org

Address: New York Public Library, Room 320
Fifth Avenue & 42nd Street
New York, NY 10018

Telephone: 212-930-0802
Fax: 212-930-0079
Email: isaacgewirtz@nypl.org

Hours: Tue.–Wed. 11 am–6:45 pm
Thu.–Sat. 10 am–5:45 pm
Closed Sun., Mon. and legal holidays

Access Requirements: After acquiring Library card in room 315, check outerwear and all containers (briefcases, computer cases, handbags, folders, etc.) in Ground Floor cloakroom, and proceed to the Berg Collection. Traceable and photo identification required. Undergraduates working on honors theses need letter from faculty advisor. No books may be brought to the reading tables, including notebooks.

Restrictions: Virginia Woolf's bound MSS are now made available on microfilm and CD. URL for Berg finding aid: http://www.nypl.org/research/manuscripts/berg/brgwoolf.xml. N.B. All the Berg's Woolf MSS are on microfilm and 90 percent of them are

GUIDE TO LIBRARY SPECIAL COLLECTIONS 109

Holdings Relevant To Woolf:
: on CD published by Research Publications and available at many research libraries.

: Manuscripts/typescripts of all of the novels except *Orlando*, including: *Between the Acts, Flush, Jacob's Room, Mrs. Dalloway* (notes and fragments), *Night and Day, To the Lighthouse, The Voyage Out, The Waves, The Years*; 12 notebooks of articles, essays, fiction and reviews, 1924–1940; 36 volumes of diaries; 26 volumes of reading notes; correspondence with Vanessa Bell, Ethel Smyth, Vita Sackville-West and others. Su Hua Ling Chen's Bloomsbury correspondence.

Recent Acquisitions: Proof copy of *A Room of One's Own* (July 1929); ALS Vanessa Bell to Vita Sackville-West, April 29, 1941 [in Marler, *Selected Letters* 478-80]; Frank Dean, *Strike While the Iron's Hot: Frank Dean's Life as a Blacksmith and Farrier in Rodmell*, ed. Susan Rowland (S. Rowland, 1994) [includes map, accounts of search for VW's body and of her funeral]; Vita Sackville-West, *Marian Stranways*, autograph manuscript, [1913].

Name of Collection: The British Library Manuscript Collections

Contact: Manuscripts Enquiries

Address: 96 Euston Road
London NW1 2DB
England

Telephone: 0207-412-7513
Fax: 0207-412-7745
Email: mss@bl.uk

Hours: Mon. 10 am–5 pm; Tues.–Sat.: 9:30 am–5 pm

Access Requirements: British Library Reader Pass (signed I.D. required and usually proof of postgraduate academic status, or other demonstrable need to use the collections—see www.bl.uk). In addition, access to most literary autograph material only available with letter of recommendation.

Restrictions: Paper Copies, Microfilms, and Photography of selected items available upon receipt of written authorization for photo duplication from the copyright holder.

Holdings Relevant to Woolf: Diaries 1930–1931 (microfilm); *Mrs. Dalloway* and other writings (1923–1925) three volumes; letter from Leonard Woolf to H. G. Wells (1941); two letters from Virginia Woolf and three letters from Leonard Woolf to John Lehmann (1941); letter written on behalf of Leonard Woolf to S. S. Koteliansky (1946); notebook in Italian kept by Virginia Woolf; notebook of Virginia Stephen (1906–1909); "A sketch of the past revised ts" (1940); letters from Virginia Woolf in the correspondence files of Lytton and James Strachey; letter from Virginia Woolf to Mildred Massingberd; letter from Virginia Woolf to Harriet Shaw Weaver (1918); letters from Virginia Woolf to S. S. Koteliansky (1923–1927); letter from Virginia Woolf to Frances Cornford (1929); letter from Virginia Woolf to Ernest Rhys (1930); correspondence of Virginia Woolf in the Society of Authors archive (1934–1937); letter and postcard from Virginia Woolf to Bernard Shaw (1940); three letters (suicide notes) from Virginia Woolf (1941). "Hyde Park Gate News" 1891–1892, 1895 (add. MSS 70725, 70726). Letters of Virginia and Leonard Woolf to Lady Aberconway, 1927–1941. Letters from Virginia Woolf to Macmillan Co. 1903, 1908. Collection of RPs ("reserved photocopies"–copies of manuscripts exported, some subject to restrictions).

GUIDE TO LIBRARY SPECIAL COLLECTIONS

Name of Collection: Harry Ransom Center

Contact: Head, Research Services

Address: Harry Ransom Center
The University of Texas at Austin
P.O. Box 7219
Austin, TX 78713-7219

Telephone: 512-471-9119
Fax: 512-471-2899
Email: reference@hrc.utexas.edu

Hours: See web site for most current information: www.hrc.utexas.edu

Access Requirements: Completed online research application; current photo identification.

Holdings Relevant To Woolf: The manuscript collection includes the typed manuscript with autograph revisions of *Kew Gardens*, and the typed manuscript and autograph revisions of "Thoughts on Peace in an Air Raid." The Center holds 571 of Woolf's letters, including correspondence to Elizabeth Bowen, Lady Ottoline Morrell, Mary Hutchinson, William Plomer, Hugh Walpole and others. Further mss. relating to Virginia Woolf include letters to her from T. S. Eliot and reviews of her work. A substantial collection of the first British and American editions of Woolf's published works, as well as 130 volumes from Leonard and Virginia Woolf's library and a collection of books published by the Hogarth Press, is also housed.

An art collection holds a landscape painting of Virginia's garden and a series of Cockney cartoons in a sketch book, signed "V.W." The center also has extensive holdings of materials related to Leonard Woolf, Ottoline Morrell, Mary Hutchinson,

Lytton Strachey, Dora Carrington, E. M. Forster, Clive Bell, Roger Fry, Vanessa Bell, Bertrand Russell, Elizabeth Bowen, William Plomer, Stephen Spender and Hugh Walpole.

Name of Collection: Monks House Papers/Leonard Woolf Papers/Charleston Papers/Nicolson Papers

Contact: University of Sussex, Special Collections

Address: The Keep
Woollards Way
Brighton & Hove
BN1 9PB

Telephone: 01273 482349
Email: library.specialcoll@sussex.ac.uk
URL: http://www.thekeep.info

Access Requirements: By appointment. Identification to be presented on arrival. Registration and material requests should be made through our website.

Restrictions: Photocopying strictly controlled.

Holdings Relevant To Woolf: The University of Sussex holds two large archives relating to Leonard and Virginia Woolf: The Monks House Papers, primarily correspondence and MSS of Virginia Woolf, including the three scrapbooks relating to *Three Guineas*, and Virginia Woolf's engagement diaries from 1930 to her death in 1941; and The Leonard Woolf Papers, primarily correspondence and other papers of Leonard Woolf. (Monks House Papers are available on microfilm in many research libraries.) The Charleston Papers consist in the main of letters written to or by Clive and Vanessa Bell and Duncan Grant which had accumulated in their home; the library houses Quentin Bell's photocopied set; letters from Roger Fry, Maynard Keynes, Lytton Strachey, Virginia Woolf,

GUIDE TO LIBRARY SPECIAL COLLECTIONS

Vita Sackville-West, E. M. Forster, T. S. Eliot, Frances Partridge and others. The Maria Jackson letters comprise some 900 letters from Maria Jackson to Julia and Leslie Stephen. The Nicolson Papers complement these three Sussex archives relating to the Bloomsbury Group, and consist of Nigel Nicolson's correspondence relating to his editorial work as principal editor of the six-volume *Letters of Virginia Woolf*, published between 1975 and 1980.

The Bell Papers. A. O. Bell's correspondence relating to her editorial work on Virginia Woolf's diaries, a parallel collection to the Nicolson Papers. Collection level description may be accessed at www.archiveshub.ac.uk

Name of Collection: The Lilly Library

Contact: Joel Silver, Director
Cherry Williams, Curator of Manuscripts

Address: The Lilly Library, Indiana University
1200 East Seventh Street
Bloomington, IN 47405-5500

Telephone: 812-855-2452
Fax: 812-855-3143
Email: liblilly@indiana.edu, silverj@indiana.edu, chedwill@indiana.edu

Hours: Mon.–Fri. 9 am–6 pm; Sat. 9 am–1 pm; *Closed Sundays and Major Holidays*

Access Requirements: Valid photo-identification; brief registration procedure.

Restrictions: Closed stacks; material use confined to reading room; wheelchair-accessible reading room and exhibitions (but no wheelchair-accessible restroom).

Holdings Relevant To Woolf:	Corrected page proofs for the American edition of *Mrs. Dalloway*; letters to Woolf from Desmond and Mary (Molly) MacCarthy; 77 letters (published in *Letters*) from Woolf to correspondents including Donald Clifford Brace, Robert Gathorne-Hardy, Barbara (Strachey) Halpern, Richard Arthur Warren Hughes, Desmond MacCarthy and Molly MacCarthy; "Preliminary Scheme for the formation of a Partnership between Mr Leonard Sidney Woolf and Mr John Lehmann to take over The Hogarth Press" (includes contract signed by Lehmann, Leonard Woolf, and Virginia Woolf and receipt for Lehmann's payment to Virginia Woolf to purchase Virginia Woolf's share in the Hogarth Press); photographs of Virginia Woolf, Leonard Woolf, Lytton Strachey, Strachey family, Roger Fry, and Vanessa Bell (Hannah Whitall Smith mss.); (Richard) Kennedy mss. (four hand-colored lithographs of Virginia Woolf: artist's proofs for RK's portfolio, VIRGINIA WOOLF: "AS I KNEW HER"; Sackville-West, V. mss. (10,529 items: includes the correspondence of Vita Sackville-West, and Harold Nicolson); MacCarthy mss. (ca. 10,000 items: papers of Desmond and Molly MacCarthy); correspondence between LW and Mary Gaither regarding publication of *A Checklist of the Hogarth Press* (1976, repr. 1986); Todd Avery, *Close and Affectionate Friends: Desmond and Molly MacCarthy and the Bloomsbury Group* (The Lilly Library/Indiana University Libraries, 1999).
Name of Collection:	The Morgan Library & Museum
Contact:	Reading Room
Address:	225 Madison Avenue New York, NY 10016
Telephone:	212-590-0315

GUIDE TO LIBRARY SPECIAL COLLECTIONS 115

Email: readingroom@themorgan.org
URL: www.themorgan.org

Access Requirements: Admission to the Reading Room is by application and by appointment. See www.themorgan.org/research/reading.asp for application form.

Holdings Relevant To Woolf: Virginia Woolf. Autograph manuscript notebook, 1931 Sept. 24. 1 item (52 p.); 265 x 208 mm. Contains drafts of "A Letter to a Young Poet," a brief letter to the press entitled "The Villa Jones" [ff. 3–5] and a monologue by a working-class woman [ff. 44–46]. MA 3333. Purchased on the Fellows Fund with the special assistance of Anne S. Dayton, Enid A. Haupt, Mrs. James H. Ripley, Mr. and Mrs. August H. Schilling, and John S. Thacher, 1979.

Virginia Woolf. Autograph letters signed (2) and typed letter signed, dated London [etc.], to E. McKnight Kauffer, 1931 Apr. 4–23, and undated. 3 items (4 p.). Concerning a drawing of her and a bibliography of her works. MA 1679. Purchased in 1959.

Vanessa Bell. 84 autograph letters, 3 typed letters, 7 postcards, and 3 telegrams. Most, but not all, are written by Vanessa Bell to John Maynard Keynes. Concerning Duncan Grant, Roger Fry, Clive Bell, the Bell children, Leonard and Virginia Woolf, Lytton Strachey, John Maynard and Lydia Lopokova Keynes, David Garnett, Ottoline Morrell, and others. MA 3448. Items in this collection are described in 97 individual records (MA 3448.1-97). Purchased on the Fellows Fund, special gift of the Gramercy Park Foundation (Mrs. Michael Tucker), 1980.

Name of Collection:	1. Katherine Mansfield Papers 2. Arts Club of Chicago Papers
Contact:	Martha Briggs, Lloyd Lewis Curator of Modern Manuscripts
	Liesl Olson, Director, Scholl Center for American History and Culture
Address:	The Newberry Library, 60 West Walton Street, Chicago, IL, 60610
Telephone:	312-255-3554 (Briggs) 312-255-3665 (Olson)
Email:	briggsm@newberry.org olsonl@newberry.org
Hours:	Tuesday-Friday: 9-5 Saturday: 9-1
Access Requirements:	The Newberry's reading rooms are open to researchers who are at least 16 years old or juniors in high school. Before using the collections, all researchers must apply for and receive a reader's card. Issued in the Reference Center on the third floor, cards require a valid photo ID, proof of current home address, and a research interest that is supported by the Newberry's collections.
Holdings Relevant To Woolf:	The papers of the Arts Club of Chicago—since 1916, a private club and preeminent exhibitor of international art—contain material related to Bloomsbury artists and how they were received in Chicago. The papers of Katherine Mansfield contain manuscript copies of some of Mansfield's most important work, and outgoing correspondence—the bulk to artist Dorothy Brett and Lady Ottoline Morrell. There are a few incoming miscellaneous letters, printed works, photographs and memorabilia.

GUIDE TO LIBRARY SPECIAL COLLECTIONS 117

Name of Collection: University of Reading Special Collections

Contact: Special Collections Service

Address: Special Collections Service
University of Reading
Redlands Road
Reading RG1 5EX

Telephone: 0118-378-8660
Fax: 0118-378-5632
Email: specialcollections@reading.ac.uk
URL: http://www.reading.ac.uk/special-collections/

Access Requirements: Prior appointment suggested to consult material. Permission required to consult or copy material in the Hogarth Press, Jonathan Cape, and Chatto & Windus collections from Random House:

Random House Group Archive & Library
1 Cole Street
Crown Park
Rushden
Northants. NN10 6RZ

rushdenqueries@randomhouse.co.uk

Holdings Relevant To Woolf: Hogarth Press (MS 2750): editorial and production correspondence relating to publications of the Press including Woolf's own titles. Production ledgers 1920s–1950s. Correspondence between Leonard Woolf and Stanley Unwin about progress with his collected edition of the works of Freud. Order books – e.g. lists of booksellers, book clubs and how many books they have ordered for a particular title. Newscuttings—press clippings of advertisements for Hogarth Press books including Virginia Woolf publications.

Chatto & Windus (CW): small number of letters 1915–1925; 1929–1931.Various letters and notes by Leonard Woolf; outgoing letters to Leonard Woolf: 22 November 1927 (CW A/119); outgoing letters to Virginia Woolf: 29 January 1936 (CW A/172), 22 December 1931 (CW A/135), 31 December 1931 (CW A/135), 15 December 1920 (CW A/100), 20 December 1920 (CW A/100).

George Bell & Sons (MS 1640): 5 letters from Leonard Woolf 1930–1966.

Routledge (RKP): Reader's report by Leonard Woolf on George Padmore's "Britannia rules the blacks" (1935); "How Britain rules Africa." 1 letter from Leonard Woolf (June 1941) from Miscellaneous publishing correspondence 1941-1942 Wi-Wy RKP 174/15. Draft introduction by Leonard Woolf to *Letters on India* by Mulk Raj Anand (1942) and 1 letter to Leonard Woolf from Mulk Raj Anand 1942-1943 RKP 178/3. Correspondence concerning the publication of *The War for Peace* by Leonard Woolf, 1939-1940 RKP 160/5. 1 letter from Virginia Woolf declining an invitation from Routledge to write a biography of Margaret Bondfield, 25 May 1940 RKP 160/5.

Megroz (MS 1979/68): 2 letters from Leonard Woolf, 1926.

Allen & Unwin (MS 3282): Correspondence with Leonard Woolf c.1914-1918 (re. his book *International Government*), 1923-1924; 1939-1940; 1943; 1946; 1950-1951; 1953; 1965 (concerning ill-founded rumors about the Hogarth Press); 1967 (concerning a reprint of *Empire and Commerce in Africa*).

Jonathan Cape (MS 2446): All correspondence from file JC A43. Correspondence between

Jonathan Cape and Virginia Woolf and Cape and A. C. Gissing concerning Virginia Woolf's introduction to George Gissing's *Ionian Sea* to which A. C. Gissing objects. 1 postcard (1935), 1 letter (1933), 2 letters (1932) from Virginia Woolf. 1 letter (1932) from Virginia Woolf declining to write an introduction to Jane Austen's *Northanger Abbey*. 4 letters (1931) from Virginia Woolf declining to write an introduction to one of Miss Thackeray's books.

Letters from Vanessa Bell: 1 letter from Bell CW 152/2; 1 letter from Bell CW 171/10; 2 letters from Bell CW 578/1; 1 letter from Bell CW 59/9; 1 letter from Bell (1936) CW 61/10. Artwork by Vanessa Bell for various Virginia Woolf titles.

Artwork by Angelica Garnett, Philippa Bramson and others for various books in the Chatto & Windus archive.

Name of Collection: Frances Hooper Collection of Virginia Woolf Books and Manuscripts.
Elizabeth Power Richardson Bloomsbury Iconography Collection.

Contact: Karen V. Kukil, Associate Curator of Special Collections.

Address: Mortimer Rare Book Room
William Allan Neilson Library
Smith College
7 Neilson Drive
Northampton, MA 01063

Telephone: 413-585-2908
Fax: 413-585-2904
Email: kkukil@smith.edu
URL: www.smith.edu/libraries/libs/rarebook

Hours:	Mon.–Fri. 9 am–5 pm
Access Requirements:	Appointment to be made with the Curator.
Holdings Relevant To Woolf:	The Hooper Collection emphasizes Woolf as an essayist but also includes many Hogarth Press first editions, limited editions of Woolf's works, and translations. The collection includes page proofs of *Orlando*, *To the Lighthouse*, and *The Common Reader*, corrected by Woolf for the first American editions, a proof copy of *The Waves* that Woolf inscribed to Hugh Walpole, and the proof copies of *The Years* and of *Flush*. The Collection also has one of the deluxe editions of *Orlando* that was printed on green paper. Other items include twenty-two pages of reading notes from 1926, three pages of notes on D. H. Lawrence's *Sons and Lovers*, thirty-three pages of notes for *Roger Fry*, a six-page ms. "As to criticism," a five-page ms. of "The Searchlight," and a fourteen-page ms. of "The Patron and The Crocus." The Hooper Collection also owns 140 letters between Woolf and Lytton Strachey as well as other correspondence, including a 13 February [1921] letter to Katherine Mansfield and ten letters to Mela and Robert Spira.

The Richardson Collection is a working collection of books and materials used by Richardson in preparing her *Bloomsbury Iconography*. It includes Leslie Stephen's photograph album, ninety-eight original exhibition catalogs dating back to 1929, clippings and photocopies of such items as reviews of early Woolf works, and Bloomsbury material from British *Vogue* of the 1920s. The Collection also has three preliminary pencil drawings by Vanessa Bell for *Flush*.

The Mortimer Rare Book Room also owns Woolf's 1916 Italian ms. notebook and her corrected typescripts of "Reviewing" and "The Searchlight." In addition, there is a 1923 photograph of Woolf at Garsington. Original cover designs for Hogarth Press publications include *The Common Reader*, O*n Being Ill*, and Duncan Grant. The Mortimer Rare Book Room also has a Sylvia Plath collection that includes eight of Woolf's books from Plath's library, several of which are underlined and annotated, as well as Plath's notes from her undergraduate English 211 class at Smith (1951–1952) in which she studied *To the Lighthouse*. The collection also includes Woolf's 26 February 1939 letter to Vita Sackville-West, a 1931 bronze bust of Virginia Woolf by Stephen Tomlin, a 1923 Hogarth Press edition of T. S. Eliot's *The Waste Land*, a 1919 Hogarth Press edition of *Paris* by Hope Mirrlees and first editions of Vita Sackville-West and Katherine Mansfield publications. Additional Bloomsbury items include *Original Woodcuts* (Omega Workshops, 1918), Vanessa Bell's original woodcut for the cover of *Monday or Tuesday* (1921), and exhibition catalogs for *Manet and the Post-Impressionists* (Grafton Galleries, 1911), Friday Club Members (Mansard Gallery, 1921) Paintings and Drawings by Vanessa Bell (Independent Gallery, 1922). Additional photographs include the Mary L. S. Bennett (née Fisher) Family Photographs. Online exhibitions are available on the Mortimer Rare Book Room's website.

Name of Collection: Literature & Rare Books, Special Collections, University of Maryland Libraries

Contact: Lauren Brown, Manager Special Collections

Address: University of Maryland
2208 Hornbake Library
College Park, MD 20742

Telephone: 301-405-9212
Fax: 301-314-2709

Email: askhornbake@umd.edu

Hours: Dates and hours of operation subject to change. Regular hours are Monday-Friday, 10 am to 5 pm. Extended hours are available on select days during the academic school year.

Contact Lauren Brown or email askhornbake@umd.edu before planning a research visit.

Access Requirements: Photo ID.

Holdings Relevant To Woolf: Papers of Hope Mirrlees contain five autograph letters and postcards (1919–1928) from Virginia Woolf to Mirrlees. Also in the collection are 113 letters from T. S. Eliot to Mirrlees, and three letters from Lady Ottoline Morrell to Mirrlees. A finding aid is available at http://hdl.handle.net/1903.1/1536.

Name of Collection: Woolf/Hogarth Press/Bloomsbury

Contact: Lisa J. Sherlock

Address: Victoria University Library
71 Queens Park Crescent E.
Toronto M5S 1K7
Ontario Canada

Email: victoria.library@utoronto.ca
URL: http://library.vicu.utoronto.ca/special/bloomsbury.htm

Hours: Mon.–Fri. 9 am–5 pm

Access Requirements: Prior notification; identification.

Restrictions: Limited photocopying.

Holdings Relevant To Woolf: This collection, the most comprehensive of its kind with nearly 5,000 items, contains all the work of

Virginia and Leonard Woolf in various editions, issues, variants and translations; all the books hand-printed by Leonard and Virginia Woolf at the Hogarth Press, including many variant issues and bindings, association copies and page proofs; a nearly comprehensive collection of Hogarth Press machine printed books to 1946 (the year Leonard Woolf and the Press joined Chatto & Windus) including presentation copies, signed limited editions, page proofs, variants as well as substantial amounts of ephemera, such as the *Catalogue of Publications to 1939* with annotations by Leonard Woolf. The collection is also very strong in Bloomsbury Art and Artists, especially the decorative arts, including important examples of Omega Workshops publications and exhibition catalogues. Materials include the catalogue of the second post-impressionist exhibition, 1912; catalogues relating to Vanessa Bell and Duncan Grant exhibitions; bronze medal of Virginia Woolf by Marta Firlet; oil on canvas portrait of Amaryllis Garnett by Vanessa Bell (c.1958); Portrait sketch of Leonard Woolf by Vanessa Bell; Duncan Grant- and Vanessa Bell-designed Clarice Cliff dinner plates; original Vanessa Bell and Duncan Grant sketches and designs for dust jackets, novels, and other special projects; bronze busts of Lytton Strachey and Virginia Woolf by Stephen Tomlin (1901–1937); as well as the Marcel Gimond bust of Vanessa Bell and the Tomlin bust of Henrietta Bingham. Original correspondence and mss. material includes that by Vanessa Bell; Leonard Woolf; Ritchie family re: Anne Thackeray Ritchie/Stephen family; Duncan Grant; Quentin Bell; S. P. Rosenbaum mss. Letters from E. M. Forster, Bertrand Russell, James Strachey, Raymond Mortimer, David Garnett, Nigel Nicolson and others in the Bloomsbury Circle; as well as biographers, scholars and bibliographers such as Joanne Trautmann, Carolyn Heilbrun, J. Howard Woolmer, Leon Edel, Leila Luedeking, P. N. Furbank, Noel Annan and others. Large Ephemera Collection includes items revealing Virginia Woolf's effect on popular culture.

Name of Collection: Library of Leonard and Virginia Woolf (Washington S U)

Contact: Trevor James Bond
Head, Manuscripts, Archives, and Special Collections

Address: Washington State University Libraries
Pullman, WA 99164-5610

Email: tjbond@wsu.edu
URL: www.wsulibs.wsu.edu/holland/masc/masc.htm

Hours: Mon.–Fri. 8:30 am–4:30 pm

Access Requirements: Letter stating nature of research preferred; student or other identification.

Restrictions: Materials must be used in the MASC area under supervision. Photocopying or photographing is permitted only when it will not harm the materials and is permitted by copyright.

Holdings Relevant To Woolf: WSU has the Woolfs' basic working library including many works which belonged to Woolf's father, Sir Leslie Stephen, and other family members. Over 800 titles came from their Sussex home, Monks House, including some works bought at auction soon after Leonard Woolf died in 1969. Later additions include: 1,875 titles from his house in Victoria Square, London; 400 titles from his nephew Cecil Woolf; and over 60 titles from Quentin and Anne Olivier Bell. WSU has been actively collecting: all works in all editions by Virginia Woolf; all titles by Leonard Woolf; dust jackets; works published by the Woolfs at the Hogarth Press through 1946; books by their friends and associates, especially those by Bloomsbury authors and about Bloomsbury artists; relevant correspondence and original works of art. Original artwork by Vanessa Bell; scattered letters by Vanessa Bell, E. M. Forster, Roger Fry, Leslie Stephen, Lytton Strachey, and Leonard Woolf. Original artwork by Richard Kennedy for illustrations in his book *A Boy at the Hogarth Press*; scattered letters by Roger Fry, Leslie Stephen, Ethel Smyth, and Leonard Woolf. Virginia Woolf's initialed copy of *Cornishiana*; Leonard Woolf's annotated copy of *An Anatomy of Poetry* by A. Williams-Ellis; Leslie Stephen's copy of *Lapsus Calami and Other Verses*, inscribed by James Kenneth Stephen. Several letters from Virginia Woolf, including two written in 1939 to Ronald Heffer, and a letter to Edward McKnight Kauffer. New in the Hogarth Press Collection are a copy of E. M. Forster's *Anonymity, an Enquiry*, bound in cream paper boards, and what Woolmer calls the third label state of Forster's *The Story of the Siren*. The Library of Leonard and Virginia Woolf is once again shelved separately so that scholars visiting Pullman may see the collection apart from the other rare book collections.

Name of Collection: Yale Center for British Art

Contact: Elisabeth Fairman, Senior Curator of Rare Books and Manuscripts

Address: 1080 Chapel Street
P.O. Box 208280
New Haven, CT 06520-8280

Telephone: 203-432-2814
Fax: 203-432-9613
E-mail: elisabeth.fairman@yale.edu

Hours: Tue.-Fri. 10 am-4:30 pm

Access Requirements: Permission needed in order to reproduce.

Holdings Relevant To Woolf: Rare Books & Mss Department: 94 letters from Vanessa Bell and Duncan Grant to Sir Kenneth Clark; Prints & Drawings Department: 4 drawings by Vanessa Bell; 4 drawings by Duncan Grant; 6 drawings by Wyndham Lewis; 1 drawing by Frederick Etchells; Paintings Department: 1 painting by Vanessa Bell, 4 paintings by Duncan Grant (including portrait of Vanessa Bell); 3 paintings by Roger Fry. 6 letters from Lytton Strachey (to Clive Bell, Siegfried Sassoon, et al.).

Reviews

Virginia Woolf, *The Common Reader* (1ˢᵗ and 2ⁿᵈ series in one volume). Translated and Edited with Notes by Natalya Reinhold (Moscow: Nauka, 2012) 776pp.

Virginia Woolf, *Night and Day*. Translated and Edited with Notes by Natalya Reinhold (Moscow: Ladomir, Nauka, 2014) 502pp.

Natalya Reinhold is one of Russia's most prominent specialists on Virginia Woolf. She was the first to translate Woolf's feminist manifesto *A Room of One's Own* into Russian in 1992. A few years before that, in 1983, she translated a selection of Woolf's key essays on Russian literature. She conducted the first conference on Woolf to take place on the territory of the former Soviet Union after its fall—an international symposium, *Woolf Across Cultures*, which gathered in Moscow in 2003. She also edited the collection of papers presented at that conference, which was remarkable for its scope and diversity (Pace UP, 2004). Among Reinhold's latest feats is a Russian translation of *Night and Day*—the only novel of Woolf's that remained untranslated into Russian until now.

In 2012, Reinhold also translated and edited the first complete Russian version of *The Common Reader* and *The Common Reader: Second Series*. Thanks to her, not only the contents of these two volumes are now accessible to Russian readers: she accompanies them with a detailed commentary, "Virginia Woolf and her *Common Reader*," and has also included a number of other essays.[1] Reinhold is the leading authority on the reception of Woolf in Russia: her article in the collection *Woolf Across Cultures* (also included in this volume) describes in detail the reasons why the first Russian translations of Woolf's works appeared only in the last quarter of the twentieth century.

The appreciation of Woolf's writings had a delayed start in Russia due to the ideological restrictions of the Soviet regime. As a passionate admirer of Woolf's work, Reinhold is determined to compensate for this delay by ensuring that Russian readers immediately see Woolf in a rich historical context. In her edition

---

[1] The additions are "Tolstoy's 'The Cossacks'"; "More Dostoevsky"; "A Minor Dostoevsky"; "A Russian Schoolboy"; "Tchehov's Questions"; "Valery Brussof"; "A View of the Russian Revolution"; "The Russian View"; "The Russian Background"; "Dostoevsky in Cranford"; "'The Cherry Orchard'"; "Gorky on Tolstoy"; "A Glance at Turgenev"; "Dostoevsky the Father"; "A Giant with Very Small Thumbs"; "The Novels of Turgenev"; "Uncle Vanya"; "Mr. Bennett and Mrs. Brown"; "A Letter to a Young Poet"; "A Room of One's Own."

of *Night and Day*, as well as her own essay on the novel, "Virginia Woolf's *Night and Day*: Moments of Being," she has included excerpts from Woolf's essays "A Sketch of the Past" and "Old Bloomsbury," as well as Katherine Mansfield's review of *Night and Day* (none of these texts has been translated into Russian before). Woolf's autobiographical texts will demonstrate to Russian readers how deeply *Night and Day* is rooted in Woolf's personal experiences, including her Victorian childhood and her later participation in the London intellectual scene. Mansfield's review takes us back to the time when *Night and Day* had just been published and Woolf's contemporaries were actively debating its value as a novel. It will remind the Russian reader that in her lifetime Woolf had to endure mixed responses even in her own country.

In Reinhold's edition of *The Common Reader 1* and *2*, we find a similarly wide range of additional materials illustrating Woolf's work as a literary critic. For this edition, Reinhold prepared the first Russian translation of Woolf's major essay "Mr. Bennett and Mrs. Brown" where Woolf famously observed that "on or about December 1910 human character changed." It is hard to believe that this important literary manifesto of the twentieth century was first translated into Russian only in 2012. One may wonder whether this essay, along with Woolf's other critical works, remained unknown to Russian scholars until their first Russian translations. The answer is no: Russian researchers and students of English literature were, of course, aware of Woolf's works, as long as they could read them in the original. What Reinhold has done is to make Woolf's writings accessible to a wide Russian reading public—the Russian common reader.

Most poignant to the Russian reader will be to see translations of Woolf's essays on Tolstoy, Dostoevsky, Chekhov, Aksakov, and other, less known, Russian authors. Not only is Reinhold the first to translate these works into Russian: she is the first to present them as one unified whole—as a mini-collection of Woolf's works on Russian literature. These seventeen essays—mostly Woolf's reviews of Russian writers whose works appeared in English translations between 1917 and 1926—are a standing reminder of Woolf's open-mindedness about foreign cultures. They remind us how, in her search for new and original ways in novel-writing, Woolf sought inspiration beyond her home border. These "Russian" essays offer us insight not only into Woolf's thoughts on Dostoevsky or Tolstoy, but also—and maybe even more importantly—into her personal beliefs as a writer.

Translating Woolf's essays is not a straightforward task. Both series of *The Common Reader* are rich with quotations from a multitude of authors—Chaucer, the Elizabethans, Montaigne, Defoe, Jane Austen, to name but a few. Woolf extensively quotes from their works, letting the style of their writings speak for itself. In this respect, translating Woolf's essays is similar to translating James Joyce's *Ulysses*: the translator has to re-create a whole choir of voices. Reinhold accomplishes this task brilliantly: for each author that Woolf quotes she finds—where possible—an already existing Russian translation and uses it in order to render Woolf's intertextual references into Russian. As a result of this painstaking work, she introduces the Russian reader not only to Woolf's voice, but also to the entire tapestry of voices present in *The Common Reader*.

As in any work of an encyclopaedic scope—and that is definitely the scope we find in Reinhold's commentary for *The Common Reader 1* and *2*— there are some minor oversights. The reason they are worth mentioning is their relevance to the Russian theme in Woolf's *oeuvre*. Discussing Dostoevsky's tendency to overpopulate his novels with minor and often outlandish characters, Woolf notes in her essay "The Russian Point of View": "The simple story of a bank clerk who could not pay for a bottle of wine spreads, before we know what is happening, into the lives of his father-in-law and the five mistresses whom his father-in-law treated abominably, and the postman's life, and the charwoman's, and the Princesses' who lodged in the same block of flats […]." Reinhold interprets this allusion as Woolf's collective reference to several episodes in Dostoevsky's novels *Crime and Punishment*, *The Idiot*, and *The Gambler*. While the images of a "charwoman" and the Princesses could be vaguely inspired by those novels, the image of the "father-in-law and the five mistresses" is Woolf's direct allusion to Dostoevsky's short story "An Unpleasant Predicament." It is also a distorted allusion, as in Dostoevsky's story the five women in question are not anyone's mistresses, but the father-in-law's relatives and lodgers. Woolf referred to these characters in her review of "An Unpleasant Predicament," written in 1919 and titled "Dostoevsky in Cranford." When re-working this piece in "The Russian Point of View," she exaggerated the intricacy of Dostoevsky's plot to the point of absurdity. Here she was following one of her own rules of essay writing: in "The Modern Essay" (1922), she observed that "literal truth-telling" is "out of place in an essay."

To go back to Reinhold's remarkable achievement of translating *Night and Day*, as well as both series of *The Common Reader* and several other key examples of Woolf's literary criticism, it needs to be briefly remembered why Woolf's works remained untranslated in Russia for such a long time. As Reinhold herself points out in *Woolf Across Cultures*, Woolf—along with other modernist authors, such as Joyce and D. H. Lawrence—was classed as "decadent," "highbrow," and thus contrary to the Soviet ideology. To ignore this label and proceed with translating an anti-Soviet author could be suicidal under Stalin's rule. For instance, Valentin Stenich (aka Smetanich), one of the first translators of Joyce in Russia, had been on the black list of Stalin's secret police for many years. Not only did he translate works by experimental authors, such as Joyce, Dos Passos, and Brecht—he was also an aesthete, a dandy, and a non-conformist who did not join the Communist Party even when it became almost compulsory under Stalin. In the end, the secret police accused him of terrorism and plotting against the Soviet government (standard accusations that the regime used when it needed to exterminate somebody). Stenich was sentenced to death and shot in 1938. There were no volunteers to risk their lives by translating the supposedly anti-proletarian Woolf in the Soviet era. Enthusiasts of English literature waited until the country reached relative ideological freedom. The first novel of Woolf's to be translated into Russian was *Mrs. Dalloway*, which came out in Moscow in 1984. It was followed by Russian translations of *Flush* (1986), *To the Lighthouse* (1988), *Jacob's Room* (1991), *Orlando* (1997), *The Waves* (2001), *The Voyage Out* (2002), *Between the Acts* (2004), and *The Years* (2005). Reinhold's translation of *Night and Day* is the final step in making Woolf's novels accessible to Russian readers.

Having established the historical significance of Reinhold's editions of Woolf, it is also important to address the problem of translating Woolf into Russian. From her work with Koteliansky, Woolf knew very well how difficult it is to reproduce a literary text in a different language. In "The Russian Point of View," she observed that in translation, literature gets "stripped of its style" and as a result, "nothing remains except a crude and coarsened version of the sense." Exactly how much of Woolf's style does Reinhold manage to preserve in her translations? This question is difficult to answer, as translation is always a process of interpretation, where personal understanding of words and their connotations comes into play. Reinhold is a sensitive and skilful translator whose command of both English and Russian is indisputable. A proof of this is her rendition of the title of Woolf's second novel. In her afterword to the translation, she points out that "night and day" has several meanings, one of which is "all the time, constantly." She perceptively links this meaning of the title to Woolf's quotation from Dostoevsky in Chapter 10 of *Night and Day*: "It's life that matters, nothing but life—the process of discovering—the everlasting and perpetual process, not the discovery itself at all." Reinhold explains that in Russian this sense of perpetuity is conveyed by a similar expression, but with a reverse word order—*Den' i noch* (literally "day and night"), and so this is the title under which the Russian reader will know Woolf's novel.

Another proof of Reinhold's translating skill is that the reader of her version of *Night and Day* is instantly swathed in the atmosphere of Edwardian London. Reinhold's translation of *Night and Day* is reminiscent of Galsworthy's *The Forsyte Saga* in the way it allows the reader to imagine the smells and sounds of Edwardian streets and households. It also has a similar narrative rhythm—measured and continuous, which corresponds with the novel's title. In *Night and Day*, Woolf still pays a lot of attention to the "fabric of things" (to use her expression from "Mr. Bennett and Mrs. Brown"), so Reinhold is right to preserve these stylistic parallels with Galsworthy—the writer whom Woolf later described as the most factual of the Edwardians.

Before proceeding to a word-by-word analysis of Reinhold's achievement, it needs to be mentioned that there are two main methods of translation. One can be called poetic: it leaves everything that is unexplained or subtly implied in the original similarly ambiguous. The other method is more explanatory: it is used when the translator wants to bring hidden meanings of the original to the surface and make the author's intentions more outspoken. In her translations of Woolf's works, Reinhold frequently uses the second method. Her choice is justified in two ways. Firstly, some of the meanings that Woolf leaves between the lines in her writings would be completely lost in a Russian translation, unless they were made more pronounced than they are in the original. Secondly, some of the meanings in Woolf's texts (particularly in *Night and Day*) refer to customs and practices of Edwardian England: they need an overt translation, because otherwise they would mystify the modern-day Russian reader, due to cultural and historical differences.

Reinhold's use of the explanatory method of translation, even though justified, still results in the inevitable transformation of Woolf's style. Woolf's prose—her novels as well as her essays—is highly poetic: even in the more traditional *Night and Day*, she leaves many meanings unspoken. To take the first line of the novel: "It was a Sunday evening in October, and in common with many other young ladies of her class, Katharine Hilbery was pouring out tea." Woolf leaves it up to her reader to imagine what happens on an October evening in terms of outdoor luminosity. She also leaves it assumed—rather than openly stated—that Katharine Hilbery's social status is a prominent one. Compare this sentence to the version of Woolf Reinhold presents to the Russian reader: "The end of Sunday was approaching, it was getting dark—in respectable homes at this October time young ladies usually pour tea—and Katharine Hilbery was busy precisely with this: a family tea-party." It is not entirely fair to judge a translation by rendering it back into the original language, but this is the only way to let the English reader imagine the transformation that Woolf's style goes through when translated into Russian. The problem is not that her prose becomes more wordy, although it is a fact that to convey the same idea, the Russian language uses more words and is less economical than English. The problem is more about the pace of Woolf's narrative: in translation, it becomes more diffused.

This is particularly noticeable when it comes to Woolf's similes. We can see this if we compare the penultimate sentence of Chapter 1 in *Night and Day* to its Russian translation:

> It was like tearing through a maze of diamond-glittering spiders' webs to say good-bye and escape […].

> To say good-bye and leave was equal to the attempts of the fly, who got caught by a spider, to free itself from the maze of the web, woven into a shining, diamond-shaped polyhedron.

Reinhold inevitably has to re-phrase the whole sentence, because Woolf's text would not make sense to the Russian reader if translated literally. However, it may be suggested that in order to preserve the poetic subtlety and economy of Woolf's prose, some meanings can be left implicit—or even left out—in Russian translation.

Another example is the enigmatic closing sentence of Woolf's essay "The Russian Point of View," and its Russian translation: "But the mind takes its bias from the place of its birth, and no doubt, when it strikes upon a literature so alien as the Russian, flies off at a tangent far from the truth." Compare this to what it approximately sounds like in Russian: "But perhaps this is the reaction of a foreigner, for whom it is difficult to abandon the prejudices absorbed with mother's milk, and so his evaluation of a literature as distant and alien as Russian most likely misses the target, without touching its true essence." In Reinhold's translation, Woolf's statement sounds less tentative than in the original. Throughout her essays on the Russians, Woolf is careful not to present either her—or anyone else's—opinion on Russian literature as the only authoritative one. The word "foreigner," absent in Woolf's statement, immediately defines the speaker as an outsider in relation to the world of Russian letters. In the original, there is only one word, "alien," that points to this divide between the speaker and the Russians; in the translation, there are three such words—"foreigner," "alien," and "distant." The presence of gender in Russian nouns is another problem that translators of Woolf encounter. This is particularly significant in Woolf's case as she often provides either a proudly female or a neutral first-person plural (as in "we") perspective in her literary essays. Throughout "The Russian Point of View," Woolf speaks on behalf of "us," her fellow English readers, irrespective of their gender. In Reinhold's translation, the words "foreigner" and "his evaluation" define the speaker of the essay as male, and since it is the closing sentence of the essay, it casts a certain strange light on Woolf's gender-neutral discussion of Russian literature.

The transformations that Woolf's style undergoes in Reinhold's translations are largely inevitable and are caused by the syntactic and morphological differences between English and Russian. What is truly miraculous and exemplary of Reinhold's skill as a translator is how she manages to convey the irony and sarcasm ubiquitous in Woolf's literary criticism. A perfect example of Woolf's sharp wit is "Mr. Bennett and Mrs. Brown," where she describes Edwardian novels as "the most dreary, irrelevant, and humbugging affairs in the world."

She proceeds to paint a scathing portrait of the English reading public as "a very suggestible and docile creature," who is ready to believe that women have "tails" and men have "humps." Reinhold masterfully recreates these sneers in her Russian translation of the essay: she makes Woolf's language even more colloquial and idiomatic than it is in English. For example, in the Russian translation the English reading public does not stop at saying, "No; she [Woolf's Mrs. Brown] is a mere figment of your imagination": she goes on to say, "Do not hold your breath, I will not believe [in Mrs. Brown]—forget it!"

To conclude, despite the difficulties of rendering English texts into Russian, Reinhold succeeds in preserving the heart and soul of Woolf's writings. English readers can rest assured that in Reinhold's versions of Woolf's novels, "[l]ife is not a series of gig lamps symmetrically arranged; life is a luminous halo, a semi-transparent envelope surrounding us from the beginning of consciousness to the end." Translating Woolf in Russia is more than a literary act: it is an act of healing the cultural memory of an entire country. Reinhold's translations are worthy contributions to this process.

—Darya Protopopova, *UCL - Institute of Education*

*Translation as Collaboration: Virginia Woolf,
Katherine Mansfield and S. S. Koteliansky.*
Claire Davison (Edinburgh: Edinburgh UP, 2014) x + 194pp.

Claire Davison's *Translation as Collaboration: Virginia Woolf, Katherine Mansfield and S. S. Koteliansky* delves deeply into the co-translations of Virginia Woolf, Katherine Mansfield, Leonard Woolf, and John Middleton Murry executed in collaboration with the Russian émigré S. S. Koteliansky. Among Davison's goals in her five-chapter study is that of illuminating the difference in concerns of these writer-translators from those of their peers, such as Constance Garnett, suggesting that their co-translations not only influenced their own modernist project but also anticipated contemporary translation theory. By comparing French and English translations of various passages drawn from the works of Leo Tolstoy, Anton Chekhov, Fyodor Dostoevsky, and several of their contemporaries, Davison provides a detailed analysis of translation choices privileged in particular by Mansfield and Virginia Woolf and what their translations reveal about their own ongoing concerns as they set out as writers and publishers between 1915 and 1923. As Davison writes, "The code-switching experiments that both Woolf and Mansfield try out by expanding translation conceptually as metaphor show them experimenting intuitively with the sort of creative outsidedness conceived philosophically by Bakhtin, and more recently by Heinz Wismann—not just cultivating an awareness of foreignness but unthinking oneself through foreignness" (32). Davison has structured her study to demonstrate through juxtapositions of many specific excerpts of translations just how these co-translations of the Russians offer new insight into understanding the texts of the Russians, be it in their consideration of gender, focalization, dialogism, the performative aspect of translation, the liminal space that the act of translating occupies, or the unruliness of language that many translations seek to tame yet which come alive when translators leave their rough edges intact.

Davison's first chapter, "Unknown Languages and Unruly Selves: Thinking through Translation," underlines the goals of Koteliansky, who, as a Russian émigré, saw an opportunity that "via translation he could feed the public's interest in Russian literature and the arts" (21) and also earn a living. Though his English was often weak, by collaborating with Woolf and Mansfield, "both passionate readers of Russian literature," Koteliansky "became" a translator whose "working praxis reveals a purist's commitment to the original text, and an accompanying sense of translation as a hermeneutic quest" (22). Woolf, on the other hand, is portrayed as a writer for whom translation is "a transformative encounter *across* languages—those we are born or educated into, or those encountered later, however briefly . . ." (27). Mansfield is shown to be multi-lingual, even if her knowledge of different languages was imperfect, and she is less driven by class consciousness than Woolf is, which would account for some of the differences in their attitudes toward translating. According to Davison, "in Woolf's overall thinking on translation, knowledge, presumption and mastery impede and mutilate meaning, while impure, imperfect translations blossom into poetry" (28), while "Mansfield demonstrates a positive delight in translation as improvisation and play, illustrating rather than debating the pitfalls and serendipities to be found when language travels" (30).

In her second chapter, "'Representing by Means of Scenes': Translating Voices," Davison focuses on how Woolf, Mansfield, and Koteliansky see translation as "a theatricalisation or multiplication of borrowed voices" (52), which she considers a product of the changing environment in which modernism is born, citing the "unprecedented clamour of voices" engendered by radio broadcasting, the battle for women's suffrage, representative democracy, and the beginnings of experimental psychology (55). Here Davison successfully demonstrates differences between "dialogized, performative conceptualisations of translating" (56) that characterize Woolf's and Mansfield's co-translations as opposed to the more classic and literal nineteenth-century translations of the Russians into French. Davison's study is certainly thorough, replete with a multitude of examples to reveal in minute detail significant differences in syntax, word choice, and point of view that suggest how these canonical Russian authors can be differently read.

In "'The queerest sense of echo', or Translating Imprudent Movables," her third chapter, Davison, drawing on the work of Emily Dalgarno, demonstrates how Woolf made use of her endeavors as a translator as a way of separating herself from realism and "extract[ing] the feminine consciousness from supposedly gender-neutral or male-focused classics" (85). She sees Woolf and Mansfield as "queering translation's pitch" (85) as they cross boundaries and shift emphases in an attempt to convey "Dostoevsky's destabilising, dialogic workings" (87) and "deliberately shifting voices" (89). Davison sees Mansfield and Woolf as similarly attentive to "emerging spaces and marginal selves" in the Russians' presentation of female characters, but without an equivalent dwelling on how the Russians construct male characters, despite their prominence in the novels' plots (95). Davison has chosen fascinating examples of the way this shift in focus allows marginal female characters a subjectivity that could easily be "lost in translation." Both Woolf and Mansfield are presented as appreciating the transgressiveness of Dostoevsky's and Chekhov's texts, which they seek to convey in their translations.

Moving into the concerns of publishing and marketing in "Editors' Choice: Craftmanship and the Marketplace," her fourth chapter, Davison illuminates the editorial choices that "were an essential part of the overall translation strategy, marking another break with the dominant modes of translation and publishing policy one generation earlier" (112). Instead of making translations "smooth and readable," writes Davison, "[t]he Koteliansky co-translations mediate between cultures differently" by providing "notes, essays and biographical insights," as the Woolfs' Hogarth Press translations did (112-113). The roles of the co-translators and their copy-editors, who often smoothed out the deliberately rough edges of the translations; the readings Virginia Woolf did of Leonard's co-translations and vice versa (often not credited) and Mansfield's co-translations for which Murry often took credit after his wife's untimely death; the titling of texts and the liberties taken; and the ethics of writing and publishing are among the various topics carefully examined by Davison, who always returns to the crucial question of which choices have been made and how they influence both the reading of the translations as well as the emerging modernist texts of the translators themselves.

In her final chapter, "Biographical Writing in Translation, or variations on the Meaning of 'Life,'" Davison considers the proliferation of collaborative translations of biographical texts that present "alternative methods for exploring creative lives" (143). According to Davison, the writing of "lives" by the Russians not only "inspired the co-translators to try out new methods in their translations," but also influenced their own conceptions of biography itself (143). Davison argues through numerous examples that these translations of "lives" that the Woolfs, Mansfield, Murry, and Koteliansky undertook were influenced by the "translator-as-biographer's own lives" (156) and that they sought to portray "the mind of the writer" rather than simply the writer (157).

Claire Davison's *Translation as Collaboration* will be especially appreciated by scholars whose background includes translation theory, as it is driven by its many examples and comparisons of different translators' choices, strategies, and praxis and its effort to demonstrate these co-translators' departure from earlier modes of translation, anticipating much more recent contemporary trends in translating. Scholars of the evolution of Woolf's and Mansfield's modernist ventures will also find much that is useful in this study's examination of their interaction with the texts of Tolstoy, Chekhov, and Dostoevsky and the nature of their co-translation. I should add that it would help Davison's readers to have a reading knowledge of French as many passages throughout this study are not translated yet are used to demonstrate the differences that occurred in French translations of these same authors. Nevertheless, for those whose interest encompasses the crucial role of modernist collaborative translations of major Russian authors, Davison's study will surely be seen as groundbreaking and significant.

—Helane Levine-Keating, *Pace University*

Virginia Woolf and Music. Ed. Adriana Varga
(Bloomington: Indiana UP, 2014)
xvi + 329pp.

In his Preface to *Virginia Woolf and Music*, Mihály Szegedy-Maszák writes: "Music played a very important role in the life of Virginia Woolf" (ix). Like the "and" of the title, it is difficult to discern precisely *what* the "role" of music was, but the contributors to this volume offer thirteen possible answers. Szegedy-Maszák frames this collection with a brief outline of some of the major challenges that will be familiar to any scholar interested in the influence of music on Virginia Woolf's writing: the fact that Leonard and Virginia listened to a tremendous amount of classical music from their personal gramophone collection; the apparent conservatism of the Woolfs' taste in music (preferring the music of the sixteenth through nineteenth centuries instead of the twentieth); and the absence of references to modernist—or even contemporary—composers in her prolific personal and public writings. As with a number of other studies of music and modernism, the two central challenges that emerge are the fact that much work has been done on the connections between the visual arts and Bloomsbury specifically, as well as modernist literature more generally; and the messiness of attempting to draw parallels between Woolf's modernist literary innovations and the parallel musical innovations taking place at the time, which she appears to ignore or reject. The contributors to this volume address these challenges in a number of ways, either constructing complex circumstantial cases to account for a lack of primary evidence, or confronting this lack head-on. Szegedy-Maszák concludes that one of the merits of the collection is that "it offers a comparison between Virginia Woolf's art and the music of some of her contemporaries," but the majority of the essays here do much more than merely compare Woolf's writing to contemporary music (x). The best contributions to *Virginia Woolf and Music* make a compelling case for the indisputable role music played in Woolf's aesthetic innovations.

In her Introduction, Adriana Varga expands on Szegedy-Maszák's discussion of how this volume fills a gap in Woolf studies by explaining that it focuses on "how Woolf's use of music led to her breaking with traditional forms of representation in her novels at various stages of her aesthetic development and by exploring the inter-arts and interdisciplinary aspects of her modernist fictional experimentation" (13). Varga emphasizes Virginia Woolf's "musical culture," particularly the influence of Bloomsbury, "as well as the rich and deeply musical nature of her works from several different perspectives" (13). "Different" here seems to mean inter- or cross-disciplinary, and the confluence of these perspectives is both challenging and fruitful. The perspectives represented here include: contextual (Bloomsbury, modernism, and early twentieth-century culture); biographical; and comparative (Woolf's use of music as metaphor, motif, and trope, and connections between classical, modernist, and contemporary music and Woolf's fictional and critical writings). Varga uses these perspectives to organize the collection loosely into three sections, though their contents frequently overlap. As a whole, the collection is quite successful in "reconsidering and opening up the question of how Woolf made music bear on her writing" in order to "advance the discussion about music in the Bloomsbury environment and the evolution of Woolf's own musical knowledge and textual praxis, interweaving modernist poetics with classical and contemporary music" (17).

Part One, "Music and Bloomsbury Culture," provides a cultural overview and introduction to what is termed Woolf's "musical culture" (14). The insistence on Bloomsbury in this section is a bit misleading, given the fact that Varga and the other contributors emphasize Woolf's *departure* from Bloomsbury tastes, especially their preference for the visual arts over music. Why do we need this "setting," if Varga is taking pains to demonstrate that Woolf's tastes were, in fact, unique amongst the Bloomsbury set, and that they can be traced to her musical experiences in her formative (pre-Bloomsbury) years? In "Bloomsbury and Music," Rosemary Lloyd offers a possible answer: setting Woolf's responses "against, or at least in the context of, those of the wider Bloomsbury circle illuminates her own independence of spirit and her originality" (42). Lloyd explains that for most of Woolf's Bloomsbury contemporaries, music was secondary to the visual arts, but Woolf was the exception to this rule: "The sensitivity to the radical changes in the plastic arts that the group embraced, promoted, and delighted in, together with that sharp awareness of the changes in social mores that Virginia Woolf playfully dates to around December 1910, seems to have found an equivalent in music only in the case of a few of the Bloomsberries, most notably Virginia Woolf herself" (40). What emerges from Lloyd's survey of the attitudes of the Bloomsbury Group to music is that there is no "Bloomsbury" attitude toward music; the passionate responses of Leonard Woolf, George Moore, and Saxon Sydney-Turner are counterbalanced by those who have considerably less enthusiasm, notably Roger Fry.

The second half of Part One, Mihály Szegedy-Maszák's "Virginia Woolf and Musical Culture," focuses on the important role music played in Woolf's life and writing. Both Lloyd and Szegedy-Maszák rely on evidence from Woolf's early musical experiences, and both point out striking absences from Woolf's diary: Woolf makes no mention of most major twentieth-century works such as those by Schoenberg, Webern, and Berg; nor does she mention "the most outstanding operatic performances of the interwar period," or any of the most significant ballets of the early twentieth century, all of which were performed in London (63). Szegedy-Maszák carefully catalogues Woolf's encounters with Wagnerian opera in her "formative years" in order to make the oft-repeated point that Woolf was relatively unfamiliar with contemporary music, while taking issue issue with those critics who would dismiss her early influences, trading Wagner for Bach as a sign of "maturity." Contrary to what critics have argued, Szegedy-Maszák sees continuity between Woolf's early musical experiences, her Bloomsbury-inspired interest in Wagner, and her later interest in the works of Beethoven, particularly his late quartets. Like the other contributors to this volume, Szegedy-Maszák is careful to state that the relationship between Woolf's musical canon and her style and the structure of her novels "must not be confused with a unidirectional causal one," but returns repeatedly to the argument that "a major artist never forgets the inspirations of her early years" (46, 68).

The essays in Part Two, "*Ut Musica Poesis*: Music and the Novel," explore the music-literature relationship in Woolf's fiction, focusing primarily on the novel. One key element of this substantial second section is that Woolf is never attempting to reproduce or imitate musical form; this seemingly basic stance is what comprises "second-wave" Woolf studies. Varga traces the text-music relationship in "Music, Language, and Moments of Being: From *The Voyage Out* to *Between the Acts*" by discussing "Woolf's interest in exploring the interconnections of rhythm, sound, and language" in three novels (15). Varga presents a clear, stark evolution in Woolf's use of music, and argues that music can be linked to the highly experimental forms of Woolf's later fiction, and that it reconfigures the relationship between reader, text, and context. Jim Stewart, too, discusses Woolf's first novel in "The Birth of Rachel Vinrace from the Spirit of Music," but focuses on circumstantial evidence framing the novel's composition, as opposed to the musically rich passages Varga attends to. Stewart hypothesizes that Woolf's early interest in ancient drama, especially Greek choruses, "informs the larger, agonistic rhythm of *The Voyage Out*," and argues that the key insight for the young Woolf—derived from Wagner—was "that writing is a form of rhythm and that rhythm enables risks" (119, 120). Stewart also offers a key phrase for thinking about Woolf and modern music, stating that her writing has an "accidental sympathy" with modern music such as Stravinsky's *Rite of Spring* (120). In "'The Worst of Music': Listening and Narrative in *Night and Day* and 'The String Quartet,'" Vanessa Manhire nicely summarizes a number of the larger arguments in this section, such as that Woolf's "groundbreaking reworking of narrative conventions depends heavily upon her explorations of the ways in which music works, especially for its listeners" (134). Manhire focuses on "scenes of musical performance as well as Woolf's questioning of music's representational capacities," using stylistically disparate texts to show how Woolf explores music "as a potential model for the representation of interiority," and "as a vehicle for the exploration of language" (134). The connection between music and linguistic expression, and the function of interiority, is one made by many of the contributors to this volume, and Manhire clearly lays out the various ways in which Woolf uses music to problematize the relationship between the external world and the world of the mind.

This simultaneous reliance on historical forms and innovative aesthetics carries us into the second half of this section. In "Flying Dutchmen, Wandering Jews: Romantic Opera, Anti-Semitism, and Jewish Mourning," Emma Sutton focuses more narrowly on *Mrs. Dalloway*'s intertextuality with Wagner's opera *Der fliegende Holländer*, particularly the figure of the Wandering Jew, and the Jewish mourning practice of shivah. Sutton's argument is based on the identifications of "theatrical allusions" and "theatrical vocabulary" throughout the novel that both rely on and reject the Wagnerian model of tragedy. Like Manhire, Elicia Clements focuses on performative elements in Woolf's novels in "The Efficacy of Performance: Musical Events in *The Years*." Clements argues that music is not always about aesthetics, but also acts as a link between subject matter and method: in *The Years*, the political and the musical converge through Woolf's foregrounding of aurality. Even more importantly, Clements argues that Woolf values music because it is performative, analyzing representations of musical performance in *The Years* to "demonstrate that Woolf deftly integrates aspects from the art forms of music, drama, and literature to elaborate practices of aesthetic efficacy" (181). Clements identifies Woolf as "a proto-interdisciplinary thinker" who deployed music in her novels on a crucial level, who uses music as an "interventionist strategy" (185). Like Stewart, Clements highlights Woolf's affinity for Greek history and culture, and argues that *The Years* makes a direct connection to Greek drama. In a more fragmented collection of vignettes, Thompson ties music to narrative method in "Sounding the Past: The Music in *Between the Acts*," interpreting *Between the Acts* as an "experiment with historically infused genres," recapitulating Woolf's engagement with the past and her explorations of alternatives to traditional historiography (216). Oddly, given its placement at the end of this section, Thompson spends multiple pages providing a general overview of word and music studies in order to establish "the tracing of ekphrasis" as most pertinent to Woolf's approach to her final novel. Such a survey of the field would have been most helpful in the introductory contextual section, in order to frame some of the most important debates about the relationship of text and music, but embedded as it is here, it does nothing more than tangentially relate to Thompson's discussion of a single novel.

Part Three, "Music, Art, Film, and Virginia Woolf's Modernist Aesthetics," explores inter-art connections between Woolf's fiction and twentieth-century music, the visual arts, and film. Sanja Bahun, in "Broken Music, Broken History: Sounds and Silence in Virginia Woolf's *Between the Acts*," opens with a compelling juxtaposition of Schoenberg's description of his objective in music composition alongside Woolf's proclamation about the simultaneity of impressions and the importance of this interiority to the novel in her essay "Modern Fiction." Bahun seeks to address the lack of "traces of her interest in modernist classical music" by making such connections between the aesthetic practices of not only Woolf and Schoenberg, but also Woolf's "mature" art and modernist music more generally (230). She argues that "the semi-ironic, agonistic, 'bared' and 'barred' expression of history in Woolf's last novel is coterminous with the modernist formal experimentation in classical music" (233). Here, she is extending Daniel Albright's "proposition to emancipate a theory of comparative arts so as to disclose mutually illuminating conjunctions of the modernist arts" (233-4). In the penultimate chapter, "'Shivering Fragments': Music, Art, and Dance in Virginia Woolf's Writing," Evelyn Haller cites connections among aspects of art—such as sound in music, language, sculpture, painting, and movement in dance—and focuses on the aurality of Woolf's novels. Haller takes this practice of cataloguing Woolf's mentions of music, also utilized by Szegedy-Maszák, to the extreme: she presents ten fragments, accompanied only by some variation of the remark: "Virginia expresses it best" (265). The final chapter in this collection, Roger Hillman and Deborah Crisp's "Chiming the Hours: A Philip Glass Soundtrack," analyzes the interplay between music, image, and text at work in all three stages of the adaptive process leading to Stephen Daldry's 2002 film *The Hours*. In a fine example of word and music studies at their best, Hillman and Crisp demonstrate how Glass's music creates the underlying connection between the narrative strands of the film. As with so many of the essays in this volume, Hillman and Crisp are concerned with how the film conveys the dimension of interiority found in Woolf's novel, by combining visuals and music.

    Though not crystallized around a central theme or argument, what emerges from this study is a productive and thought-provoking series of gesturings-toward. Amongst all of these intersections and divergent paths, perhaps the most important contribution this volume makes—not only to Woolf studies but to word and music studies—is its rejection of vague musical metaphors to describe the literature in question: "musical emotion" and literary "counterpoint" are rejected in favor of "the musicality of prose," as supported by Woolf's own musical imagery and the "rhythm" of her language. Varga opens the volume with Woolf's well-known statement, written in a letter to violinist Elizabeth Trevelyan: "I always think of my books as music before I write them" (1). For Varga, Woolf's "synesthetic experiences," what Woolf comes to call "moments of being," owe as much to music as to the visual arts she is more commonly associated with. Varga and her fellow contributors do much here to urge our (re)consideration of music alongside the other arts in our understanding of Woolf's synesthetic moments, and make a series of compelling cases for how an understanding of Woolf's musical background, tastes, and numerous metaphors enriches our understanding of her aesthetic.

While this volume may raise many more questions and problems than it answers, the act of opening up space for critical interventions and reconsiderations of modernist music and other arts is a necessary one, and should be welcomed by scholars interested in Woolf, as well as in modernism and music more generally. As Eric Prieto has pointed out, the search for "absolute" or "definitive" criteria of musicality is bound to fail. One of the central tasks for someone attempting an interdisciplinary analysis of a work is "to seek out new and unfamiliar metaphors," and "to try to explain these metaphors in ways that shed light on the underlying concerns that motivate their use," particularly in terms of what *new* kinds of information are being imparted (Prieto 55, 52). These arguments are essential for an understanding of the connections between music and Woolf's aesthetic development.

—Sarah Terry, *Oglethorpe University*

Works Cited

Albright, Daniel. *Modernism and Music: An Anthology of Sources*. Chicago: U of Chicago P, 2004. Print.

Prieto, Eric. *Listening In: Music, Mind, and the Modernist Narrative*. Lincoln: U of Nebraska P, 2002. Print.

Modernism and Melancholia: Writing as Countermourning. Sanja Bahun (New York: Oxford UP, 2014) xviii + 236pp.

The basic premise of Sanja Bahun's monograph is that there exists a "profound structural link between modernist fiction and the symptomatology of melancholia" (44). While melancholia, at least since Freud's "Mourning and Melancholia," has usually been defined "through an opposition to a normative response to grief—mourning," Bahun argues that it is more productive to approach the two "as a bifacial dynamic" (7) and "aesthetically resonant suspension" (39). Mourning, then, "may be defined . . . as a specific *culturally constructed type of behavior*" (15), while melancholia is "a symptom-cluster" (9) that gives shape to "the modern inability to mourn" (18). Simultaneously condition and critical tool, discourse and creative spur, modernist melancholia, in Bahun's telling, is distinctive, as "[f]or the first time in the history of representational arts, the melancholic dynamics are not—or not only—depicted . . . but *performed*" (10). And it is this literary performance of melancholic symptoms that, borrowing from anthropology, she terms "countermourning": "a mourning that refuses—to mourn" (18). Guided by a clinical and theoretical discourse that runs from Kierkegaard through Freud and Klein to Bakhtin and Kristeva, Bahun sees modernist experimentation with the novel's character, chronotope, and language as activating the "melancholic function of porosity" (53), generating a creative and critical aperture to exploit the permeable borders between subject and object, individual and community, past and present, sound and meaning. Modernist writers, she stresses, were well-aware of the insufficiency of language and representation, yet they persisted, poignantly (and perhaps heroically), in finding ways to enact their (melancholic) historical condition, even as the performance, "rather than curing," actually "*sustains* the melancholic symptom" (39).

Modernism and Melancholia's three representative countermourning novels are Bely's *Petersburg*, Kafka's *The Castle*, and Woolf's *Between the Acts*. While the book is marred by a number of flawed readings and suspect interpretive moves, Bahun puts her finger on something vital when she articulates the complex ethical posture and "poetic politics" (39) of countermourning novelists. With "melancholic insistence," their texts contest "the sites of forced 'wholeness'" (39) in dominant cultural and historical narratives, creating the potential "to liberate the subject . . . from the shackles of 'totality'" (46). At the same time, they reveal, "performatively, that we can (and should) aspire to resurrect what has been obscured in cultural memory but that we can never (and should not) 'write in' those gaps" (62). The larger stakes of Bahun's enterprise, then, consist in showing that melancholia provides a "structural template" (196) for revising conventional accounts of historical agency—or lack thereof—in modernist literature. In itself, the idea is provocative and worth sustained consideration; however, Bahun casts her melancholic net so widely that by the end of her methodological chapter, we might ask which modernist figures—novelists, poets, and philosophers alike— were *not* "countermourners." Her brief readings of Joyce's *Ulysses* and Ford's *The Good Soldier* are mostly convincing, but many of her examples (Proust, Musil, Stein, etc.) are less so, being based on highly selective renderings and questionable generalizations. There are also basic errors, like calling T. S. Eliot a novelist (44), and dubious assertions, such as when Bahun identifies Nietzsche and Mallarmé as a melancholic couple because they made "revolt-ridden proclamations" "about the arbitrariness of signs" (64). Furthermore, Bahun's proclivity for the sweeping gesture often exaggerates the novelty of her undertaking. "Rarely do we investigate mourning" (15), opens her first chapter. While "we" might wonder who is expected to read the book, more puzzling is that the work of someone like Jahan Ramazani goes essentially unacknowledged. Ramazani, after all, investigated much similar terrain two decades ago, coining the term "melancholic mourning" (4) to describe the highly ambivalent work of modern elegists.

In "Virginia Woolf and the Search for Historical Patterns," Bahun elucidates the "poetic politics" of *Between the Acts*, the imperative, inflected by "moderate optimism and despair" (157), to actively engage "the culture of the death drive" (155) and "address the anguish of the present moment in such manner that occlusions and gaps . . . are rescued from the abyss of non-knowledge" (186-87). The "project of reclaiming the obscure" (188), then, is focalized in Miss La Trobe's pageant—both through its "immoderate aspirations . . . to reenact . . . the entire English history and the history of English literature" and its intermissions, the "moment[s] of extended stasis, *between the acts*" (159). Formally and thematically, the correlation between theater and life or history is crucial for Bahun, as "the dynamics of the theatrical *agon* and its suspension *stasis*" become "a structural analogue for the way in which history unfolds" and "organize the narration" (166). The essential interplay of agon and stasis, she suggests, is enacted in Isa's and Giles's strained relationship, but also through the "dialogue, possibly confrontation" (161) the text generates between the two paintings in the Oliver family drawing room, those of "the long lady and the man holding his horse by the rein" (*BTA* 36). Juxtaposing the portraits of the garrulous ancestor and silent woman, Woolf stages a "drama" or "plot," "[n]arrating the troubled continuities between art and history" (161), as well as the gendered relationship between official history and the obscured one(s). The "problematization of genre boundaries" (168), coupled with an agonic, or relational, view of history, thus emerges as "a superior 'melancholic strategy'" (167), one that allows Woolf to reshape the indefinite borders between the inner and outer, individual and social, as a locus of creativity and "to instantiate—rather than represent—occlusions in official historical record" (168). At the same time, taking her cue from "A Sketch of the Past," Bahun insists that *Between the Acts* "mounts an all-encompassing search for hidden patterns" (158), seeking, however "temporarily" or "chimerically" (177), to "forge an aesthetic whole that would meaningfully speak to whatever link is still binding people" (157). The competing impulses towards wholeness and fragmentation, union and dispersal, she adds, are iterated and heightened through the enactment of "anticipatory grief" on the precipice of World War II (although she mistakenly sets the novel during the *Sitzkrieg* [12, 159, 163]). *Between the Acts*, she writes, "shapes itself into a performance of what Freud deemed a particularly poetic form of melancholia—'anticipatory grief;' an impulse to foretaste mourning, melancholically to probe an impending historical catastrophe" (156). In one sense, anticipatory mourning, with its "complex temporality of affects," brings "the incipient and ominous" (164) into the present; yet, being oriented toward the future, it also, albeit equivocally, leaves open and indeterminate the question of what is to come. Woolf, Bahun notes, had few illusions about art's capacity to heal historical wounds or prevent future catastrophes. As such, the activation of the creative and emancipatory potential of melancholia in her last novel ought to be seen as a poignant, self-aware, and inconclusive effort "to speak to, or motivate, the vastly diversified whole that is humankind" (174).

Bahun's chapter on Woolf seems indicative of the book as a whole: there are powerful, oftentimes elegant, big ideas, which, in many cases, don't quite square with the particulars. Along with simple misstatements about the novel, the case for Woolf's deliberate "reappropriation" (201) and "gendered reading of Freud's theory of the drives" (46) is, to a significant extent, stitched together by late diary snippets mentioning Freud and Bahun's own suppositions. Woolf's question in the November 14, 1940 letter to Ethel Smyth: "Why am I so much shyer of the labourer than of the gentry?" (*L6* 445), is dislocated from its actual context in order to engineer a connection between class and Woolf's "aestheticized experience of the air raids" (155). Most problematic, though, are the strained affiliations between the literary text and melancholic symptom. We are told that Giles's lack of metaphorical acuity—"Only the ineffective word 'hedgehog' illustrated his vision of Europe, bristling with guns, poised with planes" (*BTA* 53)—accords with "the melancholic impasse as an anti-metaphor, an annulment of figurative language" (184). ("Hedgehog," whatever its limitations, is a metaphor.) Another instance concerns La Trobe's unsuccessful theatrical experiment, "The Present Time. Ourselves" (*BTA* 178). Here, while the spectators fidget and chat because "nothing whatsoever appeared on the stage" (*BTA* 179), La Trobe, in humiliation and rage, "damn[s] the audience," thinking: "This is death, death, death" (*BTA* 180). Bahun, though, radically revises the affective tenor of both La Trobe and the audience: "Every stasis entails a risk, La Trobe realizes as the audience's intense despair engulfs her: one may become overwhelmed by reality, fall into autistic stillness, or be driven into melancholic asymbolia" (182). From impatience and irritability to "intense despair," "autistic stillness," and "melancholic asymbolia," the link, to put it mildly, is incongruous.

In her conclusion, Bahun proposes that the countermourning "paradigm," if used responsibly, may be productively extended "to other geocultural contexts and temporalities" (201). This would involve, she says, "identifying such or similar writerly response to a comparable set of affects and describing it in its own terms *before* recasting it in the vocabulary of the imported conceptual scaffold" (201). It seems only fair to ask that whoever takes up such a project—be it Bahun or someone else—faithfully adhere to this directive.

—Kelly S. Walsh, *Yonsei University*

Works Cited

Ramazani, Jahan. *Poetry of Mourning: The Modern Elegy from Hardy to Heaney.* Chicago: U of Chicago P, 1994. Print.

Woolf, Virginia. *Between the Acts.* San Diego: Harvest, 1970. Print.

———. *The Letters of Virginia Woolf, Volume VI: 1936-1941.* Eds. Nigel Nicolson and Joanne Trautmann. New York: Harcourt, 1980. Print.

Ecocriticism and the Idea of Culture: Biology and the Bildungsroman. Helena Feder (Burlington, VT: Ashgate, 2014) viii + 179pp.

Ecocriticism and Women Writers: Environmentalist Poetics of Virginia Woolf, Jeanette Winterson, and Ali Smith. Justyna Kostkowska (NewYork: Palgrave Macmillan, 2013) vi + 189pp.

I started reading *Ecocriticism and the Idea of Culture: Biology and the Bildungsroman* with great interest because the premise of the book is intriguing and promising: that the *bildungsroman*, as the narrative of the development of the individual as s/he takes her/his place in culture, necessarily engages Western humanism's narrative of the origin of culture itself and Western culture's construction of the nature/culture distinction. I am disappointed, unfortunately, in the results of Feder's work.

In the introduction, subtitled "Biology and the Idea of Culture," the reader learns that the book focuses on animal studies and cultural biology rather than ecocriticism (which Feder barely discusses); this focus is not of itself wrong or misplaced, but makes the title of the book misleading. Feder calls on such scholars as Stacy Alaimo (*Bodily Natures*), Cary Wolfe (*What is Posthumanism?*), Frans de Waal (*The Ape and the Sushi Master*), and N. Katherine Hayles (*How We Became Posthuman*), as well as Freud in *Civilization and its Discontents*. Central to the introduction is a discussion of primatology used to argue that nonhuman animals have culture; Feder goes on to argue that "the story of individual acculturation" is "also the story of 'nature,' of our knowledge of human animality and nonhuman agency or subjectivity" (19). Feder concludes the introduction by saying that her goal is to produce "an analysis of human culture informed by the existence of nonhuman cultures" (a worthy goal) and by summarizing the thesis of her book: "the Bildungsroman reveals an awareness of nature's agency, and human and nonhuman similarity" (27).

The body of the book focuses on François-Marie Voltaire, Mary Shelley, Virginia Woolf, and Jamaica Kincaid and consists of four chapters, "*Candide* and the *Dialectic of Enlightenment*," "Ecocriticism and the Production of Monstrosity in *Frankenstein*," "Placing Modernity in *Orlando*," "and "Consuming Culture in *A Small Place* and *Among Flowers*." The conclusion, subtitled "Dehumanization, Animality, and the Bildungsroman," discusses what Feder calls a "discourse of animality" that is hegemonic in Western culture and undergirds both exploitation of animals and discrimination and violence against human "others." Feder argues that a "fantasy of detachment" that depersonalizes human others and nonhuman animals underlies Western notions of the human, culture, and society and allows us to avoid or forgo extending "fellow-feeling" to certain other beings. This basic argument makes sense; however, Feder relies over-much on strings of quotations from others; more explanation from Feder herself would have made the argument clearer and stronger. The majority of the conclusion discusses animal studies and animal rights and unfortunately misses the opportunity to explain fully the significance of literature, and the *bildungsroman* in particular, to the current rethinking of the "human" and the "animal."

The chapter on Woolf reads *Orlando* as a *bildungsroman* that challenges both rationalism and human distinctiveness from the rest of nature. Feder proposes that "Orlando is not only writing 'The Oak Tree,' he is the oak tree. Unlike the great house, the other symbol of his identity, the oak tree embodies living process, doubled by Orlando's continuously composed poem as a narrative of his travel and development" (83). Feder also suggests that Orlando's obsessive metaphor-making about landscape could signify not only "a Keatsian pursuit," but also "a way of seeing that reaches through what Woolf called 'the cotton wool of daily life' toward . . . 'some real thing behind appearances'" (84). This "real thing," suggests Feder, could be an understanding of all bodies as ecosystems in themselves and as "connected materially, cellularly, to other larger ecosystems" (84). Unfortunately, she does not make a case, based in the text of *Orlando*, that this understanding of the world and the human relation to the more-than-human world is, in fact, what Orlando or *Orlando* is expressing. Feder also points to some interesting ideas about the role of biology in biography, but again the discussion stays at the suggestive level and demonstration is lacking. To argue, for example, that the passage of the novel that says "[o]nce look out of a window at bees among flowers, at a yawning dog, at the setting sun . . . and one drops the pen" means that nature "is an active participant in the composition of 'The Oak Tree'" (91) just does not follow.

The level of Feder's scholarship on Woolf is poor, to the extent of citing an epigraph as found in a title that does not exist: *Journal* (Feder 82). The quotation so cited is actually from *A Passionate Apprentice: The Early Journals, 1897-1909* (ed. Mitchell A. Leaska), a title that is not included in the book's bibliography. When Feder quotes this same passage in the text of the chapter, she cites it as coming from Jan Morris's edited collection *Travels with Virginia Woolf*. Apparently Feder did not read the journal entry in Leaska's scholarly edition, in which case she would have realized that she has mis-ordered the quotation (putting a later passage before an earlier one and using ellipses between them as if the two passages are separated by only a few lines) and thus her interpretation of it is suspect (Feder 81). Indeed, too often, Feder cites scholars and primary texts at second hand (from reference books or other scholars). More substantively, perhaps, Feder engages with little prior scholarship of any kind on Woolf. In terms of ecocriticism of Woolf, the only study Feder mentions is Carol H. Cantrell's article, "'The Locus of Compossibility': Virginia Woolf, Modernism, and Place" (1998), an important article certainly; however, this leaves out the significant work of Louise Westling, Bonnie K. Scott, and L. Elizabeth Waller among others, as well as the essays in Kristin Czarnecki's and Carrie Rohman's *Virginia Woolf and the Natural World* (2011).

Justyna Kostkowska's *Ecocriticism and Women Writers: Environmentalist Poetics of Virginia Woolf, Jeanette Winterson, and Ali Smith* is a more useful and satisfying book. Like Feder, Kostkowska places her study in an extra-literary context, in her case the current environmental crisis and the need to develop a "more ecologically sound society;" at the same time, she engages significant theories and methods in ecocriticism, unlike Feder. The focus of her book as a whole is to show that "ecologically progressive models of narrative, ones that model healthier ecological relationships, already exist" and thus that literature has ecological value (1).

In the introduction, Kostkowska points out that recently ecocriticism has started to pay attention to literary texts that are not "nature writing," *per se*, and places her study in this branch of the field. Citing previous criticism, including Laurence K. Buell's field-defining book *The Future of Environmental Criticism: Environmental Crisis and Literary Imagination* (2005), she aims to "offer evidence that the ecological, world-changing potential of fictional texts in fact equals and in some ways exceeds that of nature writing" (2). Kostkowska argues that the human drama of fiction need not make nonhuman presence in a fictional text secondary nor mean that the nonhuman serves as mere setting or background to the human plot. Rather, experimental fiction can represent the mutual interrelation of the human and nonhuman and can critique the notion of the "environment" as separate from the human world. Working from Buell's theory of literary texts as ecosystems, she investigates "how texts as discursive environments can constitute models for a symbiotic rather than ecologically competitive coexistence, where cooperation replaces hierarchy and value dualisms" (6). Kostkowska draws on such ecocritics and philosophers as Timothy Merton (*Ecology Without Nature*), David Abram (*The Spell of the Sensuous*), and Greta Gaard ("Toward a Queer Ecofeminism"). Kostkowska's central thesis in the book is that the texts of Woolf, Winterson, and Smith are "examples of ecofeminist praxis" through their use of "pluralist, democratic, and nonauthoritarian narrative forms" (5). The major narrative strategies that Kostkowska identifies in these works are innovations in point of view, chronology, and characterization, as well as genre blending, poetic language, and "metafictionality" (9).

Chapter One of *Ecocriticism and Women Writers* focuses on Woolf's "Kew Gardens" and *Jacob's Room*, while Chapter Two analyzes *Mrs. Dalloway* and Chapter Three *The Waves*. Chapters Four through Six discuss Winterson's *Written on the Body*, *The Powerbook*, and *Lighthousekeeping* respectively. The next two chapters are devoted to Smith's novels *Hotel World* and *Like*, and the final chapter discusses Smith's short stories which Kostkowska calls "ecological 'realityfiction'."

Kostkowska finds the roots of the formal innovations of *Jacob's Room* in an ecological "shift of vision" that Woolf achieves in the late nineteen-teens and in her short story "Kew Gardens." Woolf's diary entries about Asheham, her country house from 1911 to 1919, show, says Kostkowska, that Woolf developed a habit of close attention to nonhuman nature. Then, in "Kew Gardens," she makes a shift away from a human-centered view of the world. Comparing this shift in point of view to Woolf's critique of androcentrism, Kostkowska connects "Woolf's attention to the natural world in this period and her revision of the traditional nineteenth-century narrative" (15) and connects Woolf's feminism and what Kostkowska calls Woolf's "ecological imagination." "Kew Gardens" is an experiment in multiple points of view and presents the lives of snails and people as equally present and important; thus, Kostkowska argues, Woolf "present[s] an ecological vision that contemporary ecophilosophers such as Anthony Weston have termed 'multicentrism'" (19). Kostkowska reads *Jacob's Room* as an extension of this ecological experiment in multicentrism, "dislodging the centralized, androcentric view of the world/text in several ways: by direct narrative comment; by frequent featuring of nonhumans as subjects; by the dispersal of the single narrative point of view to reflect situated knowledge; and by building a microcosmic organic structure for the book through significant repetition" (20-21). The discussion of *Jacob's Room* that follows this assertion provides convincing close readings of the text; here we get the textual analysis and argument that is missing from Feder's discussion.

Important to Kostkowska's analysis of both *Jacob's Room* and *Mrs. Dalloway* is her interesting point that Woolf's invention of a third-person narrator who moves among multiple focalizing perspectives (usually but not always human) can be understood as an expression of an ecological awareness that everything and every being is connected. She argues that "*Mrs. Dalloway*'s narrator is a revolutionary presence hitherto unprecedented in the history of the novel . . . . an expression of Woolf's project of decentering the patriarchal 'I,' the omniscient speaking subject. Woolf replaces the single master perspective with an inclusive voice that frequently 'steps aside' to allow multiple character voices through" (32). This multiplicity of perspectives makes the novel "a dialogic, polyphonic, and therefore ecological text: one that presents multiple entities in relationship" (33). Kostkowska also understands Woolf's method of connecting the characters through their overlapping walking routes through London as a way of presenting the environment as what makes the characters all "part of one system" (34). Noting that *Mrs. Dalloway* uses various "environmental elements" as "connectors," Kostkowska argues that the novel becomes an ecological space of multiple relationships in which the reader must participate by making many of the connections her/himself. Thus, Kostkowska concludes that *Mrs. Dalloway* "models a web of relationships in a diverse ecosystem that includes the characters' minds and their physical environment, the text itself through metafictional allusion, other texts through literary allusion, as well as an elaborate net of connections establishing communication with the reader's world" (40).

In her analysis of *The Waves*, Kostkowska focuses on the body/mind and human/nonhuman dichotomies but arrives at a similar conclusion about this novel: it models, like *Jacob's Room* and *Mrs. Dalloway*, an interconnected world. She reads the six figures/voices in the novel as six characters who represent both the diversity and the oneness of human beings and whose development approximates the development of human language and cognition. In Woolf's focus on writing to a rhythm in *The Waves*, she attempts to step beyond plot, to reach for an "embodied language," and to enmesh the human characters with the nonhuman world. The interludes also serve to "show the human speakers as one with the nonhumans" (42). I find intriguing, though ultimately not fully convincing, Kostkowska's argument that *The Waves* presents verbal language as inevitably separating human beings from the world around them, and "true interaction with the world cannot happen through language" (46); to me, the novel conveys a more nuanced and paradoxical view of language. Kostkowska's subsequent argument, based on Paul

Ricoeur, that "the metaphors we create can be said to reveal reality as it really is" (53), is insufficiently developed and seems to contradict her assertion that verbal language separates human beings from the world. On the other hand, her argument that Woolf's use of soliloquy means the six characters are "speaking out to the world" (47), consistently reaching out to the world beyond themselves, is interesting and suggestive (55).

Grounded in close textual analysis of the novels as well as Woolf's diaries and essays, informed by eco-philosophy, ecocriticism, and feminist standpoint epistemology, Kostkowska's readings are fruitful and worth engaging with. While she herself could have engaged a bit more with other Woolf critics and could have grappled more substantively with some of the philosophy she alludes to, her book should be read by anyone interested in Woolf and ecocriticism and ecofeminism. Her discussions of Winterson and Smith are also worth reading and her suggestion that Woolf is "an ecofeminist foremother" and influential as such for Winterson and Smith is worth exploring further in future research.

A final note regarding both books: should we expect that scholars will use the editions of writers' works produced by their colleagues? Neither Kostkowska nor Feder use the recent scholarly editions of Woolf's novels. I also wonder about Kostokowska's choice to use a Dover reprint of *Monday or Tuesday* rather than Susan K. Dick's *The Complete Shorter Fiction of Virginia Woolf*. To complete my curmudgeonly recital, there were too many editorial mistakes in both these books, such as works cited in the text that were not in the bibliographies, parenthetical citations that did not indicate which of two or three works by the author listed in the bibliography was being cited, and the occasional dangling modifier and typo. I imagine these editorial problems arise at least in part because of the disinvestment in editorial staff by academic publishers in recent years, a warning sign regarding the state of scholarly publishing these days.

—Diana L. Swanson, *Northern Illinois University*

The Bloomsbury Group Memoir Club. S. P. Rosenbaum.
Edited with an Introduction and Afterword by James M. Haule
(NY: Palgrave Macmillan, 2014) 203 pp.

Before his untimely death in 2012, S. P. Rosenbaum had completed polished drafts of five chapters of his history of the Memoir Club, begun writing a sixth, and had outlined the entire book. James M. Haule has performed a meaningful tribute to Rosenbaum, the preeminent historian of the Bloomsbury Group, in bringing as much of this work as possible to publication. A talk given by Rosenbaum at Cornell in 2009 during a symposium in conjunction with the exhibition *A Room of Their Own: The Bloomsbury Artists in American Collections* provides Haule in his introduction with an overview of Rosenbaum's intentions, among which is to restore their original Memoir Club context to some well-known autobiographical and biographical essays. Rosenbaum also wanted to provide a thorough history of the Club, from its origins in Molly MacCarthy's 1920 invitation to a number of friends to its "definitive end" with the death of Clive Bell in 1964. As is well known, the Club was one of several schemes MacCarthy invented in the hope of getting her husband, Desmond, to write the novels she and their friends believed he had it in him to write (he never did). Rosenbaum identifies about ninety papers from the Club's history of which roughly twenty-five remained unpublished at the time he was writing this book. In an Afterword, Haule says that Rosenbaum planned a companion volume of selected Memoir Club papers—such a collection would certainly be welcome, were someone to realize Rosenbaum's intentions.

The history of the early years of the Club is told with wit and grace in a narrative that reflects Rosenbaum's intimate familiarity with numerous archives as well with the details of the lives and cultural contexts of all of his subjects. His first chapter, "Outlines," explains that the Club from its beginnings was intended to share "recollections for the amusement of intimate friends" (17), a characteristic that distinguishes the tenor of its productions from the rather anxious, confessional vogue of contemporary "life-writing" (a term that Rosenbaum somewhat disparages, as he believes his subjects would have as well). The "Memoir Club habit" (18) did not have to be learned: it was rooted in the familiarity and bonds among the friends and lovers, husbands and wives, who constituted the Club. Rather than the perennial questioning of who was or was not a "member" of the Bloomsbury Group, the Memoir Club provides a useful alternative means of discerning the shared ethos that has come to be described by the shorthand term "Bloomsbury."

In his second chapter, "Ancestral Voices," Rosenbaum names Montaigne as "in several ways ... one of the most significant precursors of the Memoir Club" (27). The essayist's "mixture of frankness and reticence" and "the short, tentative, reflective and reflexive prose genre that he originated" (27) seem to be the model for the Memoir Club papers. As Alex Zwerdling has also pointed out in "Mastering the Memoir: Woolf and the Family Legacy" (*Modernism/modernity* 10.1 [2003]: 165-88), the men and women of the Memoir Club were extremely well versed in an autobiographical tradition that stretched back through their families into the early eighteenth century. "Ancestral voices, public and private, echo around the founding of the Club," writes Rosenbaum, pointing out that the variety of forms of family life-writing "are reflected in the intimate domestic character of the Club's memoirs" (28). In these forms were expressed "evangelical, utilitarian, liberal, and aesthetic values which the memoirists inherited and transmuted" (28). Rosenbaum singles out Leslie Stephen as a particular influence on the Memoirists. "Until you 'can take delight in the queer results which grow out of them,'" Woolf's father wrote in *Hours in a Library*, "'you are hardly qualified to be a student of autobiography'" (32).

Having deftly summarized Stephen's extensive biographical and autobiographical writings, Rosenbaum connects Stephen's biographies of his own relatives with the Memoir Club's productions "through the practice of domestic life-writing and the great value they all placed on human affections" (36). Other "ancestral voices" discussed in this chapter include E. M. Forster's writings about his Thornton heritage, and the autobiography of Roger Fry's father, a private manuscript used by Fry's sister Agnes to prepare her own *Memoir of the Right Honourable Sir Edward Fry* (38). Among the better-known productions of their forebears was Lady Strachey's edition of the journals of her aunt, *Memoirs of a Highland Lady*, which is "regarded as an invaluable social document of late eighteenth and early nineteenth highland life recalled by a woman" (42). The Club's members were aware not only of the Puritanism of their Victorian heritage, but also self-consciously used their own frankness and uninhibited love for one another as a rebellion against it. In just a few pages Rosenbaum lays out a wonderful panorama of the network of various kinds of life-writing that was the Memoir Club's inheritance, stretching back to *The Receipt Book of Elizabeth Raper and a Portion of her Cypher Journal*, an eighteenth century diary (1756-1770) by Duncan Grant's great-great-grandmother published in 1924 in a handsome edition by the Nonesuch Press (43).

According to Rosenbaum, the most important modern precursor of the Memoir Club was the Apostles, the Cambridge Conversazione Society to which several of its first members had belonged. The influence, however, has more to do with candor and tone than with content, and the account of the Apostles is less rich and less satisfying than the preceding section about ancestors, perhaps inevitably as so much about the Apostles' practices are obscure. The narrative seems less sure here of how to make the connection to the Memoir Club.

Having established the context and origins of the Club, Rosenbaum presents in Chapter Three a detailed account of its first year. There is very little on record about the reception of the Memoir Club papers, apart from the accounts in Virginia Woolf's diary, the source upon which Rosenbaum inevitably relies. Woolf's diary provides tantalizing glimpses of what was read at the first meeting: a paper by Vanessa Bell, now lost, during which, Woolf writes, her sister was "overcome by the emotional depths to be traversed and unable to read what she had written" (57). Rosenbaum notes Woolf's emphasis in her diary on *performance* in the

Club's proceedings, and in his Cornell talk cautioned later interpreters against overlooking the amused response the Memoirists would have expected and, indeed, relied upon from their audience. The first year seems to have been a particularly rich one. Roger Fry's still unpublished memoir is the first complete paper from the Club which survives. Molly MacCarthy's memoirs were the first of the papers to be published (serialized in *The Nation* by Leonard Woolf and subsequently in the book *A Nineteenth Century Childhood* in 1924).

Forster appears to have read the most memoirs over the years, including that which Rosenbaum describes as the most candidly sexual, an account of his affair with a barber, "Kanaya." He was "the only one of the original continuing members (six of whom were married couples) who had not had a sexual relationship with another member" (62), and periodically agonized over his membership, saying he would resign, only to change his mind soon thereafter. It was Forster who remarked in relation to Fry that "the Bloomsbury undertone" could be summed up by saying that "It's not the Subject that matters, it's the Treatment" (69). This Rosenbaum believes "is the most interesting thing Forster has to say about Bloomsbury" (69), an insight that explains an important criterion by which the Memoir Club papers were judged by their listeners.

Also in the first year, Virginia Woolf delivered "22 Hyde Park Gate" to the Club, described, rightly, by Rosenbaum as "the most controversial of her autobiographical writings" because it includes the much-interpreted description of George Duckworth as the Stephen girls' "lover." Rosenbaum asks his reader to put aside all commentary and try to imagine the paper as a performance for intimate friends, reclaiming its comedy. In his Cornell talk, as quoted by Haule in the introduction, Rosenbaum said, "More than one of Virginia Woolf's interpreters ... have cut themselves handling the irony in her memoirs" (14). It does not seem to me impossible that Woolf could have *relied* upon an amused response to her shocking revelations about her half-brother as a way of displacing the discomfort such information would undoubtedly evoke among her friends and relatives: there are many uses of humor, after all. Still, Rosenbaum's account of the memoir's description of George is judicious and fair, providing as context details from other places where Woolf wrote about her half-brothers. That Woolf presented George "comically" seems undeniable, even if it does not have to be exclusive of other shades of meaning attendant upon her narrative.

In Chapter Four, "Private and Public Affairs," Rosenbaum begins with Clive Bell ("who has often been underrated") telling the story of his youthful sexual initiation by his parents' neighbor Annie Raven Hill, wife of the eminent *Punch* cartoonist Leonard Raven Hill. Desmond MacCarthy remarked on Clive's affectation to the absent Molly (whose increasing deafness made her unable to participate in the Club she had founded). Public recognition of the Memoir Club was initiated by the 1949 publication of J. M. Keynes's *Two Memoirs*. In 1957,

Vanessa Bell read excerpts to the Memoir Club of letters Keynes had written to her and Duncan Grant about his secret negotiations during the Versailles Peace Conference in 1919. Rosenbaum argues that Keynes's "Dr Melchior: A Defeated Enemy" changed the nature of the Memoir Club (95) by showing that their productions "could be about serious issues without forsaking humour or intimacy" (95). The summaries Rosenbaum provides of the various papers, although written with economy and clarity, do tend to sag somewhat in the accumulation and it is of course difficult to go on hearing how brilliant or witty the original being summarized is. Some of the papers that were unpublished when Rosenbaum was writing are now, though, available, and so it is possible to augment his accounts by consulting the originals.

During what Chapter Five names its "Hiatus: 1922-1928," the Club received no mentions in writings by its members, but they continued to produce works that Rosenbaum argues were influenced by its ethos, including the three novels by Woolf in this period to which, he notes, death is central. The chapter becomes something of a hiatus itself as Rosenbaum reviews Woolf's extensive writing about life-writing, gives an account of Fry's "L'histoire de Josette" (used by Woolf in her biography of Fry) that was never read to the Memoir Club, and then considers several other autobiographical works by Forster. He notes that Forster did not deliver any memoirs to the Club about his experiences in Egypt, although he wrote quite a bit about them elsewhere (e.g. in the memoir of and for Mohammed el Adl; in *Pharos and Pharillon*; and in *Alexandria: A History and a Guide*). This section on Forster is interesting and insightful but contributes little to our understanding of or knowledge about the Memoir Club.

In 1928, Molly MacCarthy announced that the Club would gather once more to hear a paper by Virginia Woolf on the beginnings of Bloomsbury. The truncated sixth chapter takes its title from Woolf's "Old Bloomsbury," a paper long held to date to 1922 but which in fact, as Rosenbaum makes clear, was read to the Club on July 4, 1928. The memoir initiated a concern with origins that was taken up by other members, including Desmond MacCarthy, Clive Bell, Vanessa Bell, Leonard Woolf, and Duncan Grant. Rosenbaum's engaging history breaks off with the intriguing question of how and when Keynes's wife, Lydia Lopokova, was admitted, for she read no papers to the Memoir Club (153).

The book concludes with two appendices: a paper Rosenbaum was to have delivered at a 2013 conference in Paris on "Woolf Among the Philosophers" concerning the influence of Cambridge philosophy on Virginia Woolf, and as thorough a list as possible of the Memoir Club papers and their archival locations or places of publication. If another scholar were to follow Rosenbaum's map and continue this absorbing story into the 1960s it could only enhance this fascinating chapter in Bloomsbury's history and afterlife.

—Mark Hussey, *Pace University*

Virginia Woolf: Art, Life and Vision. National Portrait Gallery, London, July 10 to October 26, 2014.

Virginia Woolf: Art, Life and Vision. Frances Spalding (London: National Portrait Gallery, 2014) 190pp.

The exhibition *Virginia Woolf: Art, Life and Vision*, at the National Portrait Gallery (NPG) ran for just over three months in 2014—the first UK exhibition to focus entirely on Woolf's work and life. Curated by the leading Bloomsbury scholar Frances Spalding (sole author of the catalogue) the exhibition was an outstanding success garnering glowing reviews in the popular press, the online *Huffington Post* and *Net-a-Porter*, the luxury fashion site, and scholarly journals including *Apollo*.[1] Although personally disappointed not to see Bryan Ferry (lender of *Still Life with Bust of Virginia Woolf, Charleston* c. 1960 by Duncan Grant[2]) at the private view, I was delighted to read that night a five-star review in the less than liberal *Evening Standard* (although the review, curiously, had Virginia and Vanessa moving to Golden Square in 1904 rather than Gordon Square). The praise was a welcome antidote to some wholly unjustifiable criticism of Richard Shone's wonderful *The Art of Bloomsbury* exhibition at Tate Gallery, London, from November 4 to January 30, 2000—the first comprehensive look at Bloomsbury.

The fifteen-year gap between these exhibitions has witnessed an exponential growth in Woolf scholarship evidenced in the annual International Virginia Woolf conferences, as well as public interest culminating in the 2014 Charleston-inspired Burberry collection, and a London collection of book-themed painted benches which included the *Mrs. Dalloway* bench created by One Red Shoe (www.booksabouttown.org.uk). A BBC drama series about Bloomsbury, *Life in Squares*, is planned for 2015. Woolf herself, as we know, was not positive about the NPG. As an adolescent visiting with her father (a Trustee) in January 1897, Woolf wrote "It was rather dull, and we spent our time in yawning" (*PA* 16). In "Pictures and Portraits" Woolf felt "it needs an effort, but scarcely a great one, to enter the National Portrait Gallery," and attacks the gallery for not owning a portrait of Harriet Taylor Mill, "a paragon among women" (*E3* 164). Woolf's concern about the gallery's unequal representation of women underlies her support, in a letter to Theodora Bosanquet

---

[1] According to a source at the NPG visitor numbers were 61,826.

[2] A smaller version of this painting, Duncan Grant's *Interior at Charleston with Bust of Virginia Woolf* (1955), was for sale on the NPG web site at £250,000. Stephen Tomlin's bronze bust of Woolf (1931) in a casting (1998) from the third and final casting was £200,000. The NPG also printed a limited platinum edition (45 prints) of two portraits of Woolf by George Beresford, with 20 allocated to a "Collectors Edition" at £1,000 and the rest at £600.

in 1932, for the proposal to buy "a picture of Katherine Mansfield for the National Portrait Gallery" (*L5* 135).

Woolf herself refused to be painted for the NPG in 1934 partly due to the ten-year delay, required by the gallery, between sitting and hanging the portrait (Harvey 2010). "So why should I defile a whole day by sitting?" (*L5* 277). But Woolf was an assiduous visitor to exhibitions (including the NPG), beginning with visits to the Royal Academy in 1897 to see a Lord Leighton exhibition ("they were mostly very ugly"), and later to a G. F. Watts exhibition ("weak & worthless" [*PA* 53 and 218]). In 1906 Woolf, "with Nessa," felt "Furse is better than the Sargents to my thinking (*PA* 270).[3] In 1918 she records, "I have begun my artistic education again,"[4] and made a visit to the Victoria and Albert museum to see Rodin— "not as good as Epsteins" (*L2* 284).

Woolf, with equal pleasure, visited exhibitions of more popular interest—as a child going to Earls Court and Olympia, "without any stretch of the imagination one can think oneself in Venice" (*PA* 180). With Leonard, Woolf visited the British Empire Exhibition 1924-25 about which she wrote "Thunder at Wembley" (*E3* 410-14). In 1938, Woolf was a patron of an exhibition of Picasso's *Guernica* and other works at the New Burlington Galleries to support the National Joint Committee for Spanish Relief. But Woolf's favorite exhibitions were those which included her sister Vanessa's paintings. In 1923, Woolf attended a London Group exhibition at Heals and, writing to Vanessa, "thought your big picture [*Charleston Interior*] very lovely…But its like putting a necklace of daisies round the neck of an elephant, praising you" (*L3* 44).

Miraculously *Virginia Woolf: Art, Life and Vision* encapsulates all these very different facets of Woolf and does bring us "closer to Woolf" (Spalding quoted in Barkway 55). The exhibition displays one hundred and forty-four artifacts and rare archival materials in a variety of media: manuscripts, drawings, paintings, photographs, books, sculpture, and ephemera, many never exhibited before. The catalogue illustrates one hundred and thirty artifacts. Two very large photographs dominate the entrance—a glamorous 1927 photo of Woolf (see Humm 83), and the other of the remains of 52 Tavistock Square after a direct hit from a bomb in October 1940 (17). Immediately juxtaposed are *Vogue* photographs of Vanessa Bell and Duncan Grant's sitting-room decorations (1924) of Tavistock Square, so that although both exhibition and catalogue follow Woolf's life chronologically,

---

[3] Charles Furse and John Singer Sargent. The picture by Furse was *The Return from the Ride*.

[4] From 1916, during World War 1, the Tate, Wallace Collection, London Museum, and National Portrait Gallery were all closed. The Victoria and Albert Museum was not closed but visiting was restricted and some valuable statues were sandbagged, and others taken into the London underground.

important connections (as here) and themes in Woolf's career are very vividly displayed and contextualized.

Organized into five sections, the exhibition starts with "Diaries" (entitled "Prologue" in the catalogue) containing the Gisèle Freund photographs of the Woolfs taken in Tavistock Square, and Woolf's manuscripts and published diaries. Section One, "Who Was I Then?," contains the George Beresford photographs of Woolf and her father, the Julia Margaret Cameron photographs of "famous men and fair women," the Talland House photographs, Stella Duckworth's photo album and the manuscript of the Stephen children's *Hyde Park Gate News*. Poignantly, Stella's appointment diary notes Virginia's first breakdown, and all the photographs are suitably juxtaposed with Bell's much later painting *The Memoir Club* of 1934.

Section Two, "Experiments and Reforms," opens with Quentin Bell's manuscript drawing of the "Arrival at 46 Gordon Square" from the *Charleston Bulletin Supplements* (c. 1923). Violet Dickinson's 1936 album of typescript copies of Woolf's letters follows, together with portraits of Virginia Woolf by Grant and Bell. The 1911-1912 sequence of Woolf's portraits by Vanessa Bell demonstrates Bell's move from figuration to abstraction. There are artifacts from the writers and key figures in Woolf's life: Lytton Strachey's letter confirming his withdrawal of his marriage proposal to Virginia, a portrait of Caroline Emilia Stephen (who bequeathed Virginia £2,500), Saxon Sydney-Turner, Roger Fry, James Strachey and Leonard Woolf, together with Leonard and Virginia's letter to Lytton Strachey making public their engagement simply as, "Ha! Ha! Virginia Stephen Leonard Woolf 6th June 1912" (77). The most disturbing exhibit here, which I had never seen, is Woolf's personal copy of *Spring Morning* (1915) a book of poems by Frances Cornford, with her angry scrawled child-like drawing and the annotation, "Darwins ought not to be allowed to paint or write but only to sit in the fields naked," written during Woolf's breakdown (88). Close by is Leonard Woolf's heart-breaking letter to Violet Dickinson describing the horrors of the breakdown.

Section Three, "Painting and Writing Have Much to Tell Each Other," might well be the title of the whole exhibition which demonstrates vividly how writing and art interweave in Woolf's life and work. Several Hogarth Press first editions including *Two Stories*, *Kew Gardens*, Eliot's *Poems*, *Prelude,* and *Paris* sit alongside Hope Mirrlees's portrait (1919) by Simon Bussy and a photograph of Mansfield (Adelphi Studios 1913). The very fat volume of *Ulysses*, juxtaposed with the very slim Hogarth Press editions, illustrates better than explanations can why the Hogarth Press could not publish *Ulysses*, even if the Woolfs and printers had been willing (and they were not). In Mark Gertler's portrait of Samuel Koteliansky (1930) "Kot" is a strikingly powerful figure. The Hogarth Press unpaid bill of £3.4.0 sent to Lytton in 1924, "causing the devil of a bother in our books," makes the publishing display very accessible to a general viewer.

Section Four, "Street Haunting and Novel Writing," with more Hogarth Press first editions, expertly situates Woolf's manuscripts in her contemporary context, for example with illustrations of the London underground. A photograph of Vita Sackville-West is followed by a glorious sequence of Ottoline Morrell's photographs of Woolf, exquisitely dressed by Nicole Groult, the sister of designer Paul Poiret. The sequence is given whole pages (six with "bleeding") in the catalogue, and by flicking rapidly Woolf comes alive, almost jumping from the page. The past continues to mark Woolf's present here with a 1926 *Vogue* photograph of Woolf wearing her mother's dress.

The final section, "Thinking is My Fighting," illustrates Woolf's more political work of *Three Guineas* and support for the Spanish Republic and anti-fascism. Woolf's intensely moving two suicide letters, together with her walking stick left on the bank of the Ouse before her suicide, are unbelievably poignant—underpinned by Leonard's sad letter to Anna Freud following Freud's death (160). A copy of Hitler's *Sonderfahndungsliste* ("Black Book") of 2,820 people to be rounded up after the invasion of Britain, with Leonard and Virginia at numbers 115 and 116 respectively, is almost too shocking to read in its precise listing of the Woolfs as "*Schriftsteller* and *Schriftstellerin*."

The exhibition is an extraordinary achievement capturing, as it does, Woolf's greatness as a writer as well as her awareness of modernity in all its facets. The modernism of Woolf's writing is highlighted, but the exhibition would equally appeal to those unfamiliar with her work. The catalogue is, as you would expect from Spalding, highly scholarly and beautifully written. There is a helpful annotated and illustrated chronology, picture credits, a list of further reading, and a useful index (not always included in catalogues). Typically modest, Spalding is generous in her acknowledgements, but the exhibition is undoubtedly a personal triumph.

——Maggie Humm, Emeritus, *University of East London*

Works Cited

Barkway, Stephen, "Virginia Woolf Today." *Virginia Woolf Bulletin.* 47: September, 2014. 49-56.

Harvey, Benjamin. "Virginia Woolf, Art Galleries and Museums." *The Edinburgh Companion to Virginia Woolf and the Arts.* Ed. Maggie Humm. Edinburgh: Edinburgh UP, 2010. 140-159.

Humm, Maggie. *Snapshots of Bloomsbury: the Private Lives of Virginia Woolf and Vanessa Bell.* New Brunswick NJ: Rutgers UP, 2006.

Modernism, Middlebrow and the Literary Canon. Lise Jaillant (London: Pickering & Chatto, 2014) xi + 211pp.

Modernism, Middlebrow and the Literary Canon, the seventh volume in Pickering & Chatto's *Literary Texts and the Popular Marketplace* series, offers a book historical view of modernism. Lise Jaillant's study of the Modern Library, a cheap reprint series created in New York in 1917, provides ample evidence for the argument that modernism was not just the province of highly educated elites or well-heeled purchasers of expensive hand-printed books. The Modern Library, as Jaillant suggests, combined "New York glamour and intellectual sophistication with a very affordable price" (2). Jaillant makes it clear that this was an important cultural institution for the American reading public through the 1920s and 30s, and her detailed and archivally rich study more than lives up to its fascinating subject.

Jaillant begins by offering a broad overview of the Modern Library's history, situating her work in the context of the new modernist studies and related studies of middlebrow culture of the early twentieth century. She offers a careful analysis of the Modern Library's marketing, its advertising, its design principles, its cultural influence, and, with the necessary qualifications about sparse evidence, its readers. One of the most compelling aspects of the book is Jaillant's focus on the Modern Library's pedagogical aspirations. The series was designed, she suggests, to allow its purchasers to become well-read autodidacts. The Modern Library acted as a kind of affordable curriculum, the authority of the publisher's imprint suggesting titles that would contribute to a reader's sense of having gained a coherent rather than a haphazard understanding of the contemporary literary world. The photograph Jaillant includes of the Modern Library's custom-built bookcase to house its series shows the publisher attempting to cultivate reading and buying habits by offering interior design appeal as well as a literary education. Jaillant's book is illustrated throughout with dust jackets and images from the archives. The well-chosen illustrations support her arguments: seeing the strikingly similar looking covers for the anthology *Fourteen Great Detective Stories* and James Joyce's *Portrait of the Artist . . .*, for instance, affirms the Modern Library's emphasis on continuities rather than distinctions between genres.

According to Jaillant, the Modern Library series is a quintessential middlebrow endeavor. Following Catherine Keyser's definition of the term ("mass-market venues and middle-class audiences to formal characteristics of literary style" [5]), Jaillant explains that the Modern Library series popularized literary modernist texts by producing them at an affordable price point and marketing them as aspirational possessions for middle-class book buyers. This is, as Jaillant herself notes, a positive spin on middlebrow culture, and it is an approach that admits modernist literary works into what might be described as a middlebrow publishing endeavor. Woolf's own characterization in her wry essay "Middlebrow" is famously less charitable: middlebrows are difficult to define because they are "neither one thing nor the other"; they are overly concerned with propriety and manners; they are possessed of a muddled and tasteless approach to art. And yet, when it comes to book buying, Woolf suggests that middlebrows are drawn to dead writers and repackaged versions of the Classics. The Modern Library, with its specific mandate to promote living literary culture, would not quite fit Woolf's mocking characterization. Jaillant offers a new way of looking at the "betwixt and between" that emphasizes the ways in which middlebrow and highbrow can work together.

After a thorough introduction, Jaillant examines some of the modernist texts from both sides of the Atlantic that were published in the series, contextualizing them alongside some lesser-known titles with which they appeared. The authors she focuses on are H. G. Wells, whose work she reads alongside Science and Sex titles; Sherwood Anderson, whose reputation was much enhanced by the publication of *Winesburg, Ohio* in the series; Joyce, whose *Portrait* she somewhat surprisingly reads alongside detective fiction; Willa Cather, whose *Death Comes for the Archbishop*, shows the maturation of the series in the 1930s; William Faulkner, whose introduction to the Modern Library edition of *Sanctuary* famously describes the book as "a cheap idea"; and, of course, Woolf.

The Woolf we meet in Jaillant's chapter is well established in England by the time *Mrs. Dalloway* appears in the Modern Library series, but her reputation in America is up for grabs. It's 1928, and *Mrs. Dalloway* already has what one of the advertisements describes as a "small but enthusiastic fan base" (85). Jaillant points to 1928 as another important date in the history of modernism (after the much discussed 1922) because by this time modernist texts were beginning to move from smaller venues to larger-scale commercial operations. In other words, modernism was going mainstream. Also in 1928, Harcourt and Brace published *Orlando* in the United States and touted it as a text that would make Woolf a less intimidating writer (Jaillant quotes amusingly blunt advertisement copy—"Now She Can Be Popular!"—to show just how clear the publishers were about wanting to expand modernism's public). Attacks against Woolf's snobbery and highbrowism by the likes of Q. D. Leavis and the anonymous reviewer to whom Woolf responds in "Middlebrow" were reframed in the American press as positive values: Jaillant points to a *New York Times* review of *Orlando* as the newest book on the scene and the one that promises to break down the barriers between high and low cultures. Free of highbrow associations, Jaillant suggests, Woolf is able to focus on her pedagogical approach to reading without encountering preconceptions about her own sociocultural position.

Woolf's interest in autodidacticism for the common reader comes across in her preface to the Modern Library edition of *Mrs. Dalloway*. As Jaillant points out, Woolf seldom wrote prefaces at all, since they tended, she thought, to unduly influence reader experiences. The *Mrs. Dalloway* preface contains a description of Septimus as Clarissa's double that was immediately taken up by critics in their analysis of the text in the 1930s. However, what interests Jaillant about the preface is its direct address to the common reader that seems to undermine the very authority of the preface even as it affirms Woolf's belief in free interpretation: "it would still be for the *reader* to decide," Woolf writes, " what was relevant and what not" (89). The contradictory nature of Woolf's preface—which simultaneously renounces the idea of guiding a reader's experience and at the same time suggests an interpretation—supports Jaillant's argument that the Modern Library series often shows the complexity of cultural categories as these are mediated by publishing practice. Slightly less convincing is her conclusion that the presence of Woolf's preface in the Modern Library series and her advocacy of the "common reader" may have caused the decline of her reputation as an essayist after the Second World War as the series began to be seen as a more crassly commercial endeavor. Interesting as the *Mrs. Dalloway* preface is, the suggestion that it was influential enough on its own to significantly alter Woolf's reputation on both sides of the Atlantic seems like an overstatement of its importance.

The chapter illuminates a frequently overlooked context for Woolf's reception in America in focusing on the Modern Library, and will be of particular interest to Woolf scholars who work on the 'brows', reading, paratextual evidence, publishing, and pedagogy. At times in the chapter it is clear that Jaillant is a modernist book historian rather than a Woolf specialist. The comparison between Woolf's reception in an English context and her reception in America here would have benefited from further development, especially on the English side where more work has been done. In particular, Jaillant still seems to characterize the Hogarth Press as a small press akin to a little magazine, despite the fact that by 1928 it was publishing bestsellers alongside handmade books, and, as Helen Southworth and Elizabeth Willson Gordon have recently shown, the Press was more than equal to the task of distributing its titles widely within England. Woolf herself reached a large public through the Hogarth Press, and this complicates Jaillant's notion that inclusion in the Modern Library series represented a transition from small to large circulation.

Jaillant's study offers a detailed and carefully drawn study of the Modern Library's version of Woolf and her contemporaries. Scholarly work on the institutions of modernist literary culture has tended over the past two decades to focus more on small-scale operations. Yet, the role of larger commercial publishers in disseminating modernist literature in the form of reprints deserves

further investigation, and as Jaillant amply demonstrates, the idea of a widely read modernism is not contradictory. This kind of scholarly work on publishing history and reception is especially relevant as more book history studies focus on the reception as much as the production of literature. Jaillant's study introduces us to the books that Woolf's early American public would have encountered and helps us begin to characterize those ever-elusive historical figures: her readers.
—Claire Battershill, *University of Reading*

The Work of Revision. Hannah Sullivan
(Cambridge: Harvard UP, 2013) 349pp.

Hannah Sullivan's recent monograph traces the practice of revision across several centuries, uncovering its primacy in modernism's print culture and following its reverberations later in the twentieth century. Like many of the high modernist texts it engages, *The Work of Revision* is recursive in its chronicling of textual practice. Beginning and ending with the twenty-first century, Sullivan works from a premise no doubt familiar to readers: revision is paramount. Citing contemporary writers such as Joyce Carol Oates, Michael Cunningham, and Monica Ali, Sullivan poses a series of claims about contemporary creative practice, all of which revolve around today's solemn, even compulsive, fidelity to process. This allegiance, one entangled with claims to integrity and sincerity, is relatively recent. For contrast, she points to the doctrine of Romantic-era poets, who particularly valued writing for its spontaneous provenance. Here, she echoes Keats's quip: "if Poetry comes not as naturally as leaves to a tree it had better not come at all" (3). In the early twentieth century, though, writers came to associate creative quality with revision practices that Sullivan aptly describes as "Sisyphean" in relentlessness and gravity (2). At stake here are strikingly different attitudes about textual value: whereas nineteenth-century writers had cast revision as "adornment or encrustation," their twentieth-century successors understood it in terms of "getting below the surface to the passionate heart of the matter" (33).

If earnest and diligent revision is today "an indicator of authorial integrity," this prejudice is a direct repercussion of modernism. *The Work of Revision*'s foremost argument concerns this inheritance: "the association of revision and literary value is the legacy of high modernism and the print culture that nourished it" (2). Such practices were neither understated nor incidental. On the contrary, claims Sullivan, modernists "revised overtly, passionately, and at many points in the lifespan of their texts. They used revision, an action that implies retrospection, not for stylistic tidying-up but to *make it new* through large-scale transformations of length, structure, perspective, and genre" (2). Key writers include Henry James, James Joyce, and T. S. Eliot, and Sullivan treats each as a compositional case study, unearthing examples of authorial idiosyncrasy and creative caprice along the way. Throughout, genesis is instrumental to one of the book's arguments about modernism, namely that "genetic complexity is often allied to—even, produced by—a thematic interest in complicated geneses" (5).

The monograph's first chapter, at once capacious and meticulous, charts evolving attitudes toward creativity and creative process from romanticism to the present day. Early on, revision is clearly defined, eschewing figurative connotations for plainer and more practical terms: "a study of laborious, belated, even otiose changes, made without reference to the linguistic 'felicity' or basic communicability of the original version" (15). Here, Sullivan establishes what might be called a taxonomy of modernist revision with three primary branches: addition, deletion, and substitution. So common are the first two models (elsewhere linked to maximalism and minimalism) that "they actually produce some of the difficulties and stylistic patterns we recognize *as* modernist" (16). In some cases, these models are flexible, even transformative. Early on, Henry James—whose work on *The Middle Years* (1917) is the focus of Chapter Two—followed a course of revision "primarily substitutive" but in time "became a more accretive, additive writer" (10). The book's middle chapters concern high modernist writers who were especially interested in "non-substitutive forms of revision" (10). Chapter Three explores "radical excision," a practice important to the avant garde, particularly Imagism. Sullivan explains that Eliot's *The Waste Land* was "produced through a seesaw act of compositional counterpoint"—the seesaw's other seat, of course, warmed by Ezra Pound (11). Even as Eliot created the poem in a primarily additive mode, "conjoining short drafts into an elaborate montage," the poem's genesis was also subject to the flourish of Pound's "excisive blue pencil" (11). Here we see the impact of what Sullivan terms the "Poundian aesthetic legacy," which tends to celebrate economy and control. In time, she explains, such textual practices "became identified with broader cultural and technological preferences for efficiency, hygiene, and rapidity" (10).

At its midpoint, the book turns from compression to expansion. Chapter Four focuses on revision's additive models, attending to writers who work "by accretion or extension." Whereas excision's ellipsis seems "a painful process of loss," one that demands work on the part of the reader, extension "often seems light-hearted pleasure, linguistic free-wheeling without limits" (109, 167). Joyce's *Ulysses* is central to this chapter, and here Sullivan carefully identifies and weighs Joycean models of textual extension. Chapter Five turns to the "efflorescence" of autobiography in the early twentieth century—a genre that is predisposed to revision and especially so with regard to traumatic memories (199). Joyce, for instance, was "troubled" by one of autobiography's main quandaries: "the problem of knowing where to end" (216-7). "*Portrait* has an ending," concedes Sullivan, "but what a strange, flyaway, *un*-ending it is!" (218). Joyce, Leslie Stephen, and Virginia Woolf ultimately settled on a common solution: though their autobiographical writings "begin retrospectively," they ultimately "turn into evolving, prospective diaries"—a formal choice that allows for an "unfolding, permanent present" (199).

Just as *The Work of Revision* began with allusion to modernism's legacies, Sullivan returns in her sixth and final chapter to the later twentieth century. "[A]s modernism was institutionalized and writers became college professors," she explains, "passionate correction began to seem not abnormal or excessive, but a *necessary* precondition of good writing" (238). This chapter dramatically broadens the project's temporal and textual reach. Having begun with Wordsworth and Keats, Sullivan examines Allen Ginsberg's *Howl* and the advent of Microsoft Word's Track Changes as well as the digital archives of David Foster Wallace and Michael Pietsch's editorial reconstructions of *The Pale King*. Here, then, is a wider corollary of her claim: revision also tests "the limit point of print culture, the final flowering of composition through documented paper stages" (269). Concluding this chapter—as well as the book—she claims that revision, ultimately, is "an exercise in nostalgia—an attempt to keep hold of the solidity of print" (269).

In terms of method, Sullivan is primarily a historicist, and deftly orchestrates a wide range of primary and secondary materials. Even as she acknowledges and draws from many critical methods, she is candid in stating her preference for "a historically attentive, comparative reading of manuscript materials and edition histories" (10). One of the project's critical obstacles is the thorny question of intention, one that she addresses frequently and frankly. "I believe," she writes in one instance, "that in many cases an author's intention to revise is knowable, rational, and explicable, but I am not trying to claim any one textual state as superior *in principle* to the others; nor do I believe that early and late stages are *necessarily* connected in a teleological or even causational way" (57).

Sullivan's prose is clear and elegant. Even when immersed in the particulars of genetic history, *The Work of Revision* is highly engaging. Textual minutiae and nuances of variation—surely unavoidable in an account of revision—are seldom dry or clinical because Sullivan so warmly animates them with dynamic narrative. To wit, a five-page account of additive revision includes such terms as "interleaved" (149), "heaped," "jeweled," "encrusted" (151), "grow[n] inside-out" (152), "condense[d]" (153), "riddled with outgrowths" (154), and "glutted" (154). This imaginative style is augmented by frequent illustration. In Figure 8, for instance, mirrored columns uncover Joyce's many additive revisions in the final lines of "Penelope" (181). Throughout, the project's visual apparatus—figures, diagrams, charts—is illuminating and accessible, particularly for the non-specialist reader.

Because of its impressive breadth and approachable style, this project will appeal to many. While much of the book, particularly its middle chapters, will prove valuable to modernist studies, readers of Woolf will appreciate Chapter Five's illuminating account of *To the Lighthouse* and "A Sketch of the Past." Sullivan's diligent attention to Woolf's drafts uncovers an ingenious approach to that "old impasse," the problem of autobiographical closure (221). If Lily Briscoe's conclusive brush stroke can be understood as "an allegory of *not revising*" (197), Woolf would later settle on "an extremely elegant solution to the problem of finish." Steeped in her forty years of experience as a diarist, "A Sketch" is an "embrace of provisionality as an aesthetic" (233). Returning to the question of genesis, Sullivan aptly quotes Woolf's 1939 diary, in which the writer poses telling questions, namely "what my intention is in writing these continual diaries. Not publication. Revision? a memoir of my own life? Perhaps" (232).

—Emily James, *University of St. Thomas*

Virginia Woolf and the Problem of the Subject: Feminine Writing in the Major Novels. Makiko Minow-Pinkney (Edinburgh: Edinburgh UP, 2010) 212 pp.

Virginia Woolf and December 1910: Studies in Rhetoric and Context. Ed. Makiko Minow-Pinkney (Grosmont, Wales: Illuminati Books, 2014) 213 pp.

First published in 1987, Makiko Minow-Pinkney's ground-breaking analysis of Virginia Woolf's modernist experimentalism in her five major novels was republished in 2010. Minow-Pinkney illustrates in her seminal book, which has inspired many scholars of modernism, aspiring students and Woolf enthusiasts throughout the years, that Woolf's modernist endeavors reflected in *Jacob's Room, Mrs. Dalloway, To the Lighthouse, Orlando,* and *The Waves* can also be read as "a feminist subversion of conventions" (ix). What, readers may be prompted to ask, does one mean here by "conventions"? The book's textual analyses showcase the ways in which Woolf subverts the fundamental conventions of patriarchy, reflected in the concept of narrative and the conceptualization of the subject. Minow-Pinkney's pioneering work situates Woolf in the real world of society and politics, hence retrieving Woolf and her writing from the realm of the abstract, esoteric and—to appropriate Bernard Smith's term in art history—"formalesque" modernism, one which centers on an overriding obsession with form or with quests for new form. Since, for Woolf, "[e]xperience never comes into being without representation" (12), her revolutionary project entails conveying—through self-reflexive words and through a self-critical sign(ification) system—human character as a shifting subject position, which is always in flux or in becoming, rather than as a *prêt-à-porter* archetype or identity which is fixed and stagnantly passive.

Parallels between Woolf's representation of the character and Julia Kristeva's theory of the subject are foregrounded in Chapter One, "Feminism and Modernism in Woolf," and drawn throughout the textual analysis sections. Woolf's writing depicts the positional paradoxes and difficulties which lie within the developing subject's rupture with the semiotic phase, often regarded as the realm of the mother, in order to venture out into the symbolic phase, often regarded as the realm of the father. Her writing hence reflects Kristeva's notion that the "break" required for the development of the subject, which she calls "the thetic phase," is not and should never be a clean one. Woolf's concept of androgyny is not grounded strictly upon the valorization of the feminine, but rather upon the oscillation and vacillation between the feminine and the masculine:

> Woolfian androgyny involves a *dialectic* of symbolic and semiotic, of man and woman—or, in Kristeva's phrase, 'never the one without the other'. Hence Woolf never radically destroys the symbolic and its thetic subject. For her, it constitutes one of the poles necessary for the dialectic movement of her writing, a framework to work against. (189)

This "double position" (22) is celebrated by both Woolf and Kristeva: "woman cannot but be androgynous. Even if she identifies herself with the mother in the position of the repressed and marginal, she must have a certain identification with the father in order to sustain a place in the symbolic order and avoid psychosis" (22). Woolf's refusal to offer a moment of finalization and totalization of the meaning of her story can be seen in the undecidable symbolism of a young man's room and a beaming lighthouse.

Minow-Pinkney's succinct analysis of *Jacob's Room* reveals the ways in which Woolf locates the First World War not as the "fall from grace" moment in human history, but rather as the de(con)struction of signs and subjectivity: "The war destroys Jacob, as it does the possibility of symbol" (39). Her analysis of *Mrs. Dalloway* draws attention to what lies beneath Woolf's playful façade of a conventional narrative form and of a homogeneous grand narrative. Though written in the traditional third-person past tense, the novel is subversively heterogeneous and non-linear as it is composed of the characters' intertwining lives and voices. Woolf's revolutionary representation of the subject is that which paradoxically takes place within the conventions she seeks to question and challenge, in the same way that the development of one's subjectivity takes place within the parameters of subjecthood: "This dialectic between stasis and rupture is precisely what the novel's style achieves" (81).

The chapter on *To the Lighthouse*, which contains memorable statements and poignant comments, such as "[t]he triumph of metaphor is itself a *thematic* concern of the book" (85), transforms the ways in which readers read and perceive the novel. Mrs. Ramsay's death not only symbolizes the death of the angel in the house, but also symbolizes the death of symbolism or, in other words, the impossibility of an absolute meaning. Minow-Pinkney's interpretation of *Orlando* sets in motion a reassessment of the novel that was once underrated (though students in 2015 may find this difficult to imagine!). A playful joke which offers more than a playful jest, Woolf's spoof biography reveals the multiplicity of "truth of the unconscious" (117) and the multi-layered (re)makings of the conscious. After becoming a woman, Orlando's protean subjectivity is not only a celebration of a social outsider's status, but also a confirmation of the significance of society, a homage to the society in which rapid changes can be seen reflected in new technologies and in the increasingly impersonal and transitory modern urban setting.

The pinnacle of *Virginia Woolf and the Problem of the Subject* lies in its author's analysis of *The Waves*, a novel that is often considered to be the pinnacle of Woolf's own achievement "in terms of the dialectic of symbolic and semiotic, and of the convergence of modernism and feminism" (187). Through dramatic monologue, the subject in this novel is portrayed as one which is perpetually in the process of becoming. Essentialization of identity is rendered problematic in the most dramatic sense and form. It is rendered as equivalent to the elusive Holy Grail, for which the quest generates and perpetuates myths, legends and multiple narratives which cannot do without, but which far surpass, the coveted artefact of desire itself: the desire for closure and totality.

Makiko Minow-Pinkney's *Virginia Woolf and the Problem of the Subject: Feminine Writing in the Major Novels* will continue to inspire many more generations of scholars of modernism, aspiring students and Woolf enthusiasts. This book will not fail to propel readers to take and retake the life-changing journey of the mind, fixing the Holy Grail of Cartesian subject in view while unfixing its authority through Virginia Woolf's feminist subversion and critical approach.

In her recent collection *Virginia Woolf and December 1910: Studies in Rhetoric and Context*, Minow-Pinkey offers twenty distinctive reflections and meditations on Virginia Woolf's claim that "on or about December 1910 human character changed." Contributors to this volume include Elizabeth Abel, Rachel Bowlby, Pamela L. Caughie, Melba Cuddy-Keane, Maria DiBattista, Terry Eagleton, Christine Froula, Jane Goldman, Suzette Henke, Claire Kahane, Stephen Kern, Alison Light, Minow-Pinkney herself, Tony Pinkney, Suzanne Raitt, Christopher Reed, Susan Sellers, Brenda R. Silver, Peter Stansky, and Masami Usui. Each contributor explores a variety of aspects of Woolf's landmark statement.

Minow-Pinkney illustrates that Woolf's personal life and the prevalent *fin-de-siècle* intellectual as well as aesthetic movement propel Virginia Woolf to repeatedly establish the year 1910 "as the watershed between the old era and the new" (3) in her writing. Woolf's early career as a reviewer for various newspapers and journals and the dramatic impact of Thoby Stephen's death on Woolf's life, for example, are mentioned alongside the public's increasing interest in fourth-dimensional space, a ground-breaking phenomenon in science equivalent to the Symbolist movement in literature. 1910 was also the year when the International Psychoanalytical Association was established at Nuremberg, further enhancing and emphasizing the schism between materialist ideologies and the desire to unearth the meanings beneath the surface of everyday life. Brenda R. Silver and Peter Stansky revisit and revise Woolf's iconic quotation, which takes readers far beyond the content and context of Woolf's own words, since the quotation has a life of its own in recent familiar references and even more familiar misquotations. Maria DiBattista argues that dramatic and disruptive break with the past is crucial to the modernist project: "Do you still need more evidence that insolence was a great catalyst of the change in human character Woolf discerned on or about December 1910?" (81).

Also central to the book is a study of the historical contexts of 1924, on or about the time when this seriously playful and playfully serious proclamation was made (Caughie's "On or About December 2010, Human Character Changed Again" and Reed's "On or About January 1924"), and a study of the history and concepts of "character" (Abel's "The Victorian Cook's Modern Character" and Kern's "Cézanne's Wife and Woolf's Character"). For Terry Eagleton, Woolf's most quoted testimony marks a transitional stage in the (re)conceptualization of the modernist subject: "[o]ne might claim that with modernism it was not so much that human character changed, but that the form of historical selfhood traditionally known as 'character' gave way to that rather more elusive phenomenon known as the subject" (86).

The change in and of human character, as illustrated in Woolf's juxtaposition of the Victorian cook and the Georgian cook, and of upstairs and downstairs, is examined through the paradigm of class (Light's "Pie in the Sky"). As Rachel

Bowlby points out, though the change in and of human character is a gradual one and though it takes effects on different levels without drastically disrupting the status quo, it cannot be denied that a change indeed has come:

> No more will the wives be doing housework, no more will the cooks be confined below stairs; the cook's limited liberation is measured by her becoming a consumer – of print, of clothes. (But the cook is still scouring the saucepan the wife has abandoned, while the wife will write books her husband is already in a position to write: the changes in human character are on different levels.) (59)

The issues of time and temporalization have been succinctly addressed in this collection of essays (Froula's "On Time"). Melba Cuddy-Keane's compelling story behind Woolf's anachronistic allusion to the *Daily Herald*, which did not exist in December 1910 but was first published as a strike sheet on January 25, 1911, contributes new aspects to the (re)assessment in 2014 of Woolf's 1924 announcement: "What Woolf is describing is nothing obscure or difficult; she is tracing a process most of us use: never to be the other, never fully to know the other, yet being always compelled, by our desire, to imagine the other's experiential space" (72).

Theories of psychology and utopia are also brought into the volume, adding new dimensions not only to how one reads Woolf's statement, but also to how one appreciates Woolf's life and innovation (Pinkney's "Modernism and the Gothic Utopia" and Raitt's "The Remains of Several Hearts"). Suzette Henke addresses Woolf's struggle with the Cartesian subject of self, the mental struggle that shapes the outline of her experimental fiction, through the framework of trauma theory.

Read as a hypertext, Woolf's proclamation is analyzed alongside her other works. Susan Sellers examines Woolf's quotation and its implications alongside "The Mark on the Wall," whereas Masami Usui explores the historical context which foregrounds and brings together Woolf's testimony and *The Years,* her 1937 novel: "The spring days of the 1910 section of *The Years* are the threshold to Woolf's most celebrated month, December 1910, and ultimately to the 'Present Day' section of the book" (188).

One of the most valuable aspects of this book lies in the contributors' personal meanings and accounts evoked not only by Woolf's life and her controversial statement, but also by the lives of the contributors and the lives of others which have touched their hearts. This gentle act of sharing one's celebration of lives fully lived which continue to inspire and lives worth living continually to inspire, as reflected in Claire Kahane's thank you letter to Virginia Woolf and Jane Goldman's tribute to the Scottish artists John McNairn and Caroline McNairn, can be regarded as the pinnacle of Woolf's endeavors not only as a prominent modernist writer, but also as an inspiring human being. "On or about December 1910 human character changed" can be interpreted as a solid dictum or a flippant comment, or both. Uncertainty makes up the certainty, the kind of (un)certainty which can be found in the ways in which life went on and still goes on changing not only the character of human beings, including how one perceives and understands identity as a subject in flux, but also the characters of time, society, individual hopes and dreams, which dynamically change with the dynamism of Virginia Woolf's words. As *Virginia Woolf and December 1910: Studies in Rhetoric and Context* demonstrates, Woolf's (anti)manifesto is the kind which also manifests itself in the process of becoming.

—Verita Sriratana, *Chulalongkorn University*

Modernism and the Rhythms of Sympathy: Vernon Lee, Virginia Woolf, and D. H. Lawrence. Kirsty Martin (Oxford: Oxford UP, 2013) 215pp.

Kirsty Martin's *Modernism and the Rhythms of Sympathy* presents an intently focused study of her titular themes as they play out in the works of Vernon Lee, Virginia Woolf, and D. H. Lawrence. Through detailed readings, Martin argues expansively that these writers present an embodied form of connection to others that finds representation through the poetics of rhythm. It is Martin's focus on the connection between the body and emotions, on the one hand, and the disconnection between emotions and the intellect, on the other, that defines her study vis-à-vis recent work in affect theory—which posits an enmeshment of body, emotion, and cognition—or, more importantly to Martin, Martha Nussbaum's theory of emotional ethics. Martin proposes a form of sympathy that "is emotional and intuitive and that intimates transcendence" (10) in such a way that characters' sympathetic entanglements remain in something of a pure state. Unmotivated by social forces and irrelevant to seemingly sympathetic acts of altruism, the form of sympathy Martin describes is subtly integral to modernist subjectivity and manifest in the rhythmic aesthetic she identifies in the texts she covers.

Martin does well to begin her study with Vernon Lee, whose work sets the stage for her study by presenting the word "empathy" for the first time in an English novel, in 1912 (and if this seems an extraordinary claim, the *Oxford English Dictionary* more or less corroborates it). Lee's attention, in both her fiction and personal writing, to the question of "how we feel for each other and for things" (31) provides an apt case study of the exploration of sympathy in literary form, and her work charts a course to Martin's conclusion that feelings of sympathy comprise a formal element of modernist fictions. She shows how Lee's interests in psychology, science, and music prompted her to think broadly about "the energies of the human body [and to] create a subtle understanding of emotion, sympathy, and life" (51). Woolf and Lawrence share many of these interests with Lee, and Martin presents a convincing reading of Lawrence's version of "erotic sympathy," arising as it does from the deeply embodied force of desire. Lawrence, like Lee, provides ample evidence of Martin's argument that sympathy is essentially "bodily, linked to the rhythms of the natural world" (140), whether in his description of the "carbon" nature of human existence in a letter or his portrayal of the physiological dimensions of love, pleasure, cruelty, and other feelings that bind his characters to one another.

Whereas Martin draws heavily on Lee's and Lawrence's correspondence and essays in addition to their fiction, her discussion of Woolf rests almost entirely on the five novels she plumbs for moments of embodied sympathy. Martin's most original contribution to Woolf studies is her reading of *vitalism* in her novels: by reintroducing this term from its earlier appearance in the late nineteenth and early twentieth centuries, she offers a historicized view of the ways in which Woolf weaves her characters together through poetic rhythms and webs of feeling. Martin defines vitalism as "the belief that there was a type of energy diffused in flesh, a type of vital spirit that creates and defines life" (24). Insofar as vitalism is an antecedent to affect theory, it poses an alternative to dualistic thinking about the mind and body and Martin makes a convincing case that modernist characters are possessed of essential energies that flow within and among individuals. From Clarissa Dalloway's intuitive sympathy for the distant figure of Septimus Smith to the interlocking subjectivities of *The Waves*, Woolf shows the affective workings of such abstract human connections. Martin applies vitalism to Woolf by arguing that "Woolf understood feeling as based in the physical brain and body, animated by the stirrings of energy" (99), and she combs through Woolf's novels for passages in which her poetics convey a sense of "energetic" or "vital" connection amongst characters through physiological imagery.

Martin's reading of vitalism is productive in that it draws out a pronounced anatomical trope within Woolf's prose. While much has been written on Woolf's representation of the body and of the role of the body in her writing, Martin focuses on the physiological nature of, for example, the famous "blush" and "split skin" of *Mrs. Dalloway*'s erotic moments and the physical sympathy Clarissa feels when "her body burnt" upon learning of Septimus's suicide. Martin teases out other more subtle references to embodied feelings, such as Septimus's intuitive connection to the vibrance of trees to which he feels bound by "millions of fibres," and she observes that Clarissa's momentary sense of euphoria at her party is described as a "dilation of the nerves of the heart itself." In these and other examples of an anatomical vocabulary at work in Woolf, Martin emphasizes the physiology of feeling—an analysis that works well in her reading of *The Waves* as well, replete as the novel is with organic imagery, tropisms, and rhythmic prose. While these two novels lend themselves nicely to Martin's discussion, her readings of *To the Lighthouse* and *Between the Acts*, while interesting, would be enhanced by an engagement with more a more diverse body of critical work. In the case of *To the Lighthouse*, Martin asserts an odd rejection of psychoanalytic readings that would actually support her observation that "feelings are patterned on the past" (113) more broadly, and in her reading of *Between the Acts*, Martin focuses on the extent to which the shared bodily experience of "fidgeting" connotes a rhythm of sympathy among the characters even as she argues that "Woolf had moved from a sympathy based in blood and fibre to one which emphasized culture" (128) in her last novel. The idea that Woolf creates an alternative form of community that transcends immediate or prescribed social formations is one that Jessica Berman has explored in *Modernist Fiction, Cosmopolitanism, and the Politics of Community*, in which she identifies the interconnected networks of self, society, and a cosmopolitan form of community that is as sympathetic in structure as it is political in nature. In arguing that the sympathy in the novel "might be linked more to the awareness of national identity" (126) than the embodied forms of sympathy she reads in Woolf's earlier works, Martin would do well to engage Berman and, with regard to her reading of Woolf, to take on the novel's rhythmic refrain of "dispersed are we." This paradoxical expression of a shared, and thus sympathetic, feeling of disconnection bears analysis in the context of Martin's argument.

In terms of the larger theoretical structure of her study, Martin invokes relevant psychological studies of feelings and affect by Jesse Prinz and Teresa Brennan but does not draw upon equally important work in affect theory by such theorists as Eve Kosofsky Sedgwick, Brian Massumi, Jonathan Flatley—whose *Affective Mappings* also focuses on modernism—and others who offer insights into Martin's topic of embodied emotion. Her oversight of this body of work likely stems from the extent to which her argument often assumes the form of a quarrel with Nussbaum. It is telling that the index entries on Nussbaum are similar in length to those on Woolf, and as Martin says in her conclusion, her goal is to "unsettle Martha Nussbaum's influential understanding of emotion as cognitive" (189). The force of this counter-argument throughout the book works to limit some of Martin's otherwise compelling readings of sympathy, for emotions are complex enough that the revelation that some characters' sympathies operate on a level detached from the intellect need not foreclose the role of sympathy in forming ethical judgments as well. If Nussbaum is the book's Achilles heel, though, its strengths include an original presentation of a physiological form of sympathy that Martin historicizes and brings to bear on modernist fiction.

——Erica L. Johnson, *Pace University*

Feminist Narrative Ethics: Tacit Persuasion in Modernist Form. Katherine Saunders Nash (Columbus: The Ohio State UP, 2014) x + 178pp.

Narrative ethics, defined by James Phelan as an exploration of "the intersections between the domain of stories and storytelling and that of moral values," as a field of study, "can be usefully seen as a recent development in the larger trajectory of literary ethics, one beginning in the late 1980s" (para 1, 9). The field of narrative ethics can be divided into four categories (the ethics of the told, the ethics of the telling, the ethics of writing/producing, and the ethics of reading/reception), and it is no surprise that Katherine Saunders Nash, in this study of British modernist novels, chooses to focus on the ethics of the telling, as innovations in narrative discourse (as opposed to story, or the told) have long been considered a hallmark of modernist fiction. Nash argues that traditional literary approaches applied to modernist works that tacitly persuade their audiences may miss entirely acts of telling which have profound ethical consequences and *Feminist Narrative Ethics: Tacit Persuasion in Modernist Form* bears out these claims. Nash's call for a new theory of feminist narrative ethics simultaneously focuses on novels with no or little obvious political or ideological agenda and asserts that the implied ethical strategies of these texts actually gain force by *not* focusing only on feminism. The most promising theoretical concept Nash develops is that of the "project author," and as a concept with great explanatory power for a number of different textual strategies, it is the one this reviewer hopes most to see more developed and widely applied.

Nash opens her study with a discussion of the famed "impersonality" of British novels of this period in order to set up her argument that indirection sometimes masks a persuasive argument and that the novels she examines are "paradigmatic examples of oblique authorial strategies to persuade a readership that has developed a taste for indirection to think differently about women's rights and prerogatives" (2). Nash's stated goal is to establish a new theory of feminist narrative ethics. To accomplish this, she utilizes a rhetorical approach, foregrounding the ways in which these novels "function on the multiple levels of narration, characterization, point of view, and narrative progression" in order to analyze the ethical principles underlying implied authorial strategies and their intended experiential effects on readers, designed as they are to "shape readers' reimagination of gender relations" (3, 4).

Nash proposes a new feminist narrative ethics by way of four paradigms: the ethics of distance (E. M. Forster), the ethics of fair play (Dorothy Sayers), the ethics of persuasion (Virginia Woolf), and the ethics of attention (John Cowper Powys). Acknowledging that her selected works and authors represent a wide range of aesthetic styles, purported audiences, and personal stances in regards to the women's movement (ranging from Woolf's liberal feminism to Powys's outspoken misogyny), Nash maintains nonetheless that each author employed feminist narrative ethics in their various projects, and so can be productively placed in theoretical and critical conversation. In order to make this claim, Nash argues for the necessity and utility of the implied author concept, emphasizing the explanatory power of the implied author to account for these authors' avoidance of overt didacticism and use of tacit persuasion to "compel readers to participate in the meaning-making process" (14).

"The Ethics of Distance" argues that Forster carefully constructs an ironic detachment in order to "critique gender inequity—however obliquely—as well as slyly to endorse new models for feminist relations among women and men" (16). Though his narrators never make clear pronouncements and the implied author's political beliefs are obscured, Forster does manipulate distance (especially between narrator and implied author) in order to ensure readers' deliberation and judgment. Presenting a persuasive case for reading the implied author of *A Room with a View* and *Howards End* as a stable ironist, Nash's close readings assert that the manipulation of distances is ethically productive, opening up real questions that the reader is forced to answer for herself, provoking the "reader's feminist awareness without advocating activity or intervention" (41).

"The Ethics of Fair Play" "obtains when an implied author gives her readers all the clues they need to make certain ethical deductions," regarding, for instance, the practicality of feminist marriage (16). Focalization, Nash contends, is the key technique used in service of this ethics of fair play and, beginning with the introduction of Harriet Vane in the fifth Lord Peter Wimsey novel, *Strong Poison*, focalization encourages the reader not only to anticipate the mystery's solution, but also to pay attention to the ways in which the romance plot unfolds. By breaking a cardinal rule of detective fiction and blending the genres of mystery and romance, Sayers uses focalization to advance her feminist argument. In adopting Harriet as a focalizer, Sayers is suggesting the reader inhabit her perspective and "adopt a feminist ideology through, and occasionally in spite of, Harriet's viewpoint" (65). Throughout the series, the reader is prompted to craft and then test out and revise his own "ethical judgments about gender relations in the context of a politically fraught historical moment," thereby, once again, becoming tacitly persuaded (89).

In perhaps the most intriguing chapter of the volume, "The Ethics of Persuasion," Nash makes a strong case for her scholarly method—the empirical comparison of manuscript drafts and published textual variants—in order to discover Woolf's "rhetorical purpose in revision, especially her evolving answer to the question of how one may persuade without coercion" in *The Years* (93). In order to discover this rhetorical purpose, Nash proposes a new model of authorship: the project author. Positing an "authorial figure that is dispersed beyond the bounds of the published text" allows Nash to juxtapose manuscript versions with the published novel in order to identify perplexing formal strategies, namely those of repetition, silence, and, most strikingly, compression (17). In a bravura reading of a passage in which Rose Pargiter reveals a scar, the result of a self-cutting incident occurring a hundred pages earlier, Nash showcases Woolf's deft use of compression (from the manuscript's abundant detail to the novel's sparse descriptions) as an ethical strategy. Nash's approach here is an interesting intervention into debates about self-censorship, though I remain unconvinced that *The Years* represents a break from the rhetorical strategies of Woolf's earlier novels. A more capacious study, using the project author concept to read *Melymbrosia* with *The Voyage Out*, and hence tracing processes of composition across Woolf's career, for instance, would have produced a more satisfying result for this reviewer, who is interested in the opportunities this approach affords.

Finally, "The Ethics of Attention" turns to the "ethical ramifications of observation, receptivity, and reading itself" (18). Powys's concept of "young-girl-like receptivity" "diverges radically from the equation of receptivity with passivity," and in *A Glastonbury Romance*, Nash asserts, Powys "revolutionized plot dynamics for ethical ends" by introducing an "erotics of progression" that does not align with either Peter Brooks's retrospective model in *Reading for the Plot* or Susan Winnett's prospective critique of Brooks's model, prompting attentive and receptive rather than goal-directed reading (18, 121). Though "feminist narrative ethics is not responsive to the political progress of the women's movement" in Powys's work, "it is deployed as a means of transforming gender constructs," "constru[ing] women's, and young girls', receptivity as an admirable strength and powerful asset" (118-19).

For all its merits, this study does not contextualize how this new methodological approach fits into the broader domain of feminist narratology, where discussion of the politics of sex, gender, and sexuality as it relates to real-life authors, critics, and readers, as well as to narrators and characters, is central. This study, also, does not address the need or a desire for intersectional approaches. Curiously, Kathy Mezei's edited collection *Ambiguous Discourse: Feminist Narratology and British Women Writers* (1996), the first to feature essays combining feminist and narratological approaches, is not presented as a more foundational text here.

Only Melba Cuddy-Keane (one of the contributors on Woolf), and especially her concept of the "non-coercive ethical text," is acknowledged as a strong influence. Though Nash points out in her introduction that "feminist critics and theorists have much to gain by leavening their investment in narrative politics with a more thorough consideration of narrative ethics," her readers would be better served by a more thorough contextualization of her work within the burgeoning field of feminist narratology (9).

Readers of this important contribution will appreciate Nash's lucid prose and streamlined, nuanced close readings, though readers not already well-versed in the specialized terminology of narrative theory may find certain claims less accessible. This study's stated intention, the formation of a new theory of feminist narrative ethics, is ambitious and laudable. The work undertaken here is an exciting read for the Woolf scholar, as it offers provocative accounts of specific texts as well as new methodologies for approaching covertly persuasive novels that "make few, if any, overt claims to be feminist" (143). Woolf scholars have much to gain from the insights of narratologists; this study represents exciting possibilities for the further development of theoretical frameworks examining the ethical principles underlying Woolf's unprecedented innovations in novel form.

—Annalee Edmondson, *Georgia Institute of Technology*

Work Cited

Phelan, James. "Narrative Ethics." In *The Living Handbook of Narratology*, ed. Peter Hühn et al. http://www.lhn.uni-hamburg.de/article/narrative-ethics. Web. 9 Dec. 2014.

Virginia Woolf, Jane Ellen Harrison, and the Spirit of Modernist Classicism. Jean Mills (Columbus: The Ohio State UP, 2014) xiv + 192pp.

The title of Jean Mills's book, *Virginia Woolf, Jane Ellen Harrison, and the **Spirit** of Modernist Classicism* (emphasis mine) felicitously reflects both axes of Mills's argument that reading Woolf "through the prism of Harrison's work" simultaneously illuminates Woolf's *oeuvre* and assists in "an effort to revive and reclaim Harrison's work, and to point to the degree to which her cultural, political, and scholastic example informed one of the major modernist voices of the twentieth century" (2). It also neatly avoids the fraught identification of 'Ritualist' with either Harrison or Woolf, a quagmire in which it is fatally easy to lose one's way.

Personal copies of more than a dozen of Harrison's books, some inscribed by the author, were to be found on the shelves of Virginia Woolf's library. Readers familiar with the shabby figure crossing Fernham's garden in *A Room of One's Own* will recognize it as classicist Jane Ellen Harrison, an 1879 "graduate" of Newnham College (Cambridge refused degrees to women until 1948). Harrison's unconventional preparation for being awarded the first research fellowship at that institution included sixteen years of famously public lectures popularizing Greek art and mythology. After her return to Newnham in 1898, she wrote *Prolegomena to the Study of Greek Religion, Themis: A Study in the Origins of Greek Religion, Ancient Art and Ritual,* and *Epilegomena to the Study of Greek Religion.* Harrison's capacious assembly of interdisciplinary data became a model of transformative and inspirational scholarship.

In the Introduction, Mills works her way among recent assessments of Jane Harrison (Shelley Arlen, Sandra Peacock, Annabel Robinson, Robert Ackerman, Jane Marcus, Mary C. Carpentier, and Mary Beard) with lucid economy, deftly disentangling her own purpose from theirs. She establishes the parameters of the Woolf-Harrison pairing and makes fruitful connections between Harrison's "new" classicism and Woolf's determination to find a voice of her own in literature. To these ends, Mills adapts Nancy K. Miller's "transpersonal" methodology, making connections that shift "sideways . . . away from any notion of descent to one of shared ambitions, overlapping politics, and friendships" (3). It is a "cross-reading . . . that does not rehearse a linearity of influence, but outlines . . . an active and transformative use of one body of writing by another writer" (1).

The transpersonal is a tool that enables Mills to tease out the subversive and feminist dimensions of Harrison's work which illuminate Woolf's without misrepresenting either Harrison *or* Woolf. Thus Mills can and does argue that "Harrison's research gave Woolf the necessary tools to reject patterns and structures made by others and to seek out different ways of knowing, of being, and different literary and political approaches" (5).

Historical and material evidence fit smoothly into the transpersonal. Chapter One brings Woolf and Harrison together first in 1904 when Woolf, accompanied by her tutor, Janet Case, meets "Miss Harrison" at Newnham. In teaching Woolf to read Greek, Janet Case not only uses the same texts as Harrison, but her heterodox "immersion" methods of instruction. Ultimately these early points of contact and intellectual stimulus will expand "into a relationship of shared [aesthetic and political] ideas. . . . [ideas that] resonate with Harrison's controversial theories and discoveries [apparent in] each new text she writes" (38).

Mills opens Chapter Two noting that, in the wake of the vast desolation of World War I, "many [modernist] writers turned to . . . the hero's journey, essentially a war story, often borrowed from . . . the pantheon of male Olympian gods" (62). Virginia Woolf longs for a different story to tell, of a female principle of community, a story which does *not* ignore the catastrophic consequences of heroic quests on the world and its women and children. Woolf identifies "male egotism with British patriarchy and the imperialism that brought about violence and the wars of the twentieth century" (65). She finds in Harrison a viable alternative—myths as palimpsests behind which women are present, central, and powerful in the even more ancient world of ritual (*Prolegomena*) and later as "those instincts, emotions, desires which attend and express life" and are projections "rather of the group than of individual consciousness" (*Themis*) (72).

Having organized a remarkably succinct presentation of the subversive and feminist dimensions of Harrison's work, Mills is free to display the full scope of her claim that "each one [of Woolf's novels] is an attempt to re-create 'a society,' as defined by Jane Harrison" (79). Examining each in turn, Mills makes clear how enriched a vein of interpretation is opened in reading Woolf transpersonally "through the prism" of Harrison's work. Invited back to the high table of scholarship and skillfully parsed, Harrison is demonstrably "reclaimed" as an important and valuable critical tool, especially in application to modernist texts.

In Chapters Three and Four, Mills pairs Harrison and Woolf in a slightly different way: essay to essay. Chapter Three demonstrates that *A Room of One's Own* and *Scientiae Sacra Fames* "speak to one another about feminism, politics, women's education, and women's writing as helping to form women's social identity and cultural production" (115). In both essays the personal becomes the political, one doubling the other in shared experience and imagination. They overlap at Newnham College, where J— H— haunts the grounds of 'Fernham' in Woolf's famous lines (cleverly referenced in the *Spirit* of Mills's title). Here both have had first-hand experience of the many ways in which Cambridge systematically marginalizes, excludes, and deprives women, raising the same question for both: is it worse to be locked out (of the libraries and halls of the men's colleges) or locked, as Harrison frames it, in the "wife's room, the room to which visitors are shown—a room in which you cannot possibly settle down to think, because anyone may come in at any moment" (117)? Both essays recognize that universities are hostile to women because patriarchy is hostile to any ideas which challenge unthinking male supremacy; and each offers "alternative possibilities for a woman's role and function in relation to learning, which are deeply rooted in reinterpreting ancient ritual" (122). In further consonance, Harrison and Woolf posit that the conventionally imagined distinctions between men's and women's ways of interacting with the world are social constructs which impose an unnatural and debilitating isolation, one heavily reinforced by patriarchal religions. In a different world, the one that can be recalled from ancient ritual and a social collective, everyone could, as Harrison puts it, "'worship knowledge' [chanting] together . . . men and women—today and tomorrow" (133). It is *that* world Woolf has in mind when she calls for a language, for the words that will capture "what happens when a woman walks into a room" (130).

Chapter Four juxtaposes *Three Guineas* and Harrison's *Epilogue on the War: Peace with Patriotism*. We can see in Mills's contention that chapter four

> locates Woolf's and Harrison's pacifism as part of the women's international peace movement, identifies it as a specifically feminist undertaking, and [identifies] their contributions as formative in helping to establish an intellectual climate in which the discipline of Peace studies and peace research have prospered today (134-5),

that *this* pairing is meant to do considerably more than cross-textual analysis. Mills's argument moves Harrison and Woolf onto the twenty-first century stage of formal Peace Studies. In exploring "the qualities and instincts, psychological, biological, and social, that might help to reveal the sources of violence and war" (147); in sharing a vision of war as the inevitable result of the individuating, divisive competitiveness that fosters intolerance in a patriarchal society at every level, including the way children are educated; and in establishing a radical criticism of the patriarchy which determines the conditions "of women's education, their position and function in the home, and the use of their bodies in sex and in marriage" (138-9), Woolf and Harrison re-emerge as entirely relevant to our own concerns about a world now constantly and everywhere at war.

Chapter Five, "To Russia with Love: Literature, Language, and a Shared Ideology of the Political Left," offers a graceful coda, its placement an artful tribute to Russian studies which preoccupied the end of Harrison's life after she moved to Paris in 1914. In 1924, the Hogarth Press published Harrison and Hope Mirrlees's translation from the Russian of *Life of the Archpriest Avvakum by Himself.* Harrison's friendly circle of Russian émigrés in Paris overlapped considerably with London members of the 1917 Club, which had been conceived by Leonard Woolf and Oliver Strachey. Harrison, because of her standing in both groups, facilitated the numerous connections between Bloomsbury and the Russians which "helped shape British literary attitudes toward Russia" (155). Woolf's own "perspective of Russia as soulful chang[ed] over time and bec[ame] more informed and nuanced, as she read the Russians through Harrison" (165).

In the concluding chapter, "Afterward," Mills's focus shifts back to her second purpose in adopting a transpersonal methodology: the reclamation of

Jane Harrison's rightful place of honor in classical scholarship. It is a superior kind of pleading for, having demonstrated a clear interpretive value at every point of textual intersection, Mills now surveys any number of places that Harrison *ought* to be acknowledged, yet isn't—at a recent International Virginia Woolf Conference, in Mary Beard's curious hostility to Harrison, in E. R. Dodds's *Greeks and the Irrational*, in Joan Breton Connelly's work, and so on. Brilliantly evoking the spectral J— H— of Fernham's gardens and the "darker and older shapes moving behind the bright splendours" of Greek plays (Harrison 87) is this list of haunted absence, this "s*pirit* of modernist classicism." These "oversights," Mills reminds us, constitute the "drama of denial that silences women's voices and contributions to culture, history, literature, art, politics, and to the narratives and discourses of what we commonly call civilization" (171).

—C.S.W. Schorr, *Independent Scholar*

Work Cited

Harrison, Jane. *Reminiscences of a Student's Life.* London: Hogarth Press, 1925.

Virginia Woolf's Garden: The Story of the Garden at Monk's House. Caroline Zoob with photography by Caroline Arber; Foreword by Cecil Woolf (London: Jacqui Small LLP, 2013) 192 pp.

In June 1936 Virginia Woolf was at Monk's House, in the throes of correcting the proofs of *The Years*. During these difficult days she found serenity in her garden and was able to write to Ottoline Morrell: "Here it rains, but its [*sic*] lovely in the garden; Leonard's flowers suddenly light up in the evening" (*L6* 45). This statement sums up for me Woolf's relationship with her garden: it was for enjoying, it had invaluable, inspiring aesthetic qualities, but like those flowers she mentioned, it *belonged* to Leonard Woolf and it was he who designed and worked in it. Nor, despite this book's title, is Caroline Zoob under any illusion as to the garden's "authorship." She duly credits Leonard for his creative garden-making, and his assistant Percy Bartholomew, his local Rodmell gardener. Zoob notes how Virginia Woolf, with Vita Sackville-West ("one of the most exciting gardeners of the century") on hand for gardening advice, "hardly exchanged a word on the subject in nearly twenty years" of lengthy correspondence ([92]).

Bloomsbury's gardens have been picked and harvested for the subjects of books one by one starting with Anne Scott-James's *Sissinghurst: The Making of a Garden* (1975) followed by two more on Sissinghurst and Vita Sackville-West by Jane Brown (1985 and 1990). Then it was Charleston's season, first with *Charleston: A Bloomsbury House and Garden* by Quentin Bell and Virginia Nicholson (1997), and more recently by Sue Snell in her *The Garden at Charleston* (2010). Now, with the book under review, Monk's House garden takes its turn in the spotlight. It has been left to last probably because, unlike Sissinghurst, its modest, domestic scale is not aristocratic; similarly Monk's House lags behind Charleston in visitor numbers, having a lower public and commercial profile. However, there is another crucial reason: I believe no one, since the Woolfs, has worked in it or is as familiar with its layout and its history, as its tenants of ten years, Caroline Zoob and her husband Jonathan. It was clear during my own visits to Monk's House over the years the Zoobs were its tenants that they spent innumerable hours restoring the garden not only sympathetically to the time of the Woolfs, but also creatively in their spirit. They made of it an experience where—standing on the bowling lawn, sitting in the orchard, or in isolation in one of the garden "rooms"—the visitor would feel as deep a connection to Woolf as one got *inside* Monk's House. This was quite an exceptional achievement, especially for a couple who, as Zoob herself confesses, had no particular interest in Woolf before they took the tenancy.

Yet it was Zoob's interest in researching Leonard Woolf's original planting schemes, designs, and color preferences that made the transformation possible; that, and a lot of very hard work. This book tells the story of the evolution of the garden from the time the Woolfs purchased Monk's House in 1919, when their initial enthusiasm appeared to be weighed heavily in favor of the garden over the house. Woolf told Janet Case in July of that year, "the point of it is the garden . . . there are cherries, plums, pears, figs, together with all the vegetables. This is going to be the pride of our hearts; I warn you" (20); she was right in predicting that Leonard would become both a "fanatical lover" of the garden, and "garden proud" (26).

We learn about some of the buildings that used to be in the garden. Leonard was inspired by its history and retained some of the walls and floor of what once were probably piggeries to form the Fig Tree Garden. The patterns of its old brick floor prompted Leonard to create numerous brick paths and the fact that the previous owners of Monk's House, the Glazebrooks, had been local mill owners led him to employ old millstones to form another floor as Gertrude Jekyll had done in her designs (58). An extract from a previously unpublished letter from Leonard to his builder on this subject is just one of the many little treasures this book holds, and shows the depth of Zoob's research. I was pleased to understand properly the position of Woolf's first writing room, which had been a tool shed with an apple loft above it. There is a photograph of Woolf standing outside it (51)—they later demolished it—and now the passage in her *Diary* which reads "Leonard storing apples above my head" makes perfect sense (*D2* 138).

I would like to say a word about Arber's photographs in this book, which benefit from its large format. They are taken from many different viewpoints in all areas of the garden, in varying seasonal light. The ones taken from the first floor of the house give remarkable views not available to the general visitor, for whom the upstairs of Monk's House is as off limits as a Beadle's turf. Arber's photographs are highly focused and the quality of their reproduction and color accuracy is stunning: see for example the garden taken from Leonard's study in early spring (60), or the portrait of Woolf by her sister in the dining room (141). They outshine any of the photographs in the other books I have cited. Neither will you find elsewhere better photographs of the interior of Monk's House. They bear informed captions—the author and artist dovetailing beautifully—often with judicious quotations. As well as Arber's, there is a generous selection of the Woolfs' own photographs, including a wonderful one of the two elm trees, "Leonard" and "Virginia," whose "interlacing branches," we are told in the caption, are "an instantly recognisable lodestar in even the most faded archive photograph." Of additional interest are a small number of photographs dating from the time, following Leonard's death, when the house was administered by the University of Sussex.

The book is divided into sections for each specific phase of the garden's history since its acquisition by the Woolfs, and then into chapters for each of the separate areas (or rooms) of the garden. These chapters are further illustrated with overhead plans of each garden room, sometimes with watercolors by Lorna Brown, and others with unique embroidered illustrations by the author herself. The reader is presented with a history of how the Woolfs shaped the garden, and how they designed it perfectly to suit their needs. Zoob traces the development of each area of the garden and makes good use of her technical and practical knowledge. Latin names are used sparingly so that the reader can seek direct inspiration, yet she does not allow the book to become a "How to" guide for the green-fingered.

The only mild irritation I had, a relatively minor one, was the frequent absence of the names of Woolf's correspondents when referencing the numerous quotations from her letters; and on occasion the quotations are inaccurate. I admit to being puzzled by a reference to a "wolves' heads" tapestry design on the dining room chair backs which I'd always seen as flowers in a vase (11). However, I am delighted to have the personal reminiscence by Leonard's nephew Cecil who recalls visits to his uncle and aunt in the garden shortly before the war. For those for whom a visit to Monk's House garden is easier said than done, this book is the next best experience. Monk's House remains a special place and Zoob closes the book with a poignant reflection that its real visitors can hardly disagree with: "Virginia and Leonard have themselves been absorbed into the 'tranquil atmosphere' of the house and garden. This atmosphere is not diminished because the planting in the borders is different and some trees have blown down or grown taller. The soul of the garden, which drew the Woolfs to it in 1919, is, I believe, still there" (186). We Woolfians owe the Zoobs a debt of gratitude.

—Stephen Barkway, *Independent Scholar*

Works Cited

Bell, Quentin and Virginia Nicholson. *Charleston: a Bloomsbury House & Garden*. London: Frances Lincoln Limited, 1997.

Brown, Jane. *Vita's Other World: A Gardening Biography of V. Sackville-West*. London: Viking Penguin, 1985.

———. *Sissinghurst: Portrait of a Garden*. London: George Weidenfeld & Nicolson Limited, 1990.

Scott-James, Anne. *Sissinghurst: The Making of a Garden*. London: Michael Joseph, 1975. Print.

Snell, Sue. *The Garden at Charleston: A Bloomsbury Garden through the Seasons*. London: Frances Lincoln Limited, 2010.

The Bloomsbury Cookbook: Recipes for Life, Love and Art. Jans Ondaatje Rolls (NY: Thames & Hudson, 2014) 384 pp.

Were the Bloomsbury crowd the "foodies" of their day? Jans Ondaatje Rolls makes a compelling argument that they were. A welcome addition to studies in material culture, *The Bloomsbury Cookbook* plumbs an inarguably rich archive of food references and recipes among Woolf's circle. A group known for its conviviality in both person and print will not disappoint researchers in records of dining well, the dinner parties and home meals that fortified their thinking, loving, and sleeping.

As a study of the material culture of domesticity, *The Bloomsbury Cookbook* is a necessary and delicious addition to the oeuvre. Far more focused in scope than similar collections of modern literary dishes, like *The Artists' & Writers' Cookbook* edited by Beryl Barr and Barbara Turner Sachs (1961), *The Joyce of Cooking: Food and Drink in James Joyce's Dublin* by Alison Armstrong (1986), and *Found Meals of the Lost Generation: Recipes and Anecdotes from 1920s Paris* edited by Suzanne Rodriguez-Hunter (1994), *The Bloomsbury Cookbook* is curated by Ondaatje Rolls and reflects substantial research in library archives and private correspondence. Her research sets *The Bloomsbury Cookbook* apart from its brethren.

Ondaatje Rolls, a Toronto native whose adopted home is Sussex, England, has previously authored two cookbooks for charitable purposes. All of the proceeds for the sale of *The Bloomsbury Cookbook* go to the Charleston Trust. Her name may be familiar to readers; she is the niece of writer Michael Ondaatje and the daughter of Christopher Ondaatje, author of *Woolf in Ceylon: An Imperial Journey in the Shadow of Leonard Woolf.*

The volume is produced beautifully on heavy stock, with 165 plates, two-thirds of which appear in color. Reproducing paintings (including original artwork from Cressida Bell), sketches, letters, and other ephemera, the book also integrates nearly 300 recipes, many previously unpublished. They hail from the records of Grace Higgens, cook and housekeeper at Charleston for over 50 years, and those of the best cooks in the circle: Helen Anrep, Bunny Garnett, and Frances Partridge. Generously indexed, with a separate section for recipes, the back matter includes a Bloomsbury chronology, sources for food references and the recipes themselves, and additional recipes from relevant Bloomsbury archives. A bibliography boasts a comprehensive list of period cookbooks, perhaps the most complete of its kind and a boon to the researcher of dining habits in the period.

The book is organized in seven main chapters: "Before Bloomsbury," documenting the childhoods of the Stephens and Stracheys; "Old Bloomsbury," representing the founding of the group from 1904 to the First World War; "Bloomsbury in Wartime," cooking economical and rationed dishes during WWI; "An Appetite for Bloomsbury," dining in the 1920s; "Bloomsbury Abroad," travels in the 1920s and 30s; "Bloomsbury in Eclipse," myriad recipes served at Charleston and other places in the 1930s; and "Bloomsbury's Offspring," select dishes from the following generation.

Each chapter incorporates history and personal anecdotes, some of which will be new even to seasoned scholars, as it tells the story of the decades. Tempting recipes that appear in reports of meals or adapted from fanciful metaphors follow narrative recountings. Intriguing examples include samples of university life, including Cambridge "Whales" (anchovy or sardine paste on toast) (41), adaptations of Dora Carrington's "Cowslip Flower Wine" (114) and Lytton Strachey's daily rice pudding (35-6), hearty Russian soups from Lydia (Lopokova)

Keynes (248-49), and "Tipsy Chicken" with gin (115-16). Many recreations of entire menus in the heyday of Bloomsbury bring to life the gatherings that inspired Woolf's famous comment about dining well. One example is a celebratory dinner preceding the first Omega Workshop of 1913, a lively and colorful six-course dinner that opens with a clear fish soup called "Potage Alpha Saumon" and ends with a fancy ice cream mould, "Glaces à l'Omega" (76, 80).

Unlike Armstrong's collection of Joycean recipes, *The Bloomsbury Cookbook* opts to adapt recipes from the period more often than creating new inspirations from contemporary methods. Indeed, one of the biggest strengths of the book is that Ondaatje Rolls attends carefully to her sources in the voluminous bibliography, seeking out similar recipes published close to the date of the dish. One fruitful source, *Mrs Beeton's Book of Household Management*, is used first in its Victorian long form and subsequently in bowdlerized spin-offs published as late as 1960. As a cook, moreover, Ondaatje Rolls seems to have a good palate and patience in testing and adapting period recipes from Beeton and others, which can be quite a challenge.

The cookbook, as expected, recreates not only real meals but also those made famous in the works of Virginia Woolf and others. Those teaching at women's colleges may be interested in the appetizing lady's menu from *A Room of One's Own*, surprisingly more appealing than the men's creamed soles and stewed partridges—and certainly easier to prepare (208-14). Clarissa Dalloway's dinner is presented anew, with the disappointing undercooked salmon cleverly rendered as a "Mayonnaise of Cold Salmon" (199).

Not all of the recipes are from the period, however. Ondaatje Rolls boldly chooses her own recipe for "Boeuf en Daube" (205-07). She is right to do so; it is a glorious version, scented by niçoise olives and orange. The commentary addresses the question posed by Vanessa Bell in a letter to her sister of 11 May 1927 (Regina Marler, ed. *Selected Letters of Vanessa Bell*, 318), among generations of readers of *To the Lighthouse*: "does the daube *really* need to be served immediately if it's been cooked for three days?" (No.) The daube works more effectively than another of Ondaatje Rolls's creations, "Post-impressionist Barbeque Beef," a grilled steak with garlic butter and tricolored peppercorns invented to suggest the bold colors of the art movement (72-4). The steak appeals to the contemporary palate, but seems wholly out of character in its anachronistic spicing and use of the term "barbeque," which riffs on Vanessa Bell's scandalous African costume at a fancy dress party in 1911.

With only the occasional slip, Ondaatje Rolls's whimsical sensibility, good humor, and excellent storytelling skills are distinguishing features of the entire work. The amusing anecdotal basis of many recipes themselves, rendered creatively into recipe form, make for entertaining reading. "Ottoline's Plum

Pudding," for example, represents not any particular use of fruit, but rather Lady Ottoline Morrell's hostessing abilities, as based on a quip about her luscious, plummy guests by Leonard Woolf (61-2). As a storyteller, Ondaatje Rolls rivals Alice B. Toklas, whose cookbook of 1954 similarly serves as documentation of the period and artistic currents among a circle of friends.

If the work has any weaknesses, it may be the underbelly of its strengths: the vast number of sources and archival material deployed by the author in recreating the feeling of Bloomsbury kitchens and dining rooms over three-quarters of a century. Cooking technologies and household staffing changed dramatically over the course of the century, but cookery books, especially those containing family recipes and casual meals, were slow to reflect these changes. It is arguable that because of a need for perceived stability in times of turmoil, there is less of a shift in the meals recorded in the beginning and end of the twentieth century than one might expect, as devotedly careful as the author was to her period sources. English breakfasts are English breakfasts; its teacakes are its teacakes.

The heterogeneity can be as fruitful as its sea changes, however, allowing literary historians to theorize about the unreliable temporality of intimate archives, the privileging of certain kinds of artifacts over others, especially when preserving the traditions of the home and hearth are concerned. Recipes from English households have historically tried to preserve older eras, so it is a difficult job for the historian attempting to document an impulse to "make it new." Manuscripts from seventeenth-century estates, for example, include recipes copied almost verbatim from the fourteenth century *Forme of Cury*, developed in the kitchens of King Richard II. Changes in eating habits over the span of a few decades are even more difficult to ascertain with print sources, even in those as tumultuous as the rapidly industrializing twentieth.

That said, there is enough experimentation and enough passion for culinary trends of the day to illustrate shifts in dining and even grant the label of "foodie" to the Bloomsbury Group. The flourishing of French and Italian cookery in the 1920s, in particular, especially as reflected in the receptions and travels of Vanessa Bell and Duncan Grant, emphasize the group's smart sensibilities. The recipe collections and epistolary descriptions of several denizens of the group evidence the interest in foreign food with flair. As Ondaatje Rolls notes, most only took up cooking after 1915, reflecting the simplification of the domestic structure in larger homes during the war, so the increased interest and labor devoted to cooking are signs of the times. In the efforts to maintain tradition and yet encourage the individual culinary talent, we might see more than a little modernist spirit.

—Jennifer Burns Bright, *University of Oregon*

Literary Aesthetics of Trauma: Virginia Woolf and Jeanette Winterson.
Reina van der Wiel (NY: Palgrave Macmillan, 2014) 255 pp

Literary Aesthetics of Trauma comprises a thoroughgoing treatise on British object-relations psychoanalysis applied to works of Virginia Woolf, especially *Jacob's Room*, *To the Lighthouse*, *The Waves*, and "A Sketch of the Past"; and to works of Jeanette Winterson, especially *Oranges Are Not the Only Fruit*, *Art & Lies*, and *Why Be Happy When You Could Be Normal?* Having originated as a PhD dissertation, this book maintains substantial scholarly reference, ranging from Sigmund Freud's "Remembering, Repeating, and Working Through" (1914) to the psychological theories of Melanie Klein, W. R. Bion, D. W. Winnicott, Marion Milner, Hanna Segal, and Christopher Bollas, to literary critics and cultural commentators on trauma including Mary Jacobus, Dominick LaCapra, Cathy Caruth, and Judith Herman. The literary texts appear to be deployed mainly to illustrate theories about the psychology of repairing psychic wounds.

Though van der Wiel writes in praise of formalism, I would not call her a formalist literary critic; she is primarily a psychologist. Using Wilhelm Worringer's (1908) distinction between arts of empathy and arts of abstraction, van der Wiel argues that Woolf adopted poetic prose of abstraction in order to contain the fractured emotions of grief and the loss of cultural faith and foundations occasioned by her personal losses of her mother, her half-sister Stella, her brother Thoby, and the trauma of World War I. Van der Wiel does an excellent job of explicating implications, emotional effects, and cultural resonances of Woolf's use of brackets in the "Time Passes" section of *To the Lighthouse*, and of analyzing the manuscripts, published versions, and history of this poetic experiment in abstraction, generalization, and formalism. In *To the Lighthouse*, Woolf fused her personal grief into the collective significance of the traumatic impact of World War I. Van der Wiel argues that Woolf achieved this through an experiment in abstraction as poetic containment.

In addition to Worringer's study of the psychology of style, van der Wiel works through Clive Bell's concept of "significant form," the aesthetic pronouncements of Roger Fry, and Susanne K. Langer's *Feeling and Form*, showing their congruence with British object-relations analyses of projective identification and the mother's holding environment as models for the process of obtaining the stillness of aesthetic contemplation. To achieve an artistic response to trauma, van der Wiel argues, one must distinguish between a symptom and a symbol. Whereas deconstructionists have looked to unpack the fragmented signs of trauma in the gaps, discontinuities, and inconsistencies in modernist texts, van der Wiel looks for the forms of wholeness that artistically contain traumatic emotions and give them meanings cognitively obtained through psychical detachment.

Putting forward an argument in defense of modernism, van der Wiel seeks to redeem literary formalism from previous readers such as Patricia Moran, Karen DeMeester, and Esther Sanchez-Pardo, who see Woolf's narrative possibilities as "disarmed by trauma," and who think Woolf's forms mimic the damaged psyche of a trauma survivor. Modernism in this view expresses an absence of faith in the ideologies of the past and the literary forms that emerged from those ideologies. Sanchez-Pardo claims that modernist texts attempt on many levels to deny their sense of loss and hide its sadness. These texts, says Sanchez-Pardo, "vent and contain rage, and . . . doubt any project of reparation." They "replay the shattering moments of trauma," and comment on "the very limits of representation." Van der Wiel, on the other hand, sees cognitive reparation at work in Woolf's formal experiments and thinks *To the Lighthouse* and *The Waves* manage to bring about a successful symbolization that "constitutes a process of working-through" (69).

Van der Wiel sees the baroque aesthetics of Winterson as a contrast to Woolf's modernist formalism. Winterson's maternal abandonment and adoption were her foundational trauma, and Winterson's work is "symptomatic," repeating a story of her origin as an orphan. Winterson's first novel, *Oranges Are Not the Only Fruit* (1985), fictionalized her trauma, whereas her memoir *Why Be Happy When You Could Be Normal?* (2011) retells the same story under the pressure of the real, with an ethical imperative of authenticity and witnessing. Between the semi-autobiographical first novel and the memoir, Winterson moved beyond fabrication to traumatic realism. She searched for her birth mother and portrayed the true story of finding her. Building on Roger Luckhurst's commentary on "trauma culture" (2003 and 2008) and Margaret Homans's "Adoption Narratives, Trauma, and Origins" (2006), van der Wiel sees Winterson's account of finding her biological mother as an index of renewed generativity: "Despite its historical and cultural contextualization as a trauma memoir, *Why Be Happy . . .* seems to have achieved something for its author that the compulsive return of the traumatic adoption story in the novels never could: the story is finally moving on" (213). Winterson concludes her memoir by saying she has no idea what happens next. In this "emotional ambiguity combined with a sense of the future implied by 'next,'" van der Wiel sees the promise of a psychological "working-through."

In her concluding "Coda," van der Wiel discusses the cultural shift marked by Winterson's hitherto inability to express traumatic adoption symbolically in her fiction. Van der Wiel says that in our contemporary culture, the question has radically shifted from the "*possibility* of working through trauma to its *desirability*." Whereas "moving beyond a symptomatic expression of trauma requires the cognitive transformation (symbolization) of raw emotion, in contemporary culture traumatic subjectivity has been elevated to the status of sublimity" (216). Form has given way to feeling, and we are in an era of the return of the real. The reading mode encouraged by contemporary trauma memoirs is "'complete identification, affective connection rather than aesthetic analysis'" (Luckhurst, 2008). For van der Wiel, this implies a cultural fascination with open wounds and tragic lives. Therefore, she thinks critical distance and the capacity for symbol-formation are more important now than ever.

In sum, this is a book of prodigious scholarship with a carefully considered, contemporary message.

—Dianne M. Hunter, *Trinity College*

A Mystical Philosophy: Transcendence and Immanence in the Works of Virginia Woolf and Iris Murdoch. Donna J. Lazenby (London: Bloomsbury, 2014) xii + 325pp.

In *A Mystical Philosophy*, Lazenby argues that while distancing themselves from "'traditional' models of religious belief," Virginia Woolf and Iris Murdoch "produce distinctly mystical works in ways that indicate the perseverance of irreducibly mystical categories within human consciousness" (1). Lazenby's pairing of Woolf and Murdoch is apt. As she notes, while atheists, both writers express a preoccupation with the dialectics of immanence and transcendence and emphasize the importance of aesthetics to philosophical understanding and practice. Furthermore, both women were institutional outsiders "excluded from the academic philosophical mainstream" (2). Despite their outsider status, Lazenby approaches Woolf and Murdoch as "metaphysicians in their own right" (2) who rejected the "reductive quasi-scientific models of consciousness and reality" espoused by their analytical and continental contemporaries (1). For Woolf scholars, Lazenby's book offers an important contribution to perennial debates regarding the philosophical Woolf. For example, how do we reconcile Woolf's atheism with the metaphysical musings and themes that preoccupy her non-fiction and fiction? How do we talk in intellectually rigorous ways about Woolf's metaphysical views without committing her to the kind of intellectual systems of thought she vehemently wrote against and sought to avoid? What is the relationship between the philosophical views espoused in Woolf's diaries and her memoir "A Sketch of the Past," and the novels? Lazenby claims that critical assessments of Woolf and the mystical are far from complete and she sets out to articulate the various aspects of Woolf's "*mystical* aesthetic" (212).

Lazenby's book is divided into three parts with individual chapters dedicated to Woolf and Murdoch. Part One provides a reappraisal of the ways in which the topic of the mystical has been approached in Woolf studies and assessments of

Murdoch's philosophy. Part Two explores how two different dimensions of the mystical tradition—the cataphatic and apophatic—inform the thought and writing of Woolf and Murdoch. Part Three makes a case for the contributions these two thinkers offer for a contemporary theological aesthetic. In this review, I focus on the chapters dedicated to Woolf.

In Chapter Two Lazenby contends that the topic of mysticism and Woolf has not been given sufficient critical attention and argues this is because both Woolf's contemporaries and later critics adopted a definition of the mystical that is partial or incorrect. Understandings of mysticism both in Woolf's day and thereafter have, Lazenby claims, been skewed by the dominant empiricism of the time which rejects the authority of metaphysics and aligns mysticism with the irrational, visions and voices, passivity and interiority. Lazenby discusses how vague or skewed accounts of mysticism are evident in the work of Woolf's contemporaries (she discusses Bertrand Russell's 1914 essay "Mysticism and Logic") and in contemporary critical assessments of the topic (Lazenby focuses her critique on assessments of Woolf and the mystical by Jane Marcus in her essay "The Niece of a Nun: Virginia Woolf, Caroline Stephen, and the Cloistered Imagination" and by Jane Goldman in *The Feminist Aesthetics of Virginia Woolf*). Lazenby's argument in this chapter is persuasive: there have been few in-depth critical assessments of Woolf and mysticism, operative definitions of the term are sometimes rudimentary, and in Woolf studies the mystical is too readily assumed to be incompatible with a feminist politics (a view Lazenby attributes to Goldman's discussion of Woolf and mysticism in *The Feminist Aesthetics*). As Lazenby points out, the Western mystical tradition—which has its sources in Greek philosophy (e.g. Plato) as well as the scriptures—centers on fundamental metaphysical and epistemological questions such as the relationship between the one and the many, modes of vision/knowledge and their expression, and the relationship between the numinous and the realm of everyday life. It is in relation to this much broader account of the mystical tradition that Lazenby seeks to situate Woolf's thought and writing. And from this it should be clear that the topics Lazenby focuses on in Woolf's writing, such as the tension between unity and particularity, modes of vision and expression, the interrelationship between "reality," life and art, and the nature of the self, are far from eccentric but are in fact perennial topics of interest in Woolf studies. Indeed, at base this book examines a number of familiar metaphysical and epistemological topics in Woolf's writing but refocuses the discussion by claiming Woolf's to be a distinctly mystical aesthetic.

Chapter Four focuses on the cataphatic element of Woolf's aesthetic, the cataphatic referring to that strand of mysticism which emphasizes the "constructive power of language" to express the moment of vision (72). In this chapter, Lazenby observes similarities between the mysticism of the Neoplatonic philosopher Plotinus (whom Woolf read in 1934), specifically in terms of his concept of the One, and "Woolf's visionary aesthetics" (71), all the while keeping other relevant contexts, such as Post-Impressionist aesthetics and Bloomsbury's wider philosophical milieu, in close view. The longest (and strongest) section of the chapter focuses on the well-known comments in the diaries and "A Sketch of the Past" that articulate Woolf's intimations of an underlying unity or form to life and intuitions of the numinous (her references to "reality," "it," "pattern," and so on), the relationship of this reality to the realm of everyday appearances, and the "ordering force of the work of art" (90). Here Lazenby provides a sophisticated discussion of the relationship between the one and many in Woolf's thought and how Woolf perceives art and creative expression to at times facilitate the apprehension of metaphysical order and, at other times, to be a product or reflection of that underlying form (83). In addition to analyzing, through a Plotinian lens, the concept of unity or transcendent Form and its relationship to life and art in Woolf's non-fiction and fiction (particularly *To the Lighthouse* and *The Waves*), Chapter Four also discusses the mystical self (focusing on the characters of Mrs. Ramsay and Lily Briscoe in *To the Lighthouse*), and concepts of vision and light.

In Chapter Six, Lazenby turns to the dialectical opposite of the cataphatic—the apophatic—discussing representations of the ineffable in Woolf's writing and moments in which the mystical vision resists expression. Drawing here on ideas of apophasis in Pseudo-Dionysius, Lazenby focuses her attention on the failure or limits of artistic expression as represented through the character of Lily Briscoe in *To the Lighthouse* and Miss La Trobe in *Between the Acts.* Arguing that Woolf moves to an increasingly mystical (apophatic) aesthetic in her later work, Lazenby contends that rather than a gesture of despair, expressive failure is, for Woolf, productive, and comprises an essential part of an overall dialectic in her work: "it is the tension, inherent to Woolf's thought, between the unifying and fracturing of vision, which is faithful to the dialectical interplay of the apophatic and cataphatic dimensions of mystical experience and language" (197). Indeed, throughout her analysis Lazenby emphasizes Woolf's commitment to paradox and her refusal to reconcile opposites into naive unities and contends that this is a defining characteristic of her mystical aesthetic (80).

Lazenby's analysis throughout is sophisticated and illuminating. My major criticism of this project is its limited engagement with relevant secondary criticism in Woolf studies, particularly philosophical studies. While the volume of critical scholarship on Woolf and philosophy is too large for any scholar to take on in full, several relevant studies are missing here and Lazenby's points of reference are limited in number (her key interlocutors are Ann Banfield, Mark Hussey, and Carl Woodring). In terms of scholarship on Woolf and mysticism—which is a small field—Lazenby only discusses studies by Marcus and Goldman; other scholars who have published on this topic are not mentioned. The work of Val Gough seems particularly relevant here given Lazenby's extensive discussion in Chapter Four of *To the Lighthouse* and conceptions of the mystical self which elide the issue of irony that Gough has explored. Given this project's sustained interest in modes of vision and the aesthetic, and the importance of Greek philosophy to Woolf's thought, the absence of any mention of Emily Dalgarno's *Virginia Woolf and the Visible World* is puzzling. Similarly, there are important studies (too many to list here) on Woolf's engagement with Greek philosophy (particularly Plato), gender and epistemology, and the interrelationship between Woolf's broader philosophy and her commitment to the everyday that are not mentioned but relevant to Lazenby's interests and arguments.

 A Mystical Philosophy examines in nuanced and erudite ways many of the questions and themes that lie at the heart of the philosophical Woolf. It also offers the most in-depth and even-handed account to date of how Woolf's metaphysics can be aligned with mystical traditions whilst always remaining faithful to the questioning, open-ended nature of Woolf's thought and philosophical temper. It also draws perceptive consonances between Woolf's implicit philosophy and Murdoch's philosophical project which I have not had the opportunity to discuss here. However, for a book that is at many points concerned with the issue of relationality, it is a shame that this study does not situate its analyses more firmly in relation to the rich field of scholarship on Woolf and philosophy, because there are many potential correspondences at work here that have not been pursued.

—Lorraine Sim, *University of Western Sydney*

Becoming Virginia Woolf: Her Early Diaries & the Diaries She Read. Barbara Lounsberry (Gainesville: UP of Florida, 2014) xi + 260pp.

I love books like *Becoming Virginia Woolf.* Based in archival excavation, conversations with others who have worked with Woolf's diaries, and methodical detective work. Filled with close and original readings. Secured by an unswerving focus that allows for depth and refreshing revelations. Enlivened by a portrayal of the young Virginia Woolf as a working professional whose wide reading fed everything she wrote. Supported with just enough theory and cultural history to provide readers with a framework for interpretation. Bolstered with connections to Woolf's other work. Anchored in a clear organization the reader can count on. Lounsberry ultimately helps us see, through her close attention to what she calls the first of three phases in Woolf's diary-keeping, *how* the Virginia Woolf we know actually became that writer. This book is foundational, one the rest of us will depend on for a long time.

Lounsberry argues that although scholars, critics, and biographers have mined Woolf's diaries for many purposes, "What remains now is to understand the diary as a *diary*" (1). As a result, she studies each of Woolf's first twelve diary books "(1) as a work of art itself; (2) as it relates to her other early diaries; and (3) as it intersects with her public works" (2). But Lounsberry transforms her book into something extraordinary through a deceptively simple method: she examines the "crucial role of *other* diaries in Woolf's creative life" (3). Thus, Lounsberry interweaves her close readings of Woolf's early diaries with equally close readings of the fifteen diaries Woolf read during the period (those by Sir Walter Scott, Fanny Burney, Samuel Pepys, William Johnson Cory, James Boswell, William Allingham, Lady Dorothy Nevill, Lady Charlotte Bury, Elizabeth Lady Holland, Dr. Charles Meryon [about Lady Hester Stanhope], Ralph Waldo Emerson, Mary Coleridge, Mary Berry, Edmond and Jules de Goncourt, and Stopford Brooke) and shows how those other diaries "flow[ed] through" Woolf's mind, shaping not only her own diary "but also her future public prose" (11).

The focus on these early diaries grows out of Lounsberry's lifelong work on Woolf's entire diary oeuvre; not only has she read and reread all of Woolf's thirty-eight diary books, but she has also tracked down and seems to have read the sixty-six diarists she can be certain Woolf read. Such incredible immersion in Woolf's diaries and the diaries she read, along with a deep knowledge of existing diary criticism and theory, lends great weight to Lounsberry's assertions about Woolf as a diary writer, including her argument that Woolf's diary writing falls into *three* stages, not two: the experimental early diaries (1897 through mid-1918); the mature modernist diaries (from 1919 through 1929); and her final "flowering" diaries (1930 to her death) (2).

Lounsberry calls Woolf's early diary "more structurally experimental than any of the diaries [Woolf] read" and notes that in her "first two decades as a diarist, not one of her diaries resembles another" (5). Lounsberry gives the 1897, 1899, 1903, and 1904-05 diaries chapters of their own; she then combines the Cornwall diary with the Great Britain travel diary, puts the Continental travel diary with the 1909 diary, and devotes a long chapter to the four diaries Woolf kept between 1915 and mid-1918. To help readers visualize the differing physical nature of Woolf's diary books, Lounsberry introduces each one with a material description that includes size, color, condition, ink, number of entries, and number of words. Lounsberry also identifies a developmental task and thematic identity for each book. In the 1903 diary, for example, Woolf identifies herself as an outsider for the first time, and throughout, compares London, "culture, the male literary tradition, even (social) death" with the country, "nature, the female, and the unconscious mind" (55). Lounsberry sees Woolf focusing on places in her travel diaries from 1906 to 1909, portraits in her 1909 diary, and natural history in her 1917 Asheham diary. The professional writer emerges in the 1904-1905 diary, and at the end of this experimental period, in July 1918, "town and country diaries start to merge," and Woolf's diary both expands and coalesces as her "various diary forms and styles begin finally to fuse" (226). Lounsberry's attention to the individual books means the reader can return to a sense of the diaries as they exist, not as they have been edited and combined and put into editions (no matter how accurately or judiciously).

Lounsberry's study follows Woolf in her love of "marginal" genres, honors Woolf's readings and reviews of other diaries, and highlights Woolf's theoretical comments about her own diary work. Lounsberry distinguishes between daily and periodic diarists and labels Woolf one of the great periodic diarists of the world. She helps us experience the speed, change, and *life* in Woolf's diaries, feel the pen dashing across the page, sense the protean nature of the genre. But she also comments on many other aspects of Woolf's life and work as well. Lounsberry provides a fresh perspective on the interplay of country and city in Woolf's mind, emphasizing Woolf's search for a "difficult synthesis": "country *and* London, unconscious *and* conscious, female *and* male" (225). For Lounsberry, Woolf's "drive to merge" culture and nature "are among her most significant diary acts" (223). Lounsberry also illuminates Woolf's ties to other women writers and the lessons she learned from them. Furthermore, she suggests a mother/daughter marriage market context for the nastiness in Woolf's portrait of Mrs. Loeb, sketched after a visit to the Loebs, thus asking us to see something besides anti-Semitism in it. Lounsberry blends theory, close reading, literary history, biography, and Woolf's other work in a readable narrative at the same time she achieves what she set out to do in her introduction—her argument for the diary *as* diary builds steadily and recursively. She successfully challenges long-accepted categories for Woolf's diaries and sometimes questions readings of specific diary passages; quoting one interpretation by Katherine Dalsimer, for example, she then baldly states, "This I do not find" (40). *Becoming Virginia Woolf* is clear and well-written, rewarding the reader with frequent and surprising turns of phrase (the Stephen tendency to use animal, fish, and fowl nicknames, for example, is described as "thrust[ing] the human back into nature" [8]) and thought-provoking description:

> A diary's fate, furthermore, often rides on the diarist's descendants: this has meant wholesale destruction, ripped-out pages, crossings-out, or, worse yet, rewritten passages. Vulnerable at the diarist's death, in life the diary, paradoxically, often is the stable bridge through the diarist's chaotic days. The diary is the life raft. (10)

As someone who is also working on Virginia Stephen's apprenticeship, I noted an error that's been made before and thus frequently repeated. Margaret Lyttelton is indeed mentioned often in Virginia Stephen's journals and letters, and she was Violet Dickinson's friend (75). But Margaret did *not* edit the women's supplement of *The Guardian*—her mother, Mrs. Arthur (Mary Kathleen) Lyttelton did. Stephen always calls Margaret by her first name and her editor by Mrs. Lyttelton or Mrs. L. It might also be worth pointing out that the invitation to write for *The Outlook* never panned out, and the invitation to write for the *Times* actually began Stephen/Woolf's lifelong association with the *Times Literary Supplement* (77).

The book's argument, summarized nicely in the epilogue, supports Lounsberry's claim that Woolf's "diaries disclose (when carefully studied) a clear path of development no biographer yet has shown" (225). But the epilogue's ending seems too abrupt, its references too cryptic. Perhaps Lounsberry meant this paragraph to create suspense for her next book, but it left me puzzled and searching the thirteenth diary for information about what she calls Woolf's "dispute with her women supporters" (226).

These were small matters, however. This book begs for and clearly hints at sequels, and I was pleased to learn from Lounsberry's website that she is at work on *Virginia Woolf's Modernist Diaries: Her Middle Diaries & the Diaries She Read*; I assume Lounsberry plans a third volume as well. An appendix at the end of the third volume that lists the sixty-six diarists Woolf read, perhaps in rough chronological order, would be extremely helpful. Whatever the format, though, readers can look forward to Lounsberry's future books, to rereading this one for their own work, and to dipping back into the diaries themselves. Perhaps, too, we can look forward to other scholars' projects informed by Lounsberry's method, used to such splendid effect here. Woolf's letters, anyone?

—Beth Rigel Daugherty, *Otterbein University*

Virginia Woolf: Experiments in Character. Eric Sandberg (Amherst, NY: Cambria, 2014) xiii +324 pp.

Virginia Woolf: Experiments in Character boldly takes up the problem of character and characterization in Woolf's novels. Eric Sandberg acknowledges that character "is, and has long been, out of fashion" (7) in literary studies, and that "character as such has not traditionally been the primary focus, or even a primary focus, of Woolf scholarship" (7). Nonetheless, he rightly insists that a deep-seated concern with character and character creation runs throughout Woolf's work, from her earliest book reviews to her latest fiction, providing a focus for understanding Woolf's development as a writer. Through detailed and meticulous readings of Woolf's novels (with the sole and inexplicable exception of *Night and Day*, a virtual treasure trove for his inquiry, one imagines!), short stories, early journalism, and late criticism, Sandberg attempts to show that reading Woolf's novels in the context of her own struggles to formulate and represent character offers new insight into her works. This is in one sense an unremarkable claim. (How could character *not* be important to Woolf, or reveal key aspects of her creative process?) But Sandberg is right to underscore the degree to which critical trends have moved us away from asking fundamental questions about the stories we read and the characters who occupy them.

What results is an unusual, but oddly satisfying book. The individual readings are thorough, nuanced, and closely detailed. Often Sandberg's investigations into character reveal aspects of style or inflection that are not at all obvious in individual works or scenes. At several points I was led unexpectedly to reassess my own readings in productive ways. The call to return to questions of character and representation—how both fictional and real individuals know one another and themselves, and what this means for literary creation—seems to me a healthy impulse and one for which Sandberg is to be commended.

The book begins with a provocative discussion of the common, unwitting substitution of "nature" for "character" by those quoting Woolf's famous declaration that "On or about December 1910, human character changed." Chapter One, "They Strain and Quiver: Woolf's Early Criticism and Characterization," turns to Woolf's early journalism and book reviews. Seeking a "sense of continuity" (27) from the early criticism to the later work, Sandberg purports to have found the key in the way Woolf approached the fiction presented to her for review:

> In only one of the approximately twenty works of fiction Woolf reviewed in 1905, a very short review of Edith Wharton's *The House of Mirth*... did Woolf not refer to characterization (172-173). This exception proves the rule: Woolf was keenly interested in characterization and was also extremely critical of contemporary practices, outlining what can be broken down into six types of character failure: conventional characterization, exaggerated characterization, thin characterization, excessively detailed characterization, representative characterization, and structural characterization. A brief examination of these categories of failed characterization will indicate both its importance to Woolf and provide at least a negative image of what Woolf thought character should *not* be. (27-8)

Chapter Two, "A Spectrum of Characterization," takes up Woolf's first novel, *The Voyage Out* (1919). Sandberg describes the novel as Woolf's experiment with "Theophrastan characterization"—a mode of character development that relies on external details, describing characters (or showing characters to perceive one another) in terms of type, rather than as unique individuals:

> Theophrastus was Aristotle's student and successor as head of the Lyceum, but he is best remembered for *Characters*, which represents an alternative to the influential Aristotelian vision of character (Kennedy 194). This is a collection of thirty character types, with a description—"the fraud is the sort who stands on the breakwater and tells strangers how much of his money is invested in shipping [...]"—and a definition, "you can be sure fraudulence will seem to be a pretence of nonexistent goods" (Theophrastus 117). A comparison of this Theophrastan structure and Vinrace's description of Richard Dalloway as "a gentleman that thinks because he was once a member of parliament, and his wife's the daughter of a peer, they can have what they like for the asking" reveals similarities (*VO* 30). A Theophrastan character is a type rather than a complex individual and is completely externalized. The reader's understanding of the "inner man emerges from this description of externals" (Smeed 4). (52)

I am not entirely convinced that we need Theophrastus here to recognize that Woolf is describing her characters as "types," allowing them to learn about (and generalize about) one another based on external observations and the assumptions they generate. Rather, what seems most interesting in Sandberg's description is that he has Woolf adopting exactly the "materialist" technique that she later criticizes Arnold Bennett for, working her way into characters from the outside—accessing interiors, to the limited degree possible, through external clues. Reading *The Voyage Out* from this perspective allows Sandberg to reveal some of the more intricate work Woolf does—and the risks she takes—in this early work, which is often wrongly assumed to be an attempt at Victorian conventionality on Woolf's part.

The next chapter, on *Jacob's Room* (1922), "Constructing Absent Character," is meticulously researched and cross-referenced, as all of Sandberg's readings are (perhaps to a fault—at times one feels that his own voice is crowded out by the parade of citations he includes). This chapter continues to trace Woolf's quest for the essence of character, a task complicated in this, generally considered Woolf's first "modernist" novel, by the title character's absence and definition largely through social conventions. In a series of short sub-sections—which pepper this and other chapters—making at times for a feeling of disconnection or too-abrupt transition) Sandberg details Woolf's debate with Bennett, maintaining that despite rewritings of the feud by critics as one based in class or gender divisions, the true subject as put forth by the two writers—character creation—was at the heart of the disagreement. The chapter ends with the suggestion that "one possible approach to the question of character in *Jacob's Room*" is that "character is satirical, and there is little reason to look beyond the corporal, mechanistic, and habitual" (112). Indeed, this description is close to Sandberg's ultimate take-away, in his book's conclusion, on Woolf's character-creation, which he again finds, surprisingly (and without naming it as such) to be much closer in practice to that of the Edwardians she derided than to a modernist fragmentation or experimentation with interiority: "By knowing people in a simplified way, by accepting broad outlines in place of detailed-depth psychology, by preserving a measure of autonomy in human relations, and all of this without reducing the individual to the status of a type, an ethically acceptable form of relation becomes possible" (280).

Chapter Four, "Compression and Character," turns to *Mrs. Dalloway* (1925), focusing on its use of memory as a key element of its characterization. Sandberg maintains convincingly that Clarissa Dalloway's character offers a more positive vision of the way in which society can work to solidify the self than is present in her earlier work: "Self is, the text seems to imply, temporally situated in time in a way that depends on memory and the relationship of past to present to future for its significance. It is a socially constructed artifact, the product of other voices, other pressures, and other definitions. At the same time, it takes part in a process of self-definition, of self-composition, in ways that are elucidated by extensive metaphorical structures in play in the novel" (153).

Readings of *To the Lighthouse* (1927) and *The Waves* (1931) follow, the first presented as a meditation on the relationship between fictional characters and real people (in which Sandberg's reading of Lily's attempts at characterization is of particular note), the second as a study of the development (and continuity or discontinuities) of self over time. Considerations of Woolf's last two novels, *The Years* (1937) and *Between the Acts* (1941), where these themes continue to emerge and reconfigure themselves, conclude the study, which ends with a call to return to questions of character in order to investigate what and how we know about ourselves, others, and the fictional characters we create. Sandberg has written a thoughtful, meticulous, and convincing study of Woolf's novels.

——Randi Saloman, *Wake Forest University*

Behind the Mask: The Life of Vita Sackville-West. Matthew Dennison (London: William Collins, 2014) xix + 364pp.

Prominently displayed even to this day in the Great Hall of Knole is the original manuscript of Virginia Woolf's *Orlando* inscribed "Vita from Virginia." The novel has become as inescapable an element in the great Elizabethan manor's reputation as it was in that of the house's daughter Vita Sackville-West herself after its publication in 1928, linking all three forever together. Vita Sackville-West's position as Virginia Woolf's one-time lover, and constant friend and correspondent for nearly twenty years, has kept her name in front of students of British literature, even as the literary reputation of her enormous body of writing—poems, novels, travel books, biographies, and gardening books—has waned. Contemporary visitors to Knole and nearby Sissinghurst Castle often come knowing much more about the personal legend of Vita Sackville-West, with her unusual looks, her associations with grand Tudor houses, and her litany of lovers, than they do about her actual writing. She has become a famous writer who has retained her celebrity after death, but not because of what she wrote. Despite the promise of its title, the new and charming biography *Behind the Mask: The Life of Vita Sackville-West* by Matthew Dennison, does little to alter this paradox. Dennison has authored several biographies of royalty, including those of Queen Victoria, her daughter the Princess Beatrice, and members of the Julian-Claudian imperial family, so it should come as no surprise his latest biography treats Vita almost entirely as a figure of aristocratic glamour and gossip, focusing on her storied upbringing in one of the great homes of England and her trail of extramarital loves, while giving short shrift to her writing, which Dennison disparages. While Vita was not the novelist that Woolf was (as both writers knew), the fact that this is the first biography of the former in more than thirty years makes it disappointing that Dennison is unwilling to consider her much at all as a writer.

There is, of course, much inherent interest in Vita Sackville-West's life from the more romantic aspect Dennison favors. Given that she was as fully a daughter of Knole as was possible—both her parents were Sackvilles, with her mother the illegitimate child of her father's uncle—Vita clearly felt the impulse to live up to the fantastic past she imagined of her forebears painted in the galleries by Hoppner, Van Dyck, and Gainsborough, most of whom stared down at her with the same hooded Sackville eyes she shared with her parents. A lonely child (her mother loathed the experience of childbirth and refused to repeat it), she used the hundreds of rooms filled with ancient furniture, tapestries, and stone leopards as a fount of fantasy; as Dennison notes, "Day by day Vita absorbed an inflated, erroneous sense of Knole's importance. Its place in British life—the prestige of her own family—overwhelmed her imagination" (27). Although the Sackvilles had accomplished little in history since the days of the first Duke of Dorset (so created by his cousin Elizabeth I), Vita felt compelled to live her life on the scale of her dreams about her childhood surroundings.

Certainly the fame and importance of Vita's parents during her childhood and adolescence contributed to this determination. After her father inherited it, Knole became repeatedly host to many of the great society figures of the time, including Edward VII (it was through him that Vita and her family first met his mistress, Alice Keppel, and her daughter Violet, who became one of the great loves of Vita's life). Her parents were the centers of two of the great scandalous trials of the era, first to determine her father's right to the house and the title of Baron Sackville after it was contested by her mother's oldest brother (who lost), and later when her mother, Lady Victoria Sackville-West, was sued for the fortune she inherited from her lover Sir John Murray Scott, one of the richest men of the day, by his other survivors (who also lost). Scott's bequest allowed Vita's parents to keep Knole running during their lifetime on the lavish scale that entertaining friends like "Bertie" and Mrs. Keppel required; the newspaper notoriety also fueled the sense of both mother and daughter (who became regular figures in the newspaper stories surrounding the scandal) of their own glamour and self-importance.

"*Quel roman est ma vie!*": Lady Victoria Sackville-West often repeated this phrase in her personal writings (19), but it was a sentiment her daughter Vita also came to believe—and inhabit—as she grew older. The young Vita not only began to write fantastical stories about her ancestors on the walls, but grew to have a fondness for fancy dress as well; her mother often capitalized on Vita's dramatic height, air of languor, and enormous eyes by starring her frequently in roles in the elaborate entertainments she devised for her houseguests. Twice in her youth Vita posed for now well-known portraits by famous painters (Philip de László in 1910, and William Strang eight years later) that captured this excessively theatrical air about her by depicting her in large and startling hats.

By this time, Vita had publicly been courted by some of the wealthiest nobs of her day, including the heirs to the Duke of Rutland and the Earl of Harewood. Eventually, she had settled on the diplomat Harold Nicolson, who largely let her do as she pleased, and allowed her mostly to continue the many passionate affairs (which he called her "muddles") that so characterized her entire life. The most serious of these was with her childhood love Violet Keppel, who had by this time married Denys Trefusis; Violet's insistence on intensifying their grand passion during Vita's early wedded years with Nicolson almost destroyed both marriages altogether. After much intrigue and drama, Vita decided to return to Harold and the first Elizabethan home they restored for themselves, Long Barn (since Vita's sex barred her from inheriting her beloved Knole), where she could produce her writings comforted by the stability Harold provided for her.

Yet despite this outward show of unity, the two Nicolsons continued to pursue their own love lives apart: while Harold indulged in his own extramarital relations with young men, Vita continued with her series of new "muddles" which proliferated to the extent that it becomes genuinely hard to keep her lovers straight while reading Dennison's biography. They include (among many others) the biographer Geoffrey Scott, the painter Mary Campbell, the BBC director Hilda Matheson, the heiress Dorothy Wellesley, and, most famously, Virginia Woolf. Although Vita Sackville-West claimed that she and Woolf had sexual relations only twice, and that they were traumatic experiences for Virginia, the relationship they enjoyed together became one of the most meaningful of Vita's life, especially when Woolf chose in 1928 to immortalize Vita (by then the best-selling author of her long Georgian poem *The Land*) in thinly disguised form in *Orlando*. As Dennison astutely points out, while *Orlando* (which also became a best seller) fed into Vita's fantasies of herself as the glamorous and androgynous descendant of a noble lineage, it also became "the literary equivalent of a shackle." Claiming the novel served as Woolf's "means of skewering Vita in print in order to possess at least a part of her in person and prolong indefinitely aspects of their closeness" (164), Dennison shows that *Orlando* became such a part of the public's legend of Vita Sackville-West that it came to define her; as Harold perceptively prophesied to Vita, it was a book "in which you and Knole are identified for ever, a book which will perpetuate that identity into years when you and I are dead" (187). The legend of *Orlando* brought Vita even more firmly into the public eye than before, allowing her to craft a sensational novel about the aristocratic glamour of her childhood, *The Edwardians,* that became not only her all-time best seller, but even largely helped pay for the final Tudor home she and Harold owned together, Sissinghurst, which became the locus for their magnificent experiments in gardening and landscape design during their later years.

Dennison, perhaps correctly, does not award much merit to this gossipy publishing success; but unfortunately neither does he to any of the other novels or written works Vita produced during her prodigious career. Although Dennison claims he does not second Woolf's estimation of Vita as possessing "a pen of brass," you'd be hard-pressed to find evidence much to the contrary in this biography. He accords very little (if any) attention to either of Vita's excellent novellas, *Seducers in Ecuador* or *The Heir,* or her best novel, the Galsworthyesque *All Passion Spent*. For Dennison, the only real interest of Vita's fiction lies in "its autobiographical dimension" (223): he cares about what it potentially betrays about her affairs and her tortured relationships with her family, and very little about the intelligence or craft she poured into her writings. Tellingly, there is practically no discussion of her relations with her publishers—although a full page is given over to the visit of the Queen Mother to Sissinghurst in 1953. Readers should come to Matthew Dennison's *Behind the Mask* with the expectation of finding much detail about Vita's loves, family, and houses, all told with spritely animation. They will have to return to either Victoria Glendinning's 1983 biography *Vita* or Suzanne Raitt's 1993 study *Vita and Virginia: The Work and Friendship of V. Sackville-West and Virginia Woolf,* however, to find out about the actual authorial mind housed underneath all the splashy hats.

—Jay Dickson, *Reed College*

Notes on Contributors

Kristin Czarnecki is an associate professor of English at Georgetown College, where she teaches modern British literature, multiethnic American literature, and composition. She has published articles on Virginia Woolf, Samuel Beckett, Jean Rhys, and Louise Erdrich as well as an essay for Cecil Woolf's Bloomsbury Heritage Monograph series, *Virginia Woolf, Authorship, and Legacy: Unravelling Nurse Lugton's Curtain*. She was recently elected President of the International Virginia Woolf Society.

Bethany Layne works on biofiction about Henry James, Virginia Woolf, and Sylvia Plath, and has published work on these subjects in *The Henry James Review*, *Bloomsbury Inspirations*, and *Adaptation*. Her research has been disseminated at conferences including "Contradictory Woolf," "Transforming Henry James," and "Henry James and Material Culture." She is currently working on a monograph about the role occupied in contemporary fiction by the life and works of James. She is also employed as an Associate Lecturer at Sheffield Hallam University, where she specializes in modern-to-contemporary literature.

Rebecca Wisor is assistant professor of English at the United States Military Academy at West Point. Her research focuses on the intersection between British modernism, interwar pacifism, intellectual networks, and textual studies. She is the author of two other articles on Virginia Woolf, published in *Modernism/modernity* and *Studies in the Humanities,* and she presently is at work on a study of how narrative empathy functions in Woolf's short fiction.

arizona quarterly

a journal of

American Literature Culture & Theory

The journal publishes articles from a variety of scholarly approaches to canonical and non-canonical works of American literatures and film. *Arizona Quarterly*'s Annual Symposium brings together senior scholars, advisory board members, and newly established academics, to renew our commitment to the study of American texts.

The digital edition is published online by Project MUSE, produced by the Johns Hopkins University Press. For print subscriptions and submission instructions, visit http://azq.arizona.edu/.

criticism

A Quarterly for Literature and the Arts

renée c. hoogland, editor

Criticism provides a forum for current scholarship on literature, media, music, and visual culture. A place for rigorous theoretical and critical debate as well as formal and methodological self-reflexivity and experimentation, *Criticism* aims to present contemporary thought at its most vital.

Recent and Upcoming Special Issues

- Jack Smith: Beyond the Rented World,
  A Special Issue Edited by Marc Seigel
- Andy Warhol, *A Special Issue Edited by Jonathan Flatley and Anthony E. Grudin*

For submission guidelines and subscription information, visit
http://digitalcommons.wayne.edu/criticism/

Wayne State University Press
www.wsupress.wayne.edu
800-978-7323

LEGACY
A Journal of American Women Writers

Edited by Jennifer S. Tuttle,
Theresa Strouth Gaul, and Susan Tomlinson

The only journal to focus exclusively on American women's writings from the seventeenth through the early twentieth centuries.

The official journal of the Society for the Study of American Women Writers

Legacy is available online through Project MUSE and JSTOR Current Scholarship Program. Both offer free access via library subscriptions and pay-per-view options for those without library connections. Read it at
bit.ly/LEG_MUSE
or
bit.ly/LEG_JSTOR

There are additional resources and information about publishing in *Legacy* at
legacywomenwriters.org

Follow *Legacy* on Twitter: **@LegacyWmenWrite**

For information on membership in the Society for the Study of American Women Writers, visit
ssawwnew.wordpress.com.

For subscriptions or back issues:
Visit **nebraskapress.unl.edu**
or call **402-472-8536**

UNIVERSITY OF
NEBRASKA PRESS

Mosaic, a journal for the interdisciplinary study of literature

Call for Submissions: Letters

Mosaic invites innovative and interdisciplinary submissions for a special issue on the theme of philosophy's, literature's, or any other discipline's, letters. Traditionally, letters have been regarded as "non-serious" or at least as superfluous to the critical enterprise proper (consider Kant's division of Plato the letter-writer from Plato the philosophical father). But can letters themselves be considered critical forays and/or keys to the inheritance of scholarly work? Might letters put the serious/non-serious opposition into question? For this special issue, *Mosaic* encourages submissions that bring letters to light in relation but not limited to the following themes: understanding a writer's or artist's body of work; alternate histories; friendship; auto-bio-graphy; archival and digital repository research; email and electronic posting.

If you would like to contribute an essay for review, please visit our website for details: www.umanitoba.ca/mosaic/submit. Email any submission questions to mosasub@umanitoba.ca. Submissions must be received by October 16, 2015.

Forthcoming Publications

"A matter of *lifedeath*" Conference Proceedings I-III **48.2, 48.3, 48.4 (June, Sep., Dec. 2015)** The proceedings issues will feature keynote lectures given by Andrea Carlino, Françoise Dastur, and Elisabeth Weber, along with selected papers presented by participants.

Mosaic, a journal for the interdisciplinary study of literature
University of Manitoba   Tel.: (204) 474-9763
208 Tier Building   www.umanitoba.ca/mosaic
Winnipeg MB R3T 2N2 CANADA   mosaic@umanitoba.ca

Submission Guidelines

Woolf
Studies
Annual invites articles on the work and life of Virginia Woolf and her milieu. The *Annual* intends to represent the breadth and eclecticism of critical approaches to Woolf and particularly welcomes new perspectives and contexts of inquiry. Articles discussing relations between Woolf and other writers and artists are also welcome.

Articles are sent for review anonymously to a member of the Editorial Board and at least one other reader. Manuscripts should not be under consideration elsewhere or have been previously published. It is strongly advised that those submitting work to *WSA* be familiar with the journal's content. Among criteria on which evaluation of submissions depends are whether an article demonstrates familiarity with scholarship already published in the field, whether the article is written clearly and effectively, and whether it makes a genuine contribution to Woolf studies.

Preparation of Copy

1. Articles are typically between 25 and 30 pages, and do not exceed 8,000 words. This is a guide rather than a stipulation, and inquiries about significantly shorter or longer submissions should be sent to the Editor at woolfstudiesannual@gmail.com.

2. A separate file should include the article's title, author's name, address, phone number, and email address. The author's name and any other identifying references should not appear on the manuscript to preserve anonymity for our readers.

3. All submissions must include an abstract of no more than 250 words.

4. Manuscripts should conform to the most recent MLA style.

5. Submissions should be sent as Word files by email to woolfstudiesannual@gmail.com.

6. Authors of accepted manuscripts are responsible for any necessary permissions fees and for securing any necessary permissions.

All editorial inquiries should be addressed to woolfstudiesannual@gmail.com.

Inquiries concerning orders, advertising, reviews, etc. should be addressed to PaceUP@pace.edu.

Other Woolf titles available:

"The Hours": The British Museum Manuscript of Mrs. Dalloway, transcribed and edited by Helen M. Wussow (paper 2010)

Virginia Woolf, Jacob's Room: *The Holograph Draft*, transcribed and edited by Edward L. Bishop (paper 2010)

Women in the Milieu of Leonard and Virginia Woolf: Peace, Politics and Education Ed. Wayne K. Chapman and Janet M. Manson (1998)

Virginia Woolf and Trauma: Embodied Texts Ed. Suzette Henke & David Eberly (2007)

Woolf Across Cultures Ed. Natalya Reinhold (2004)

Woolf Studies Annual 5 (1999)

Woolf Studies Annual 6 (2000): The *Three Guineas* Correspondence, edited by Anna Snaith

Woolf Studies Annual 7 (2001)

Woolf Studies Annual 8 (2002): The Fawcett Library Correspondence, edited by Merry Pawlowski

Woolf Studies Annual 9 (2003): *Virginia Woolf and Literary History Part 1*, edited by Jane Lilienfeld, Jeffrey Oxford, and Lisa Low

Woolf Studies Annual 10 (2004): *Virginia Woolf and Literary History Part 2*, edited by Jane Lilienfeld, Jeffrey Oxford, and Lisa Low

Woolf Studies Annual 11 (2005) - *Woolf Studies Annual* 20 (2014)

Woolf Studies Annual 19 (2013): *Special Focus Virginia Woolf and Jews*, edited by Mark Hussey

Virginia Woolf and Communities: Selected Papers from the Eighth Annual Conference on Virginia Woolf, edited by Jeanette McVicker and Laura Davis

Virginia Woolf Turning the Centuries: Selected Papers from the Ninth Annual Conference on Virginia Woolf, edited by Ann Ardis and Bonnie Kime Scott

Virginia Woolf Out of Bounds: Selected Papers from the Tenth Annual Conference on Virginia Woolf, edited by Jessica Berman and Jane Goldman

www.ingramcontent.com/pod-product-compliance
Lightning Source LLC
Chambersburg PA
CBHW061444300426
44114CB00014B/1835